The Home Office 1848–1914

―――――

from Clerks to Bureaucrats

―――――

The Home Office 1848–1914

from Clerks to Bureaucrats

Jill Pellew

Rutherford • Madison • Teaneck
Fairleigh Dickinson University Press

Associated University Presses, Inc.
4 Cornwall Drive
East Brunswick, N.J. 08816

Library of Congress Cataloging in Publication Data

Pellew, Jill
    The Home Office, 1848–1914, from clerks to bureaucrats

    Bibliography: p.
    Includes index
    (1.)   Great Britain. Home Office — History
    (i.)   Title.

JN 453.H7P44.   354.41063′09   82-1533

ISBN 0-8386-3165-7   AACR2

Printed in Great Britain

In Commemoration of
Two Hundred Years of
Home Office History
27 March 1782
to
27 March 1982

Contents

Foreword

by Sir Leon Radzinowicz

No piece of administrative history, however good, can expect immediately to excite the imagination or capture intellectual curiosity. But if one sets out to absorb it, without being submerged by its details, the rewards at the end will prove both illuminating and enduring.

This is especially true when a work endeavours to retrace the administrative framework of a great department of state which, by the very nature of its functions and the circumstances of history, remains at the centre of domestic affairs. And when, as in Dr Jill Pellew's book, the reconstruction is carried out impeccably, the final product becomes an indispensable source for a better understanding of the social and political evolution of the country as a whole.

The changes which took place in the organization and functioning of the Home Office during the Victorian period reflected the fundamental changes which at the time were reshaping the responsibilities of the State, extending gradually but substantially its frontiers of interference and control. As the State departed more and more sharply from its traditional liberal stance of non-interference, so did the Home Office.

This expressed itself in many ways. A particularly instructive section of Jill Pellew's book is the one devoted to the network of Home Office Inspectorates. It reveals how the machinery of the Office was moulded by the new communal concerns and aspirations, as well as by crude political exigencies. But she also makes it clear that the pace of accepted reforms, indeed their ultimate directions, frequently depended on the internal attitudes and forces of the department itself.

In contrast to the cluster of exceptionally complex and controversial issues thrown up by present-day Britain, which the Home Office is expected to anticipate, to pick up and do something about, the life of the department within the period covered by this book may appear remarkably trouble free, serene, exhibiting a contagious confidence in its future. But make no mistake, they too had their problems and their anxieties. Take the field of penal policy. The conscience-stricken probing of Sir William Harcourt and the fierce challenging of Sir Winston Churchill are striking, but by no means isolated examples. No less characteristic were the positions taken up by the permanent heads of the Office, so vividly illustrated by the sensitive Sir Godfrey Lushington and the monolithic Sir Edward Troup.

The political history of the Home Office still remains to be written. It is my hope that Dr Pellew, encouraged by the reception extended to her book, will expand her solid investigations and bring them as close as possible to the present.

I share with Dr Pellew a deep satisfaction that this book could see the light of day at the very moment when the venerable governess operating under the useful but somewhat elusive fiction 'I am Sir Your Obedient Servant' celebrates a second centenary.

Preface

This study of the Home Office was motivated by a desire to explore, in a major government department, the changing nature and role of nineteenth-century civil servants. In recent years the British civil service has come in for much criticism on the grounds of failure to adapt to changing political and social needs. Several of the features which are most criticized nowadays first emerged as characteristic of the civil service during the period of reform following the Northcote-Trevelyan report. This is not an original subject: historians, political scientists and civil servants themselves have produced many works which seek, in a general way, to answer this question. But administrative histories of individual government departments are a comparative rarity. I intend in this one to try to illustrate some of the generalizations made in less specific studies of nineteenth-century civil service reform.

I cannot claim a monopoly of Home Office study. The period 1782 to 1801 has already been examined by one historian;[1] a later period, 1822 to 1848, has briefly been portrayed by another.[2] There is an excellent detailed account of the holders and functions of each office within the department between 1782 and 1870.[3] Someone else realized before I did the significance of the period 1870 to 1896: this was a retired Home Office official, Sir Austin Strutt, who wrote a small, privately printed volume on the subject of structural change, based on Public Record Office sources.[4] I am grateful to him for his reminiscences about one or two officials who were in the Home Office during the period covered by this book, and for a useful pointer towards further research. In addition, there are two official histories of the Home Office.[5]

The Home Office between 1870 and 1896 formed the subject of my PhD thesis for the University of London in 1976. I am still inclined to think that these are the most significant years to study from the point of view of nineteenth-century civil service reform: within this period can be observed the most dramatic changes in terms of the ability of higher officials, and of office structure and work load. But it is worth setting this period in the context both of the pre-reform Home Office and of the pre-first world war era when the initial open competition entrants were in positions of authority. The starting date of 1848 has been chosen largely because the Parliamentary Select Committee on Miscellaneous Expenditure and a Home Office committee of inquiry provide useful material on the department at that time. 1914 is a terminal date not merely inspired by convention but chosen because the war brought new kinds of responsibilities to the department. Another addition to the work for the thesis has been a study of some of the Home Office sub-departments: the inspectorates. The importance of inspection as a new tool of central government in the extension of its control during the mid-nineteenth century has been stressed in recent years even though there has been considerable debate about the motivation for the growth and spread of inspection. Since the Home Office supervized several important inspectorates, a study of their functioning, effectiveness and relationship with the central department seemed imperative.

The Home Office during this period is a large subject and has provided difficulties of selection. The main emphasis of this work is on the changing educational and social backgrounds of the clerks and – to a more limited extent – of the inspectors; the changing structure of the department; and the changing functions of the upper (or first) division and lower (or second) division officials. To this discussion has, perhaps, been sacrificed examination of the formulation of departmental policies, although the latter has been presented in some detail in two specific cases showing the work of two inspectorates between 1876 and 1914. Again, twelve inspectorates provide an enormous amount of material and interest and it has only been possible to present them by drawing heavily on the various secondary sources about individual inspectorates and by being highly selective in detailed analysis. A further problem has been the lack of memoir sources and personal papers of officials: notable lacunae exist in the cases of Lushington and Troup – in a sense, the heroes of the book – and in the case of the lower division clerks where I have had to resort to generalization and occasional speculation.

Despite several years spent studying the Home Office over this sixty-six year period there still seems a great deal of territory left unexplored. Nevertheless, I hope that this work will provide a useful administrative background for the student of any of the numerous aspects of social policy which concerned the department during this period, or a useful comparison for anyone studying administrative reform in other government departments.

The research required for aspects additional to my original doctoral study has been carried out with the aid of a Social Science

Research Council grant, without which I would not have been able to continue the work. Publication of the book has been greatly facilitated by the assistance of the Home Office on its two hundredth anniversary. Various friends and colleagues have helped me enormously by reading and commenting in some cases on substantial parts of the manuscript. In particular, I would like to thank Professor Oliver MacDonagh, Professor Roy MacLeod, Dr Roger Davidson, Dr John Myerscough, Dr Peter Bartrip, Mr Gerald Rhodes, Mr R. M. Morris and Mr Philip Stevens. I would also like to thank Mr Michael Port and Mr John Sainty who helped me during the period when I was writing my thesis. I am grateful to Sir Leon Radzinowicz for his kind help and advice. In addition, my father, Professor Frank Thistlethwaite, has consistently encouraged my work. I also owe a debt to Mrs Jennifer Martin who worked hard typing out the manuscript. None of these institutions or individuals, of course, bears any responsibility for my argument or, indeed, errors.

Crown-copyright material from the Public Record Office and the Home Office library appears by permission of the Controller of H. M. Stationary Office. I owe a particular debt to the staff of the Home Office Noters' Section, especially to Miss White and Mr Millett, who have been most helpful in providing me with documents. For permission to use copyright material I would like to thank the Marquess of Salisbury, the Trustees of the British Library, the Bodleian Library, the Kent County Record Office, Sir John Ruggles-Brise, Mr Kenneth Maconochie and the Trustees of *The Times* newspaper.

Most of all I am grateful for the constant interest, tolerance and support of my husband, Mark, a modern civil servant.

Part I The End of the Old Order

1 Introduction

The interesting thing to the historian of an institution is that the institution itself is an entity – almost a *persona* – over and above those individuals who constitute its personnel at any given moment. Its ethos is derived from its designated functions, its historical development, its effectiveness and the extent of its influence, to which the accumulated actions and interactions of those who have worked in it have contributed. While to a greater or lesser degree this ethos may be given a new shift in direction by one generation of individuals passing through it, they in their turn are to some extent influenced by the institution itself. Therefore, before focusing on the backgrounds and functions of Home Office officials in 1848, we must introduce the department by looking briefly at its own early history and functions.

Although the Home Office was created in 1782, its political head and his officials had antecedents going back at least to Tudor times. In the mid-sixteenth century, when Thomas Cromwell was Henry VIII's principal adviser, the king's secretary emerged from being a confidential clerk in his household to being the recognized channel through which royal wishes could be conveyed to the privy council and the king's counsellors could consult him. The secretary was the executive member of the council, providing it with information and responsible for executing its decisions. He had his own secretaries for whose appointment and work he was responsible. His own authority always rested on his personal relationship with the king.

In the seventeenth century the title 'principal secretary' came into use; and, after a provision of 1640, it became the practice to have two principal secretaries of state, each of whom was responsible for different areas of foreign policy. Their two departments became known as the 'northern' and 'southern' departments and dealt respectively with Protestant and Roman Catholic powers. The more senior of the two principal secretaries also administered Irish and colonial business. After the revolution of 1688 the power of a secretary of state began to depend less on his personal relations with the monarch and more on his position among the dominant political leaders. On the one hand he subsumed some of the powers hitherto held by the monarch. On the other his powers were limited as the idea of collective cabinet responsibility gradually became a reality. They were also limited by various legal decisions of the eighteenth century, one of the most important of which was the outcome of the case in 1765, Entick v. Carrington: in declaring general warrants illegal, the judiciary established that a secretary of state had no extraordinary jurisdiction. The House of Commons endorsed this particular decision the following year.

In 1782 the apportionment of the main business of state between two geographical departments was abolished. One of the two secretaries of state (Lord Shelburne) was to administer domestic and colonial affairs; the other (Charles James Fox) was to be in charge of foreign affairs. Shelburne's precedence as a peer over Fox may explain the origin of the home secretary's precedence over all other secretaries of state.[1] Twelve years later a newly created secretary of state for war took over responsibility for military affairs (with the exception of troop movements and the maintenance of order within the country); and in 1801 his title became secretary of state for war and the colonies. The secretary of state for home affairs, or home secretary, was left with responsibility for all domestic affairs which did not come under the purview of another minister. For this reason he has been described as being in the position of a 'residuary legatee'.

The Home Office started with a staff of two under-secretaries, a chief clerk, ten other clerks and some domestic staff. The secretary of state, under-secretaries and chief clerk were entitled to fees on office transactions; the other clerks were paid out of the secretary of state's emoluments. This changed in 1795, following the report of a commission on fees. All officials were paid fixed salaries from a consolidated fee fund made up of fees and gratuities paid to the office (although this did not prevent their requesting gratuities for certain duties). This fund was topped up when necessary from the civil list. In 1822 there was a major revision of the establishment. The majority of clerks ceased to be paid individual salaries and were for the first time divided into 'first class', 'second class' and 'third class' clerks (known alternatively as 'senior', 'assistant' and 'junior' clerks), each class having its own salary scale including regular increments. The clerical staff, from chief clerk downwards, was permanent. The traditional position of the under-secretaries was that one invariably sat in the House of Commons; the other did not and his position was unaffected by political change. In 1831 the Treasury formally recognized one under-secretary as 'parliamentary' and the other as 'permanent' and laid down fixed salaries for them.[2]

The home secretary retained the ancient functions of the king's secretary, acting as the official channel of communication between the monarch and his subjects and preparing royal warrants, grants and appointments. He advised the king on his prerogative powers, in particular the royal prerogative of mercy. His responsibility for the maintenance of internal peace in the United Kingdom gave him extensive powers over local authorities such as lords-lieutenant and magistrates. This role was particularly important during the turbulent years following Waterloo when there was perpetual underlying fear of insurrection and when the Home Office kept up a flow of advice and instruction to fearful local authorities.

In the second quarter of the nineteenth century a new trend can be discerned as the home secretary began to acquire diverse responsibilities through acts of parliament. This was not unprecedented: in 1793 an aliens act had imposed duties on his department. But from the time of Peel's tenure of office as home secretary, the scope of departmental work steadily expanded through work imposed by the legislature. The 1829 police act gave the home secretary direct control over the first uniformed, disciplined metropolitan police force; the 1832 prison act brought certain prisons under the jurisdiction of the home secretary; the 1844 naturalization act gave him statutory powers to naturalize aliens; and so on.

Many of the new responsibilities were concerned with social welfare. Philanthropists and investigators of social problems were finding that the answers to problems arising from industrialization and urbanization lay in giving central government more power to intervene in aspects of men's lives where hitherto private enterprise and local authority had control. A good example of their influence on legislation was the 1833 factory act, which empowered the home secretary to appoint factory inspectors to enforce restrictions on hours of work and on the employment of young children. Other kinds of inspector followed in the wake of the factory inspectors. Out-departments of the office were established and staffed by a new kind of expert official who worked in the field, observing and enforcing regulatory legislation and reporting back to the secretary of state in London on a regular basis. Thus the Home Office increased in size although (at first) at its periphery rather than at the centre.

The name of Jeremy Bentham is a leitmotiv in any study of nineteenth-century government or public administration. Bentham advocated the renovation of English institutions so as to include a far wider social participation in the process of government in order to promote the interests and happiness of as much of the community as possible rather than a small aristocratic minority. The Home Office, like other government departments, was directly influenced both by Benthamite advocation of reform of the public service and the recruitment of officials through competitive examination, and by Benthamite emphasis on solving social problems through inspection, inquiry and report.

During the years following the 1832 parliamentary reform act, radical members of parliament, influenced by utilitarian strictures against inefficiency and hostility towards the running of the country by a landed elite, directed the attention of the reformed House of Commons towards the alarming growth of public expenditure. By this time salaries, voted by parliament, had generally replaced fees as the normal method of paying officials and all officials had the right to a pension. Thus they had become genuine servants of the government. The reforming Whig government of 1832 consolidated an effective system of public accounting which enabled parliament to scrutinize expenditure. A war on sinecures began in the House of Commons where members began to acquire the habit of criticizing public service waste through the device of select committees. The target of their attacks was increasingly the Treasury since it had acquired responsibility for presenting items of civil expenditure to parliament for approval. Therefore the Treasury showed a growing interest in the way in which other departments spent their resources although it had no control over ministerial appointments to office or the way in which departments were managed.

Our story starts in 1848 when expanding budgets, after Peel's 1841–6 ministry, provoked renewed and lively parliamentary debate about increases in the numbers of officials and extravagance in departmental use of funds. The continental revolutions of 1848, as Sir Charles Trevelyan, permanent head of the Treasury, put it, 'gave us a shake' and inclined him and other reformers seriously to tackle the problem of waste in government departments.[3] One outcome was a major investigation of the Home Office establishment.

2 Challenge to a traditional department of government: 1848–76

The unreformed Home Office: 1848

In the mid-nineteenth century Home Office all important decisions were taken at the top by the home secretary and a handful of advisers. These consisted of his two under-secretaries, the Home Office counsel and the private secretary. These men alone among departmental officials worked alongside the secretary of state, going over all incoming correspondence, working on legislation and advising on policy matters. The roles of the two under-secretaries had not always been differentiated but since 1831 they had become officially known as 'parliamentary' and 'permanent'.[1] The parliamentary under-secretary was a junior political colleague of the home secretary, while the permanent under-secretary was not a politician and therefore, by contrast, did not change office with him. The private secretary was his own personal appointment and since 1830 invariably came from outside the office. The counsel was the permanent legal adviser to the department. See Table 1.

The Home Office was a highly conservative department of government, as one of its important functions – 'maintenance of the King's Peace' – implied. The permanent under-secretary both absorbed and contributed towards this conservatism: always an experienced barrister, he inevitably respected precedent and tradition. Typical were the two permanent under-secretaries of 1848. Samuel March Phillipps, who retired in May of that year, had been forty-seven when appointed to the position by the Marquess of Landsdowne in 1827. The son of a gentleman and landowner, he had been educated at Charterhouse and Cambridge before becoming a barrister and producing a couple of legal works. He was succeeded by the recorder of Warwick and Lichfield, Horatio Waddington. His father had been a clergyman and, coincidentally, he too had been educated at Charterhouse and Cambridge before qualifying as a barrister. He was forty-nine when Sir George Grey[2] appointed him to the Home Office.

By contrast with their political colleagues, these men, with their experience of and loyalty towards the office, were the continuity factor which home secretaries needed. They eschewed politics; but the very fact that they were appointed by the political head of department implied that they had social if not political connections with their patron. The appointment of Waddington's successor illustrates how political affiliations operated in these appointments. Adolphus Liddell was appointed permanent under-secretary in 1867 by Sir G. Gathorne-Hardy who was home secretary in the third cabinet of the conservative Lord Derby. The Liddells were traditionally a Conservative family: Adolphus' father, son of the fifth baronet, had been created Baron Ravensworth by Lord Liverpool in 1821; and various members of the family, including Adolphus himself, had stood as Tory candidates.

Table 1   The Home Office establishment, 1848 (before Grey's reforms)

politicians	secretary of state (home secretary) (£5,000)	
	private secretary (£300)	
	parliamentary under-secretary (£1,500)	
senior advisers	permanent under-secretary (£2,000)	
	counsel (£1,500)	
permanent career officials	chief clerk (£1,000–1,250)	
	4 first class clerks (1 at £900, 3 at £600–800)	keeper of the criminal register (£300)
		assistant ditto (£120)
	4 second class clerks (£350–545)	clerk for criminal business (£550–800)
	5 third class clerks (£150–300)	assistant ditto (£300–400)
		*librarian (£600)
		*précis writer (£300)
		clerk for aliens business (£300–400)

(permanent officials encompasses senior advisers and permanent career officials)

*Posts held by one clerk
Total number of permanent officials = 22
Total cost of permanent officials   = £13,406 (annual estimates, 1849)

The distribution of the work among the home secretary's senior advisers was fairly informal but there was a rough demarcation of duties. The permanent under-secretary had a special responsibility for criminal work, and questions on specific points of law were referred to him. The parliamentary under-secretary dealt with correspondence about all parliamentary business and about Ireland, Scotland and the Channel Islands.[3] The counsel had the work of drawing up public bills, not only for his own department but – since

1842 – for thirteen other government departments as well. This made him less closely tied to the Home Office than the others.

It was possible for this small group of men to make all significant departmental decisions because the volume of incoming correspondence was still small enough for the home secretary to scrutinize the daily mail. The morning routine was described by Sir James Graham, an ex-home secretary, in 1850:

> ... the Private Secretary attends as soon as the letters arrive, the Under-Secretaries at ten o'clock, and the Secretary of State ought to be at his post about eleven, and then everything is brought before him which has arrived, either by his Private Secretary or by the two Under-Secretaries; and the answers to be given to the correspondence of the day are settled by the Secretary of State with those three officers who distribute the correspondence.[4]

Graham, who had left the Home Office in 1846, complained that this system had begun to be strained by increasing responsibilities. He had even sighed for a 'ten hour' bill for himself so that he would be prevented from working his average twelve hour day as home secretary.[5] But for all that, he was firmly against changing the system by allowing anyone below the rank of these senior advisers to have increased responsibility:

> I am most anxious to prevent the delegation of effective duties by the heads of departments to their Chief Clerks. No head of a department, who really does his duty to the public, permits any such delegation; he keeps the reins of his department in his own hands, and allows nothing that is important to be done without his knowledge.[6]

This was because his senior advisers were a breed apart from the rest of his staff – the Home Office clerks. These were a body of twenty permanent career officials headed by the chief clerk. He was Thomas Henry Plasket, who in 1848 had served the Home Office in this capacity for thirty-two years, having previously worked in lowlier posts for over twenty-one years. He had, in short, 'been educated in the office';[7] he had started in the most junior clerical grade and laboriously worked his way up to the highest. Since he had followed the classic career of the successful Home Office clerk of that time he no doubt possessed the essential qualities: an average degree of intelligence, a good memory, the ability to work carefully and accurately, and loyalty to his department.

While the home secretary required expert advice and a sharing of the decision-making load from his senior advisers, he required clerical back-up from the rest of the department. The clerks' contribution to the running of the office was based on their long service, their knowledge of precedents and attention to detail. The registry work of docketing,[8] despatching and filing letters, and the secretarial work of copying and writing them out was the standard work of government clerks. But certain aspects of their work derived from the special functions of the department and contributed to its peculiar, highly conservative character. A good deal of the work was formal. This was because of the home secretary's role as the liaison between the monarch and her subjects. All petitions to the queen went through the department; all royal appointments to office, all royal licences and commissions were drawn up by the home secretary. Enormous care had to be exercised in the actual writing out of these 'formal instruments': for 'even a clerical error in a commission would be attended with very serious consequences'.[9] Thus the clerks, working under the chief clerk who supervised this work, spent hours drawing up these official documents in their careful copper-plate handwriting. Meticulous attention to detail was also required in the keeping of records. Although it had not been one of the original constitutional functions of the home secretary, his department was becoming the repository of recorded information about crime in the form of lists and calendars of prisoners, convict transportations and criminal offences, trials and sentences. All this incoming information was carefully set out by the clerks in bound ledgers. In addition a host of returns had to be prepared during the parliamentary season.

The home secretary's advice to magistrates, local authorities and crown officers followed the tradition of English law, being based on custom, statute and precedent. It was therefore essential for him to be able to count on officials who could find or remember the relevant statutes and precedents. The modern practice of recording work efficiently so that one official might take over smoothly from another by 'reading himself in' was unknown. Instead the personal knowledge of these men was vital:

> . . . much of the business in the Secretary of State's department consists of routine and precedent; and there are men there who, perhaps, are not men of great capacity; but at the same time, from having been so many years in the office, they are in possession of information which it would be difficult to find in any other quarter. A great deal of information is not recorded; it exists only in the minds of those who have been there, and are the depositories of this information.[10]

For this reason clerks tended to remain in one department within the office and to have their own specialist functions – sometimes actually defined in their titles – which they guarded fiercely. The story is told of an aged clerk who had been a specialist in ceremonial affairs. Early in Queen Victoria's reign he was reluctantly induced to retire. 'His parting words were said to have been, "Ah, let them wait till there's a Demise of the Crown; then they'll be sorry they got rid of me." ' As the author of the story indicated, given the relative ages of the queen and the clerk, the likelihood of his still being alive at her demise was very small.[11]

Seniority gave status both to clerks and to the internal departments. The most revered department was the chief clerk's which dealt with ancient responsibilities such as communications between monarch and subjects. Lowest in status came the department which dealt with criminal business – although it exceeded the chief clerk's in potential if not actual importance – for it was the newest branch of work.[12] Plasket's age and devotion were not unusual: the précis writer, F. R. Mills, had served the office for fifty years; and one of the first class clerks, R. H. Noble, for fifty-one. Long service was expected by politicians and officials alike to be rewarded by a slow but steady climb up the career structure. For 'although some are in point of natural capacity vastly superior to others', and although the home secretary did have the right to promote on merit, in fact 'no gentleman who has conducted himself respectably has ever been passed over'. For 'it would be considered a grievance in the office if a senior clerk were passed over by a person below him on account of his possessing greater ability'.[13]

The career ladder was straightforward: the regular clerks who had no specific duties allotted to them on appointment moved up three or four simple rungs from third to second to first class clerkships and then – if longevity favoured them – to the chief clerkship. They might spend years at each stage waiting for a death or retirement (which was not compulsory) to cause a vacancy in the next grade. They were paid according to a set salary scale, although some had special allowances in addition for 'extra' work. The clerks with named functions, such as the keeper of the criminal register, had special salaries. By 1848 they were on the establishment but were not on the ordinary promotion ladder. Special allowances and individual salaries – technically abolished since salaries had replaced fees as the normal method of payment[14] – were a hangover from the old idea that a public official bought a post with specific duties attached and therefore could demand extra fees for additional work.

A factor which increased departmental tradition and loyalty was the appointment of all officials through the nomination of the head of department – the standard method of appointing public officials. This could mean a direct connection with the home secretary or connection with a departmental official. New young entrants, with little experience of the world, nominated by the august home secretary either through family or office connections, were unlikely to challenge departmental traditions. No doubt they soon assimilated the traditional respect for seniority, regard for accuracy and reverence for precedent. Anyway it was not a life about which they had much to complain. Salaries were reasonably good; clerks rarely worked more than six hours a day and could look forward each summer to a good two months' leave. Generally it was a gentlemanly existence compared with that of 'both the middle class and the working class' of 'the great body of the people in this country'.[15]

Political debate and inquiry into government offices: 1848–56

However, the apparent calm of the world of government clerks was being ruffled by external debate and inquiry. In 1848 the Select Committee on Miscellaneous Expenditure interviewed representatives from several departments including, from the Home Office, Sir George Grey (home secretary), Sir Denis Le Marchant (parliamentary under-secretary) and C. R. Fitzgerald (a second class clerk). The committee probed about the structure and functioning of the department, the responsibilities, qualifications and length of service of the clerks, the method of their promotion, and whether or not they were subject to probation. It wanted full details of salaries, being particularly concerned about a recent large increase for the Home Office counsel. Implicit in its questioning was the view that the numbers of officials should be reduced by the combination of various duties, that merit and ability ought to play a greater role in promotion, and that the allotment of work to officials should be entirely in the hands of the head of department and not pre-ordained by some specialist title.

On the whole the Home Office interviewees justified their department's expenses, practices and attitudes. Grey defended his counsel's increased salary and denied the committee's imputation that there was no need for the special office of chief clerk. He did admit that a reduction in the number of officials might be possible and even desirable but refused to commit himself on this, using a counter-argument which was to become familiar: that to reduce the number of senior posts would be unfair on the junior clerks – many of whom had spent years as such – since some of them would then have to forego the additional salary they had come to expect.[16]

By contrast, the views of the assistant secretary of the Treasury, Trevelyan, who openly criticized the administrative inefficiency of his own department for many of the characteristics it shared with the Home Office, came like a blast of cold air. (He even attacked the Home Office for its use of a 'very fine description of paper'.)[17]

Trevelyan suggested reorganization of the Treasury establishment in order to separate 'intellectual' and 'mechanical' work functions – a recommendation which, for the time being, was shelved. However, Trevelyan's views on departmental organization at this point were directly relevant to the story of Home Office reform. For by the middle of the century the foundations for Treasury control of government departments had been laid both through the reform of the system of public accounting and auditing, and through the Treasury having been granted the right to present items of civil expenditure to parliament for approval. The Treasury had become the department through which parliament attacked public expenditure and which therefore had an interest in the way in which departments spent their resources. Thus it was concerned about numbers of staff, how they were paid and the amounts they were awarded in pension just as were parliamentary select committees. One of the methods which was coming to be used by the Treasury to influence the functioning of other departments was its participation in inter-departmental committees of inquiry. In 1848 Trevelyan sat on such a committee of investigation into the Home Office.[18]

This Treasury-Home Office committee was set up by Grey who was no doubt partly stimulated by demands for retrenchment in the Commons and strongly encouraged by the Treasury. Despite his somewhat non-committal answers to the 1848 select committee, Grey emerges as an enthusiast for reform in a department whose traditions and sentiment militated against it. He was home secretary three times between 1846 and 1866 for a total period of thirteen and a half years, and during each of his periods of office there occurred departmental reform along the lines Trevelyan was advocating for all government offices. The committee consisted of three members: Trevelyan, W. Gibson Craig (junior lord of the Treasury) and Sir George Cornewall Lewis (Home Office parliamentary under-secretary). They found the pressure of work unevenly distributed, largely because of the internal prejudice against criminal work. This had led on certain occasions to the criminal branch of the office having more business than it could cope with while other clerks, who were under-employed, failed to help out. It opposed the inflexible organization which resulted from specialization on the increasingly familiar ground that an official's time should be at the disposal of the public.[19]

As a result Grey outlined a plan of reform, which was later confirmed by order in council. He was aided against possible office resentment of change by the simultaneous retirement of various longstanding officials, including the chief clerk. In an attempt to bring the hitherto unestablished criminal clerks into line with the rest of the establishment, the salary of the clerk for criminal business, G. Everest, was assimilated to that of a first class clerk and Everest was to be 'considered' as such. The posts of précis writer and clerk for aliens business were abolished and the work absorbed by the rest of the staff. Money was saved by reducing the chief clerk's salary and through the decision that a special allowance of £100 should be granted to the senior first class clerk only if he were actually in charge of a branch of office business. In addition Grey stipulated that future appointments to the establishment were to be subject to examination and to a year's probation. Promotion was to be based on merit; and, as if to emphasize this, Grey's nominee for the vacant chief clerkship, H. J. Knyvett, was not next in line in terms of seniority. These changes were approved by the Treasury.[20]

The Home Office was by no means the only department to be subjected to scrutiny. For the Treasury then proceeded, by overhauling itself, to set an example to other departments, several of which were investigated by comparable committees of inquiry between 1849 and 1854. Trevelyan sat on nine of these and his departmental investigations culminated in his wider examination of the public service with Sir Stafford Northcote which was published as the *Report on the Organization of the Permanent Civil Service* and presented to parliament in February 1854.[21]

In advocating reform W. E. Gladstone (who, as chancellor of the exchequer, had commissioned the report), Northcote and Trevelyan were strongly influenced by the current faith in examinations and selection by merit. Examinations were the natural extension of the Benthamite desire for democratic reform of institutions in the interests of efficiency and expertise. In the professions the system whereby professional bodies could examine for proficiency and prevent unqualified persons from calling themselves members of those professions was beginning to take root.[22] In the educational world reformers of public schools and other middle-class schools were urging the use of examinations.[23] After 1852, when the royal commissions on Oxford and Cambridge reported, these universities began to place a higher value on merit by abolishing ancient privileges. Nearer to the public service the examination idea triumphed in 1853 with the passing of the government of India act, which abolished the patronage of the directors of the East India Company and opened appointments in the company's service to competitive entry.[24]

The reformers started from the premise that 'the Government of the country could not be carried on without the aid of an efficient body of permanent officers . . . possessing sufficient independence, character, ability and experience to be able to advise, assist, and to some extent, influence, those who are from time to time set over them'.[25] And they found the public service 'far from perfect'. They described a situation which precisely fitted the Home Office. Men entered their careers with no qualifications other than a connection with their patron. They usually started very young and, since a civil service career tended to mean the 'secluded performance of routine duties', gained few opportunities to broaden their limited experience through their work. The system of promotion by seniority led to a deadening feeling of security and created no stimulus for men to excel. There were few really good jobs to which they could aspire since the top posts were reserved for outsiders. Naturally the civil service did not attract the best men. Moreover, it was hardly a 'service', being of a fragmentary nature and composed of disparate departments.

The reformers' prescription for these ills is well known. They wanted the reorganization of departmental work into 'intellectual' and 'mechanical' functions, each to be done by separate classes of men recruited through open competitive examination. They recommended promotion on the basis of merit and the opening of the top posts to career officials rather than outside appointees. They aimed at unity of the civil service by advocating the standardization of appointments to all departments which would make inter-departmental transfers possible.[26]

It was a scheme of which many educationalists approved. Some, like Benjamin Jowett, saw the reformed civil service staffed by men of the 'liberal' education which the public schools and ancient universities provided.[27] But within the public service itself commentators were less sanguine about the scheme. Many, like Sir James Stephen, felt that the qualities of 'self-reliance, self-possession, promptitude, address, resource, hopefulness and courage', shown by the most successful graduates of the two ancient universities, were 'gifts ill-suited, and even inconvenient to one who is entombed for life as a clerk in a Public Office in Downing Street'.[28] The Home Office was sceptical. Cornewall Lewis, ex-parliamentary under-secretary and future home secretary, was worried that examinations could not test character and trustworthiness – qualities the Home Office valued in its clerks more than intellect and ambition.[29] Waddington presented his views in a scathing letter, spiced with Latin and Greek epithets of the best 'liberal' tradition. He found the report 'mistaken and erroneous'. No doubt government clerks were men 'of excellent capacity, of untiring industry, and . . . of vigorous and sound constitutions'; nevertheless, they were a race apart from the professionally trained decision-makers at the top. Open competitive entry, he felt, would be more trouble than it would be worth.[30] To many with experience of public administration at the Home Office Jowett's vision of highly educated, ambitious clerks on the establishment appeared unrealistic and unnecessary.

For the time being the views of the conservatives held sway and the Northcote-Trevelyan scheme proved politically unacceptable.[31] But in May 1855, partly as a result of the public outcry against the Crimean disasters and maladministration in the conduct of public affairs, Palmerston's cabinet set up the Civil Service Commission. This body was to issue certificates to all nominated candidates for positions in the civil service if they passed certain tests of fitness. Successful candidates must be qualified in age, health, character and to pass an examination, the subjects of which were to be worked out between the commissioners and heads of individual departments which agreed to co-operate.[32] The nomination system was to continue: suitable candidates were still to be sent for examination by individual departments. But the establishment of the commission was the first step towards demanding not only minimum entry standards for civil servants but also comparable standards for different departments.

At the Home Office the civil service commissioners found in Grey a head of department who was 'strong for examinations'.[33] His earlier attempt to introduce entrance examinations had come to nothing; here was his chance to move away from unrestricted patronage. He not only co-operated immediately with the commissioners to establish satisfactory entry tests for Home Office clerkships, but even suggested that clerks within the office who wished to be promoted should be examined.[34] The tests were arranged in April 1856. Candidates nominated as clerks had to be between eighteen and twenty-five, be of good health, and pass tests in English language, arithmetic, geography, English history, Latin and French. They could obtain honorary certificates by taking various further subjects. Soon afterwards the examination became competitive, although the ratio of competent candidates to vacancies offered at the Home Office was not impressive.[35] Nor was the standard of examination high: 'In general the Commissioners thought the standard of their papers was lower than that set by the Society of Arts and the Oxford and Cambridge Local Examinations'.[36] The Society of Arts set examinations for adult students at mechanics institutes and the Oxford and Cambridge local examinations were for pupils at grammar and private schools; so the standard was well below that required for university degrees.

However, the examinations did secure, for the first time, a certain minimum standard for Home Office (and other) recruits to clerkships.

The new method of recruitment

The new method of recruitment caused little stir at the Home Office. Even Waddington had to admit in 1860 that he did not find the new type of clerk 'more presumptuous than other clerks'; indeed, one of them had even 'behaved remarkably well'.[37] This is hardly surprising considering that recruits were still nominated for the same reasons – their political or social connection with the secretary of state – and therefore had the same links with the office and social backgrounds as their predecessors. It is worth examining the origins of the thirty-eight clerks on the permanent establishment of the department between 1848 and 1876.[38]

Home secretaries appointed relatives of political colleagues and personal friends. E. A. S. Hobhouse, whose uncle was John Cam Hobhouse (Lord Broughton), a Whig politician, came to the Home Office under Palmerston in 1854. A. P. Graves, who entered in 1870, acquired his nomination through the historian, Sir William Napier, a friend of both Graves's uncle and the home secretary's (Bruce's) father-in-law.[39] But home secretaries also evidently responded to requests for appointments from within the office. For although none of these clerks was actually the son of a Home Office official, one or two had close relatives in the department. J. Streatfield, recruited in 1828, replaced a brother who had died. C. J. Knyvett, who entered the office in 1852, was the nephew of the chief clerk, H. J. Knyvett. Similarly, G. B. Fitzgerald was the nephew of the chief clerk, C. R. Fitzgerald, although he actually entered the office in 1868 after his uncle's retirement. Also nominated were several sons of public servants outside the department. Grey was responsible for the appointments of three: A. Maconochie, son of Captain Alexander Maconochie, the famous penal reformer who became governor of Birmingham gaol; R. C. Arbuthnot, whose father was a senior Treasury official; and C. S. Murdoch, son of a chairman of the Colonial Land and Emigration Commission.

The fathers' professions or family backgrounds are known in the case of twenty-nine of these thirty-eight clerks. Five were sons of public officials; eleven had fathers in other professions, such as the church, the law and the navy; the fathers of three were merchants or manufacturers; and three had fathers working directly in politics. The fathers of the remaining seven were all landowners with no other known occupation. (Some with listed occupations may, of course, also have been landowners – indeed, four appear in *Burke's Landed Gentry*.) At least half, therefore, were the sons of men with professional occupations. As far as social pedigree went five appear in *Burke's Peerage* and two of these succeeded to titles themselves.

It looks as though there was some change in the educational backgrounds of the clerks at about this time, although to what extent this was due to the imposition of examination in 1856 is not entirely clear. Comparing those recruited before 1856 with those recruited between 1856 and 1876 (the era of limited competition), we find that only three out of the twenty-six (11.5 per cent) in the first group had university degrees, while four out of the twelve (33.3 per cent) in the second group were graduates. As a result the average entry age rose from around nineteen and a half to twenty-one and three quarters. We have already noticed that the entry examination was by no means up to degree standard. Therefore this change cannot fully be explained by the new method of entry. It seems more likely that the apparent rise in the number of graduates (reflected also among Treasury and Colonial Office recruits)[40], was due to the university reforms following the Oxford and Cambridge university acts of 1854 and 1856. Vested interests and obsolete regulations were abolished, more relevant courses were developed for those who wished to enter the professions, and degrees could be confirmed on non-conformists which led to a wider intake of students.[41]

Less is known about the clerks' schooling although records of the well-known public schools show that three out of the first group of twenty-six (11.5 per cent) and five out of the second group of twelve (41.6 per cent) had received this type of education. An increase in the number of public school-educated officials as the period progressed, which this implies, could have reflected the increasing popularity among the professional classes of this kind of school.

Grey's reforms and Treasury attempts at control: 1856–68
In 1856 Grey once again instigated an inquiry into the functioning of his department. Again the Treasury was well represented on the committee, this time by H. B. W. Brand, a junior lord, and by George Arbuthnot, auditor of the civil list. The other member was W. N. Massey, who occupied the post of parliamentary under-secretary at the Home Office – an officer who throughout the whole period 1848–76 seems to have been particularly concerned with departmental reform.

This committee found that in those matters where enforcement was difficult without departmental co-operation the recommendations of the 1848 committee had not been carried out.

With the sole exception of Grey's appointment to the chief clerkship, 'the use of seniority had invariably prevailed' in promotion; there was no sign that probation had been enforced; and Everest's position remained anomalous. The committee recommended that these deficiencies be remedied and suggested that heads of department submit monthly reports on their clerks 'to prevent that laxity of which some examples were brought under our notice'.[42] There was a proposal to give the chief clerk additional responsibilities for office regulations and discipline, and the departmental arrangement of clerks. The committee found the registry system a 'useless encumbrance' which it wanted replaced by separate departmental registries. It suggested the creation of a new police and statistical department, to be placed under the direction of the keeper of the criminal register, S. Redgrave. Grey duly issued instructions to put these proposals into effect.[43]

Other recommendations required formal Treasury approval. On the basis that the more senior clerks should do less of the routine work, the committee wanted the number of first class clerks reduced gradually from five to three, each of whom would head a department. It was felt that this would also give the second class clerks greater responsibility for which they and the first class clerks should receive increased salaries. In addition it wanted the rationalization of the haphazardly organized salaries of the non-established 'supplementary' clerks. Somehow these proposals were either ignored or forgotten and the report lay buried in the department until the Treasury was reminded of it in 1858 by a Home Office request for a salary increase for one of the first class clerks. On referring to the report (which it took the Home Office over a year to produce) the Treasury were particularly irked to discover that there had been no reduction in the number of first class clerks and that the Home Office was using the report – whose recommendations it had not fully implemented – to justify the salary rise.[44]

There followed a long drawn-out inter-departmental row in which the Treasury's ability to control a major department of state through financial sanctions was put to the test.[45] In the Treasury's eyes the question at issue was whether or not the Home Office needed more highly paid first class clerks than was necessary to head each of its internal departments. There were then four departments which it felt ought to be headed by the chief clerk and three first class clerks. The home secretary felt he had to maintain the morale of his department whose traditional patterns of work and behaviour were being changed. Moreover, he did not like the Treasury challenge to his independence.

The Treasury would agree to the requested pay rise on condition that the number of first class clerks was reduced. An opportunity to put this into effect was about to present itself with the imminent retirement of one of these, Redgrave. Cornewall Lewis, then home secretary, agreed to replace Redgrave as head of the police and statistical department with another first class clerk, F. S. Leslie, who was not head of a department, thereby reducing their number from five to four. At the same time the other recommendations of the report about the pay scales and numbers of second class, third class and supplementary clerks would be carried out. The Treasury was prepared to agree to this proposal which would involve a pay rise for Leslie, but on condition that the number of first class clerks was reduced from four to the desired three when next there was a vacancy. Lewis refused to accept this condition. Eventually, having mildly threatened at one point to withhold consent to Leslie's pay rise, the Treasury capitulated and agreed to all the Home Office proposals without having extracted a promise from the home secretary. Its only consolation was his admission of its competence to raise the question again when a first class clerk next retired.[46]

This occurred in 1866 when Grey was once again home secretary. Notwithstanding his reforming instincts and the fact that he had commisioned the 1856 report around which the debate revolved, he retained the existing number of first class clerks by promoting one of the second class clerks. Once again angry Treasury officials referred to the report.[47] Eventually Grey proved more accommodating than Lewis: he agreed with the Treasury on yet another revision of staff and salaries, and he promised that the existing number of first class clerks would be reduced when the next vacancy occurred.[48] Thus when Fitzgerald retired as chief clerk in 1868 he was replaced by Leslie whose place was not filled by promotion from below. At last the first class clerks numbered three, each of whom (with the chief clerk) had the responsibility of supervising a department.

The most important effect of Grey's reforms was to reduce the numbers and increase the salaries of the senior clerks while conversely increasing the numbers and reducing the salaries of the juniors. Also important was the regularization of the position and salaries of the supplementary clerks who by 1870 were recruited through an examination and placed on the establishment, forming what had become known as the 'supplementary establishment' as opposed to the 'superior establishment' of the other clerks. The number of specialist clerks had been reduced so that the time of officials should be at the disposal of the departmental head and not restricted to one specific and limited job. But one specialist official, who had a potentially important function, was added in 1868. Two years earlier the exchequer and audit departments act stated that civil service expenditure had to be approved by the Treasury before it could be charged to parliamentary votes. The government established the office of comptroller and auditor-general to whom all civil departments were to submit their annual appropriation accounts. These new arrangements led to the appointment at the Home Office of an accountant, A. R. Pennefather.[49] His work was specialized, but what distinguished him from, say, the clerk for criminal business was that he was technically skilled before he entered the office. His status was low: his salary ranked him with a supplementary clerk.

The arrival of a new senior official: 1869

At the other end of the status and salary scale a new senior official was added to the permanent staff. A Treasury Minute[50] of 12 February 1869 had led to the establishment of a new parliamentary counsel's office under the direction of the Home Office counsel, Henry Thring. This left the Home Office without its own legal adviser and the home secretary immediately began to feel the need of one to advise during the passage of public bills and give opinion on private bills which affected its interests. In addition, Gathorne-Hardy's successor, the Liberal, Henry Austin Bruce, found that Liddell was not giving him the support he needed.[51]

The result of this was the appointment in October 1869, of a legal adviser, Godfrey Lushington, who was to remain a leading Home Office official for over twenty-five years. Superficially Lushington was of the same ilk as (though fourteen years younger than) Liddell with whom he was to head the permanent officials of the department for sixteen years. Both had been educated at public schools and Oxford where both became fellows of All Souls; each had had experience at the bar. Lushington, however, had been not at Eton but at Dr Arnold's Rugby where he had been imbued with the ideal of responsible service; and while Liddell had managed only a third from Christ Church, Lushington had been through Jowett's famous 'nursery of public men'[52] at Balliol and acquired a first. Lushington too had party political connections through his family but with the Whig-Liberal cause. His father, an admiralty judge, was several times Whig member of parliament; and he himself had stood unsuccessfully as a Liberal candidate. Moreover, unlike Liddell, he entered the office with the reputation of a radical. At All Souls he had been part of a young group of fellows who protested against the narrow basis on which candidates for fellowships were examined.[53] His youthful passion for reform derived partly from his friendship with the pupils of Richard Congreve at Oxford. Like them he became a positivist and was involved during the 1860s in helping the working classes through the trade union movement.

What, then, must Lushington have made of the 'Spat and Whisker Brigade' at the Home Office whose motto was once described as 'Live and let die'?[54] The ways of his popular colleague, Liddell, were described by a contemporary as 'those of a jovial schoolboy rather than a staid official': he had been known 'in the middle of a serious discussion to whistle a popular air', and he was inseparable from his collie dog which attended him in his room at the Home Office.[55] The chief clerk was said by a comtemporary to have commented, in true Circumlocution Office style,[56] 'that the way to get on in the Civil Service was to do as little as possible, and to do it as quietly as possible'.[57] These attitudes could hardly have been more alien to Lushington whose life was dominated by the gospel of work and who was found 'wanting in his bonhomie and popularity' by his more frivolous contemporaries. Meticulous and painstaking, as his very handwriting shows, 'he had about him much of the schoolmaster'.[58] He was to devote much of his leisure to office work and allegedly even spent his annual leave preparing memoranda. Above all, he was extremely able. He was to be a daunting example to the easy-going Home Office officials.

Reluctant acceptance of open competitive entry for recruits: 1873

In the summer of 1869, largely as the result of pressure on Gladstone from Robert Lowe, then chancellor of the exchequer, the Liberal cabinet debated the subject of open competitive entry to the civil service. Several ministers, including the home secretary, Bruce, proved hostile to the idea. Gladstone proposed that it should be left to departmental chiefs whether or not to recruit to their offices by open competition, and Lowe immediately decided to adopt the scheme at the Treasury. In December a Treasury Minute was drafted setting out the principle of recruiting permanent public servants by open competition. This was accompanied by a letter to all heads of department sounding out their views.[59] Bruce's negative response from the Home Office echoed an argument which had been put forward by opponents of the Northcote-Trevelyan report in the 1850s. With the premise that Home Office work required particular trustworthiness, the home secretary argued:

> The personal knowledge possessed by the Secretary of State of young men appointed by him to clerkships affords a guarantee for their character and honour which has hitherto proved sufficient, and which could not be supplied by unrestricted competition and

mere testimonials to character; while at the same time the present system of competitive examination, which however I am far from regarding as perfect, ensures a competent amount of intellectual training and ability.[60]

This was totally opposed by the Treasury, whence Lowe was pressing departments hard to embrace open competition. His permanent secretary, Ralph Lingen, urged him to 'fight for the principle that the Civil Service Commissioners can judge character and that the Public Departments must in all cases accept their judgment of it'.[61]

The views of Lowe and his senior departmental offficals carried the day with the majority of government offices. An order in council of 4 June 1870 reconfirmed the general arrangements of the 1855 order in council and directed that in future the majority of vacancies to permanent posts in all public offices should be filled with men recruited through open competition. These posts were to come under 'Schedule A'. Posts which – exceptionally – were not filled by open competition were to come under 'Schedule B'. Regulations framed by the civil service commissioners (and approved by the Treasury) subsequently divided Schedule A examinations into two categories: Regulation I, designed to test men of university training for higher administrative posts; and Regulation II, designed to test candidates with an 'ordinary commercial education' for lower, executive posts. Most departments accepted the principle and began negotiations with the Treasury about its adoption.

But there remained firm opposition at the Home Office (and Foreign Office). Bruce's personal view was probably the most important factor in the Home Office reaction. But it was, no doubt, reinforced by general departmental inertia about such a radical idea. Liddell was hardly the man to swim against traditional departmental currents. Lushington was comparatively new and did not then have the influence of Liddell in the office. Departmental heads, according to Liddell, echoed his view that the nature of Home Office work put a premium on the discretion of clerks and that the home secretary should be responsible for their nomination.[62] Maconochie, then a second class clerk, was firmly against open competition.[63]

Treasury officials took no pains to hide their displeasure at this recalcitrant attitude. In fact, there are indications that Bruce did weaken, not only by agreeing to the principle of submitting candidates for supplementary clerkships to open competition, but even to the extent of seriously considering putting the Home Office generally on the 'same footing as the other offices'.[64] But no practical results emerged from this possible shift of view and, as political fortune would have it, Bruce's seat was about to be assumed by Lowe. In August 1873 Gladstone reshuffled his cabinet, removed Bruce to the lord presidency of the council and placed Lowe at the Home Office. The new home secretary lost no time submitting his department to his cherished scheme. Within a month the Treasury received an application from the Home Office. All posts on the establishment were to be gazetted as Schedule A situations; the posts of permanent under-secretary and legal adviser were to come under Schedule B.[65] Treasury officials aggressively backed their erstwhile chief. 'Will you see that no hitch takes place to prevent the notice being gazetted in Thursday's *Gazette*', ran a minute on the Home Office letter;[66] and three days later the decision was formally announced. If there was any reluctance within the Home Office it could not withstand Lowe's determination.

It was to prove, in the long run, a momentous decision for the Home Office. In retrospect Bruce appears to have been a misguided die-hard, suspicious of a system which was, in the event, to transform the civil service into the much-admired body it became in the early twentieth century. Yet there was something to be said for his attitude. His department did not yet require brilliant graduates. Through the system adopted in 1856, which as Bruce himself put it was a 'security against dunces', it was getting the recruits it needed. These were loyal men who could reliably be put to work on sensitive matters, such as the maintenance of order in the metropolis or the rounding up of Fenian activists, and yet who would not be too highly educated to baulk at the drudgery of much of the work. Having agreed to adopt open competition, the office had no actual need of new clerks of the Regulation I category for several years because of internal reorganization. It was not until 1880 that the first of these entered the office, although the first Regulation II entrant (a supplementary clerk) was recruited in 1875.

Internal reorganization: 1876
Between 1870 and 1876 plans, memoranda and minutes circulated at a dizzy rate within the Home Office in an attempt, yet again, to reorganize the role and pay of the officials and the arrangement of their work. By 1870 the office was organized into four main departments. The domestic department was the intermediary between most of the inspectors and the secretary of state and administered a variety of other miscellaneous subjects. The criminal department – now fully established as an important part of the office – dealt with work arising from the administration of the police and

Table 2 The permanent officials of the Home Office establishment, 1870

	Office	No.	Salary (£)		
Senior officials	{ permanent under-secretary	1	2,000		
	{ legal adviser	1	1,000		
Superior establishment	⌠ chief clerk	1	1,000 × 50 –		1,200
	first class clerks	2	700 × 25 –		1,000
	second class clerks	8	350 × 20 –		800
	third class clerks	8	100 × 10 –		300*
	clerk for criminal business (equivalent to first class clerk)	1	700 × 25 –		1,000
	clerk for signet business†	1	600		
	⌡ TOTAL (higher grade)	21			
Supplementary establishment	⌠ supplementary clerks	7 { 4	250 × 10 –		350
		{ 3	100 × 10 –		200
	clerks for local taxation returns	2	150 × 10 –		300
	accountant	1	250 × [10 – 15] – 400		
	⌡ TOTAL (lower grade)	10			
	TOTAL (all officials)	33			

Cost of Home Office senior officials and clerical staff
1870–71 = £15,345 (annual estimates)

*The third class clerk acting as private secretary to the parliamentary under-secretary earned an additional £150 p.a.
†Sometimes classed in the supplementary establishment.

prisons, and from 'the general administration of criminal law'.[67] These departments together consisted of two first class, six second class and six third class clerks (now more commonly known as 'principal', 'senior' or 'assistant', and 'junior' clerks, respectively) and four supplementary clerks. The clerks' functions were as follows: all the incoming letters were docketed, registered and joined with earlier papers by junior and supplementary clerks. They were then passed up to the head of department (a principal clerk) who by this date had acquired the role of minuting on a course of action. The letters were then forwarded to one of the under-secretaries who either initialled the minutes or wrote his own, consulting the secretary of state or legal adviser about any doubtful cases. The letters were then returned to the departments where the senior clerks turned the minutes into formal replies which were passed back to one of the under-secretaries for signature, copied out into a letter book by a junior or supplementary clerk and despatched. The only clerks, therefore, whose work called for any judgment were the principal clerks who not only had to see to the running of their departments but also had to make suggestions as to administrative action. In fact the minutes of the principal clerks of this period were on the whole fairly simple: in straightforward cases they referred to precedents or gave stock replies; anything complicated they left to an under-secretary. The work of the seniors needed experience but not originality, although they did have to deputize for the principals during their two months' annual leave. The juniors were solely concerned with registry work and copying, and this could be their work for 'ten or even fifteen years'.[68]

In the chief clerk's department he, a senior, a junior, four supplementary clerks and the accountant prepared statistics and various other parliamentary returns. There was also a warrants and appointments branch, where a principal, a senior, a junior and a supplementary clerk did all the formal work for the preparation of warrants of appointment, licences, commissions and so on. In addition there was a small, temporary roads branch, concerned with the running down of the turnpike trust system. The work of all these clerks still primarily required care, accuracy and experience. It was not intellectually demanding.

Government departments were under pressure, partly from Treasury officials and partly as the result of the reforming instincts of Gladstone's first cabinet. A cabinet committee memorandum of 1869 'explicitly recognized' the principle of separating intellectual from mechanical work in the civil service, and stated that departments should have two established classes of permanent executive officers, backed up by non-permanent writers.[69] In December 1869 the Treasury formally requested departments to reduce expenditure by cutting down the numbers of their permanent staff.[70] As a result, Bruce commissioned an internal inquiry into Home Office organization. No permanent officials sat on the committee whose members consisted of E. Knatchbull-Hugesson (parliamentary under-secretary), Lord Morley (the home secretary's representative in the House of Lords) and A. O. Rutson (Bruce's private secretary). It was asked whether any reduction in staff could effectively be made and whether the work could be reorganized so as to leave the purely mechanical work to supplementary clerks and writers.

The committee was most concerned about the role of the junior clerks whose work of copying, filing and docketing was barely distinguishable from that of the supplementary clerks. It proposed the creation of a new, single departmental registry which eventually would be staffed by supplementary clerks and temporarily-employed writers under the supervision of a senior clerk. This would relieve the juniors of the tedium of entering and filing papers. The committee suggested that fewer superior establishment clerks should be engaged on routine work such as the preparation of warrants and statistics which could be done by supplementary clerks. A reduction in the number of senior and junior clerks was recommended together with an increase in pay – along the lines of a projected increase for Treasury clerks – for the remaining seniors and juniors.[71]

The committee urged principal clerks to allow their seniors and juniors more responsibility at an earlier stage in their careers. It also objected to the inefficiency, particularly in the chief clerk's department, 'of assigning to one or more clerks certain duties, at one time needing the whole, at another only part, of their official hours, and practically limiting their obligation to the performance of these duties'.[72] Clearly, despite Grey's efforts, office tradition was still holding firm – in at least one department – against this reform which, perhaps more than any of the new ideas, struck at the basis of their old existence. They may not have performed duties which demanded much intellect, but at least they, and they alone, knew their work. Now they were being asked to be adaptable: not to be the expert on one tiny area of Home Office administration, but to be able to move around and take up work wherever necessary. These reforms – the devolving of responsibility on to more junior clerks and the more effective deployment of staff by heads of department – were difficult to put into effect in the Home Office. For they depended on the discretion and co-operation of the more senior clerks and could not be effected simply by circulating a list of instructions from the secretary of state. However, Bruce – like Grey before him – did his best by urging heads of department to pay special attention to these suggestions.[73]

The most important outcome of the report was Bruce's establishment of a new central registry which, apart from three part-time junior clerks, was entirely staffed by supplementary clerks and writers.[74] So started what was to grow into an effective executive back-up service for the decision-making part of the office.[75] The proposals about staff and pay were thwarted by bad relations with the Treasury, which was already displeased about Bruce's lack of co-operation over open competition. Far from applauding his proposals for staff reductions, Treasury officials urged far more drastic cuts in superior establishment staff which should, they argued, amount in total to no more than three times the number of heads of department (or principal clerks). This would have given the Home Office a superior establishment of around twelve, rather than the proposed seventeen.

As the Treasury explained, 'These relative numbers become feasible if such second and third class clerks are relieved of mechanical work ... and are confined to the duty of assisting the senior clerk in minuting answers on the simple cases, and in preparing materials for minutes on the rest.'[76] But this kind of reduction was much further than the Home Office was willing to go. Nor was it alone in this: Rutson produced figures for the ratio of principal to other superior establishment clerks at the Foreign Office and Colonial Office and found that their arrangements were even further from the Treasury's ideal.[77] Such a change would have meant a Home Office largely staffed by supplementary clerks and writers. In terms of the work this would have been feasible, but no minister – certainly not the home secretary – was likely to want apparently to down-grade his department to such an extent. Moreover, when it referred to superior establishment staff, the Treasury explicitly meant university graduates, recruited through open competition; and Home Office clerks were not of this calibre.

Nevertheless, there was a good deal of slack which could have been taken up. Even the Home Office clerks were finding their duties irksome and their talents under-utilized: '... bets were made as to whether more vehicles would pass up the street or down the street within a specified time, or as to the colour of the horses'.[78] There are plenty of tales of cricket in the corridors and tennis in the courtyard. Some put their time to more productive use: A. P. Graves, a considerable Celtic scholar, wrote his *Songs of Killarney* and contributed to the *Spectator* and the *Examiner* while a private secretary. He found the civil service full of 'men of literary taste who combined writing in some form or other with their official duties'.[79] Other departments had their quota of bored clerks: even at the Treasury an official later recorded how he and his contemporaries 'had a good deal of time on our hands in the late 1860s'.[80] But by 1870 the Treasury equivalent of junior clerks were already preparing minutes and memoranda.

Discussion about reform continued for the next six years. It was, above all, the parliamentary under-secretaries who were set by their respective chiefs to consider the matter. Existing records show Liddell and Lushington to have concerned themselves comparatively little with departmental reorganization. The only career official who wrote substantial memoranda on it was Maconochie who was not even head of a department until 1876. Interestingly, at the Colonial Office, undergoing similar reconstruction between 1868 and 1872, attempts were made to enlist the support of the senior clerks; but they too 'had little or no interest in reorganization'.[81] This was probably the case at the Home Office. After all, every proposal for reform involved the immediate retirement of the chief clerk and two of the three principal clerks (each of whom had been in the office for over forty-five years) which may well have accounted for their lack of concern for the future of the office.

Debate crystallized into a plan – more radical in terms of cuts than Bruce's – and was submitted by Lowe to the Treasury in 1874. The office was to be divided into three rather than four departments: it was felt that the work of the chief clerk's department and the warrants and appointments branch could reasonably be merged which would allow for greater flexibility in the disposal of staff. The nineteen superior establishment clerks were to be reduced substantially by the immediate retirement of the ageing chief clerk and three others, while five others would not be replaced when they retired. This eventually would leave eleven, none of whom – apart from the two private secretaries[82] – would have specific named functions so that they could be moved around the office if necessary. Once again there was a proposal for salary increases at all levels for established clerks. The supplementary establishment was to be given greater status and form by the creation of two staff posts: the head of the registry and a senior statistics clerk. These officials, together with the accountant, would head an increased supplementary establishment, specifically designed to perform the routine work of the office.[83]

The path to reform was not to be smooth. Even Lowe's plan led to Treasury haggling over retirement terms and over suggested salaries for the supplementary clerks.[84] Then, in February 1874 the Liberal government fell and the Conservative, Richard Assheton Cross, succeeded Lowe at the Home Office. The following year Cross submitted a similar, though slightly less drastic plan than Lowe's, with one significant addition. He suggested that the chief clerkship be abolished – a suggestion mooted as long ago as 1848 by the Select Committee on Miscellaneous Expenditure. This was quite a blow at the traditional Home Office structure of which the post had been an integral part since its formation in 1782; and to reach the chief clerkship had represented the summit of a successful clerk's achievement. The chief clerk was in charge of personnel matters – not an onerous duty at that time – and, from 1866, he was formally responsible for office finances after the adoption in all government departments of the new accounting arrangements. In February 1874 the Treasury had declared that a chief clerk was unnecessary in departments where there was an assistant secretary. At that time the Home Office had no such officer. However, shortly before Cross submitted his plan, Lushington had requested a salary increase which led Cross to suggest promoting him to 'legal assistant under-secretary' – a proposal which was subsequently adopted.[85] The chief clerk's responsibilities could easily be transferred to the senior principal clerk, and thus there was no reason beyond sentiment to maintain his office. The title did not disappear until the retirement in 1885 of C. Erskine (the next in line for the post) who was allowed the old salary and title of chief clerk as a courtesy towards his expectations.

Cross's plan proved abortive for two reasons. First, discussion was widened by a proposal to amalgamate the staff of the sub-departments (including the large staff of the prisons department) with that of the central department when the office moved into new quarters further down Whitehall in August 1875. Secondly, the Civil Service (Playfair) Inquiry Commission was about to produce a report which would have a bearing on the staffing of all government departments. The commission, set up to examine the selection, inter-departmental transfer and grading of civil servants, produced its first report in December 1874.[86] The commissioners found in many departments the problems which were being discussed at the Home Office, in particular, the unclear division of labour between the lower end of the superior establishment and the supplementary clerks. They also found enormous discrepancies in salary levels in different departments. Their recommendations were based on an attempt to solve these problems. The report endorsed the Northcote-Trevelyan concept of civil service reform and, therefore, the order in council of 4 June 1870 dividing the service into two distinct classes of clerk. It recommended that Class II entrants should constitute the bulk of the civil service, should be called the 'lower division' and should be common to the whole service. Thus the problem of salary differentials would be solved at this level and redundant clerks in one department could be transferred to fill up vacancies in another. This scheme was put into effect through an order in council of 12 February 1876.[87] The salaries of lower division clerks were to start at £80 and rise by triennial increments of £15 to £200 in those offices – such as the Home Office – which worked a six hour day. Before the end of 1876 new lower division recruits began to enter the Home Office.[88]

The same year a complete reorganization of the Home Office establishment was finally achieved. The basic principles of the earlier plans of Lowe and Cross were followed: the creation of three internal departments – domestic, criminal and general; a consider-able reduction in the number of superior establishment (or upper division) clerks together with an increase in their salaries; the creation of staff officers at the head of an enlarged Class II (lower division) establishment; and the abolition of the chief clerkship.[89] A new feature was the incorporation into the establishment of the inspectors' clerks – all Class II clerks – most of whom moved with the central secretariat into the new Home Office building in August 1875, although it was decided not to include the staff of the prison department which was currently undergoing a separate review.[90]

The final reconstruction was not achieved without the customary battles with the Treasury over details. There were several months of altercation, two inter-departmental meetings and one joint report on the lower division staff before full agreement was reached. Two points of dispute are interesting in illustrating the continuing differences in Treasury and Home Office thinking about the role of officials. One difficulty was the upper division's increased salaries. Cross proposed two grades (and therefore salary scales) for the junior clerks on the grounds that the considerable reduction in the number of the more senior posts would seriously reduce the junior clerks' prospects and that a two-tier salary for them would ease this situation.[91] His argument was based on the assumption that if it were not for the reorganization all these young clerks, in the natural course of events, could have expected to proceed to the next grade. Now there would be a blockage for some of them. But the idea that clerks should be compensated for loss of promotion prospects was related to the question of whether promotion should be made on seniority or on merit. The Treasury firmly upheld merit as the criterion and therefore opposed the claim put forward on the young clerks' behalf which 'assumes an absolute right of succession from class to class by seniority only'.[92] Eventually the Treasury's pay scale was adopted but the officials whose prospects were thought to have been impaired were generously compensated.[93]

Another debate centred around the nature of the work done by certain upper division officials. The Treasury disliked the proposed staffing arrangements for the new general department in which it was intended to place three upper division clerks. It pointed out that the criminal and domestic departments were the two most important because they were responsible – in theory anyway – for drafting correspondence and controlling a large and increasing body of inspectors. It was therefore quite right that they should be staffed by upper division clerks with upper division salaries. But the general department, which was to do the registry, statistical and accounting work, was largely intended to service the other two departments and its functions were basically routine. Why, then, asked the Treasury, did it need to be staffed by any upper division clerks at all? And, if it did not, could the Home Office not further reduce its upper division?[94] Such interference in the running of his department, in Cross's eyes, went considerably beyond the Treasury's accepted powers. After all, his proposals amounted, all told, to a reduction in the total cost of the Home Office establishment. Yet the Treasury was now suggesting that the internal staffing of the department should be organized not as he, the home secretary, had suggested would be most efficacious, but simply so as to cut costs further. The argument dragged on for weeks, but Cross – to the fury of Lingen – refused to compromise and went ahead with his own arrangements for the general department.[95]

It is worth comparing the Home Office establishment of 1876 with that of 1848 and 1870.[96] In 1848 there were twenty-two permanent

Table 3   *The permanent officials of the Home Office establishment after the 1876 reforms*

	Office	No.	Salary (£)
Senior officials {	permanent under-secretary	1	2,000
	assistant under-secretary (legal)	1	1,200
Upper division {	chief clerk*	1	$1,000 \times 50 - 1,200$
	principal clerks	2	$900 \times 50 - 1,000$
	senior clerks	3	$700 \times 25 - 800$
	junior clerks	7	$200 \times 20 - 600$[†]
	TOTAL (upper division)	13	
Lower division {	clerk in charge of accounts	1	$400 \times 20 - 600$
	examiner of police claims[‡]	1	$400 \times 20 - 550$
	clerk for statistical returns	1	$350 \times 15 - 500$
	superintendent of the registry	1	$350 \times 15 - 500$
	supplementary clerks	4 {2 / 2	$250 \times 10 - 350$ / $100 \times 10 - 200$
	inspectors' clerks	2 {1 / 1	$150 \times 15 - 400$ / $100 \times 5 - 200$
	lower division clerks	11	$90 \times 15 - 250$[§]
	TOTAL (lower division)	21	

TOTAL (senior officials and clerks)   36
Cost of Home Office senior officials and clerical staff
1877–8[‖] = £15,811 (annual estimates)

*Title and salary to be abolished on next vacancy when principal clerks to be increased to three.
[†]Two junior clerks earned additional pay: the private secretary to the secretary of state, £300 p.a., and the private secretary to the parliamentary under-secretary, £150 p.a.
[‡]See p. 102
[§]This does not include 'duty pay' for which see p. 110
[‖]This was the first year the establishment changes appeared in the civil service estimates.

officials on the establishment at a cost of £13,406; in addition there were a few supplementary clerks who were not considered part of the establishment and were paid separately. By 1870 there were thirty-three officials: two senior officials, twenty-one superior establishment and ten supplementary establishment clerks at a total cost of £15,345. After the 1876 reforms there were thirty-six permanent officials: two senior officials, thirteen upper division and twenty-one lower division and supplementary clerks at minimal extra cost (£15,811 in 1877–8). Thus the long-term effect of the changes of this period was a substantial increase in the size of the establishment with very little rise in cost. This was achieved through the growth of the lower class of official who by 1876 substantially outnumbered the higher class: in fact, the ratio of upper to lower division officials was more or less reversed between 1870 and 1876.

Reform, inspired by the desire to make government more efficient, had totally changed the Home Office of Plasket and his contemporaries. Nomination had been replaced by open competition. A new and substantial executive branch had grown up below the old established clerks and had taken over many of their functions. Gone forever was the old specialization which tied a man forever to one particular job. The department was no longer the independent institution it had once been but was now equated with other senior government departments in terms of salaries and organization by that superior Whitehall body, the Treasury.[97] These far-reaching changes had been imposed on the permanent establishment by its political head and other external forces. Orders in council resulting from cabinet decisions were binding on all departments. The Treasury enforced its decisions through Treasury Minutes and through the more indirect but very effective means of persistent pressure in its correspondence whenever the subject of staff and salary changes arose. Clearly there were differences between the Treasury and home secretaries over reform: it was hard for ministers to acclimatize to the lessening of their independence and the home secretary, after all, ranked high in ministerial precedence. Moreover, however zealous a home secretary may have been about reform, this must always have been tempered by considerations such as the conservatism of the office and the need to maintain departmental morale. But the differences between the Treasury and home secretaries such as Grey, Lowe and Cross, were ones of degree rather than substance: after all it was often the home secretary who would set up a committee of inquiry which might well contain a Treasury representative.

But there were aspects of reform which had not yet been resolved and which no amount of external exhortation and pressure could enforce. There was no sign that the time-honoured system of promotion by seniority had been abandoned. Probation virtually did not exist. Moreover, no amount of encouraging departmental heads to pass down more responsible work to their subordinates was likely to have any effect until upper division officials were encouraged by the under-secretaries to do more responsible minuting. And there was still no need for this since the secretary of state and his under-secretaries could still themselves cope with most of the important minuting and bill work. Thus, although the office had been divided into upper and lower divisions in order to differentiate between 'intellectual' and 'mechanical' work, the upper division was still too large for a totally effective distinction of this kind.

How many people, one wonders, spoke up for the pre-reform clerks? Graham had done in 1830 from his experience of them in the days before they were seriously under attack: 'They labour almost unseen, without any reward except their salary. Their zeal for the public service, and their exemplary and trustworthy conduct, speaking generally, exceed any praise that I can bestow upon them.'[98] But once the onslaught on government clerks gathered momentum their champions seemed to dwindle. Most striking, perhaps, is their own apparent lack of retaliation. Either they were not given a chance or did not feel inclined to defend their existing role by arguing that, for the functions of the office as they then were, the staff was reasonably effective. No one knows what verbal mutterings and protests went on behind their desks and inkstands. But none was asked to sit on a committee of reorganization and Maconochie appears to stand alone as a clerk who put his views about reform on paper. In short, the older clerks of the Home Office were not an effective pressure group against the new ideas of the day: rationalization, examination and competition.

Part II The Development of the Central Secretariat

3 The late-Victorian Home Office and the new élite: 1876–96

The effects of open competitive entry

In 1880 C. E. Troup entered the Home Office as the first open competition recruit to a junior clerkship. He was the first Home Office member of a new generation which was beginning to permeate the whole civil service. In every department 'a ferment was at work owing to the introduction of the democratic system of entry by competitive examination, which paid no heed to family trees and recognized no aristocracy but that of brains'.[1] For Troup's contemporaries, with their laudable university degrees, were entering the civil service in search of professional careers suitable to their intellectual talent. Between 1880 and 1914 forty-five young men entered the Home Office upper division (or first division as it was formally called after 1890).[2] Three of these were promoted from the ranks of the lower (or second) division; three others transferred from other departments they had previously entered without degrees; and the remaining thirty-nine came in as recent graduates, some on transfer from other departments within one or two years of their entry into the civil service.

The popularity among university graduates of the Class I examination, with its wide range of subjects, produced, as the potential leaders of central officialdom, precisely the type of young men which Jowett had foreseen when he had designed a prototype examination in the 1850s. The Home Office was no exception to the classic predominance of Oxford men with good greats degrees: nine of the twelve graduates who entered the department between 1880 and 1896 had degrees from Oxford where all except one had read greats; and every first division graduate entrant between 1896 and 1914 came either from Oxford or Cambridge: eighteen from Oxford and nine from Cambridge, of whom at least eighteen had read greats or classics.[3] The dominance of Oxford and Cambridge recruits is well known and its causes are not hard to find. It was due partly to the 'immemorial prestige' of the two ancient universities from which men graduated at a 'more mature age', having 'the advantage of a more thorough and finished learning' which made them more acceptable than other graduates.[4] The raising in 1890 of the minimum entry age of candidates from eighteen to twenty-two made it difficult for those who graduated from other universities at a slightly younger age to join the civil service directly after taking their degrees. In addition, the exclusive and powerful standing of classical studies, particularly at Oxford, contrasted with wider courses of other universities and gave classics graduates a distinct advantage in the examination. These factors all contributed to a new tradition among Oxford and Cambridge undergraduates, which became firmly rooted during the late-Victorian period, that a prestigious career for alumni was to be found in service to the state in the upper reaches of the civil service.

It followed that a large proportion of the new type of entrant had been schooled at good public day or boarding schools which middle-class parents found the most satisfactory preparation for their sons to enter Oxford or Cambridge. Scholarships were of course available both at public schools and at Oxford and Cambridge colleges for clever boys whose parents could not afford the fees. But while the mid-century university reforms had opened up Oxford and Cambridge to the middle classes they had had the effect of restricting places for the poor: awards were thrown open to merit alone as many scholarship places traditionally reserved for poor students from specific schools or localities were swept away.[5] This naturally favoured those from privileged schools; and the older public schools themselves were becoming more exclusive, abandoning their ancient obligations to educate local children.[6] Thus the new men of the Home Office tended to come from an income group which could afford this kind of education. It was not an invariable rule: Troup himself, the son of a congregationalist minister, had been educated at a Scottish parish school and at the University of Aberdeen before acquiring 'polish' at Oxford;[7] A. J. Eagleston, whose father was once an ironmonger, had been at the City of Oxford High School from which he gained a Balliol scholarship. But on the whole the social backgrounds of the upper division Home Office clerks did not change dramatically as the result of open competitive entry. Fewer appeared in *Burke's Peerage*; fewer were the sons of public officials (and none – as far as is known – was related to another Home Office official); there was the occasional man whose father would not have been described as 'professional' or a 'gentleman'. But the men of the new generation tended, like their predecessors, to be sons of upper middle-class men, often with professional occupations.

The Home Office ranked high in terms of pay and prestige which meant that it probably attracted among the best recruits.[8] The regulations allowed candidates to choose current vacancies according to their position on the results list. It is possible, therefore, to assess the popularity of a department by examining the choices made by successful candidates. Between 1880 and 1896 six recruits entered the Home Office directly after their examination. Of the nine departments which offered vacancies only the Treasury and Colonial Office were consistently favoured above the Home Office. The latter, in its turn, was always chosen before the Post Office, Inland Revenue, War Office and Local Government Board.[9] This hierarchy is confirmed by the choices made by those who transferred early in their careers from one department to another under the provisions of Clause VII of the 1870 order in council. Departmental preference is well illustrated by the progress of E. G. Harman who moved from the Admiralty to the Home Office to the Treasury.[10]

These departmental differences left ajar the door to patronage as the entry of E. Ruggles-Brise to the department illustrates. He succeeded in the Civil Service Commission examination of 1881 but decided to take advantage of his option to turn down the department initially offered and await a better one. Within a week or two of the expiry of his six months' time limit he and his family were evidently worried. His father, Sir Samuel Ruggles-Brise MP, wrote to the home secretary, Sir William Harcourt, requesting him, if it were true that there was an imminent vacancy in his department, to let the Civil Service Commission know about it immediately so that his son's appointment should not go by default. He also persuaded a colleague, Sir John Lubbock MP, to support his son with a personal recommendation.[11] Harcourt was co-operative and Ruggles-Brise found he had been appointed to the Home Office. Later Harcourt openly claimed credit in parliament for having actually recruited him – a claim which Matthews hotly denied in view of the existence of the open competitive system.[12] Inter-departmental transfers also gave scope for a vestige of patronage: 'connection' with another department almost certainly oiled the wheels in an application for transfer. Suspicion of this in Harman's case prompted a parliamentary question to which the bland reply came that the criterion for such transfers was ability, proven by experience.[13]

The new men had all the confidence and arrogance of an elite. Troup found his new department full of 'a lot of old people drawing £1,000 a year and dozing through routine duties...who were not worth 50 shillings a week'.[14] L. N. Guillemard, who entered the office in 1886, contemptuously described it as 'the last stronghold of the die-hards of the old school'.[15] For these new recruits brilliance at examination was the criterion for ability and success: Ruggles-Brise believed that no one who could not 'take a First in Greats...can be really first rate'.[16] This was strong meat even for the under-secretaries of the day (although, fortunately perhaps for order and morale, Lushington was quite up to scratch) but it was no doubt insufferable to the older clerks who doubtless shared the view of a contemporary Colonial Office official: 'The "cocksureness" of the rising race of civil servants...is remarkable. They seem never to have heard of the saying that "we are none of us infallible, not even the youngest".'[17] If the older clerks could not combat the talent of the new arrivals, they at least tried to keep them in their place by appealing to traditional departmental mores. Once, when Troup – through circumstances of death and illness – was placed temporarily in charge of the criminal department, the dismayed Knyvett pointed out the impropriety of this:

> Mr. Troup (whom I am told is most efficient) is a 'Junior' acting as a 'Senior' clerk – whilst he has seniors in the office, who are not thus temporarily engaged as 'Senior Clerks'. If they are fit to act as 'Senior Clerks', then they, if not transferred, will likewise be in false positions; and by acquiescing in Mr. Troup's employment as a 'Senior' over their heads they may possibly be injuring their prospects in the office.[18]

Clearly the transition of the office from its traditional leisurely pattern into a modern institution of government was going to pose certain personnel problems.

A new work problem
The ideas for civil service reform had been put forward in the middle of the century before there appeared to be a need for radical change at the Home Office. Yet the considerable time lag between the publication of the Northcote-Trevelyan report and the actual recruitment to the department of upper division officials through open competition meant that their abilities began to be required before they were allowed by departmental tradition to assume responsibility. For Troup was not promoted to a senior clerkship

until 1886; and H. B. Simpson (the next to be thus promoted) not until 1894. Meanwhile, the older clerks of the comparatively small upper division had been struck by a new phenomenon: an unprecedented increase in the volume and complexity of work.

It is difficult to be precise about when the office first seriously felt the pressure of new business. In 1873 Liddell had been worried about pressure to reduce the upper division because Home Office business was 'continually increasing'. Between 1862 and 1872 the annual number of incoming papers was thought to have risen from 18,659 to 30,047.[19] He was concerned about the amount of correspondence, applications and circulars generated by the 1872 coal mines regulation act, with its stipulation that every coal mine was to be under the control and daily supervision of a manager nominated by the mine-owner and certified by the Home Office. In 1877 the equilibrium of the criminal department was threatened by the prision act of that year which brought local prisons under the central supervision and authority of the newly formed Prison Commission, a new sub-department of the office. Settlements had to be made with local prison authorities, circulars sent out, and continual correspondence from new local visiting committees answered. In 1878 the head of the criminal department, Maconochie, complained to Lushington about having to take work home in order to keep up, alleging that the state of his eyes had temporarily forced him to give up work.[20]

The domestic department became similarly afflicted. In 1881 the senior clerk, C. G. Campbell, wrote a miserable letter to Lushington from Lausanne, where he was on holiday recovering from the strain of having been in charge of his department while the principal clerk, C. Erskine, was on leave. (A gentlemanly two months' holiday remained an annual feature, despite these crises.)

> When Erskine returned I could not have done another day's work, and I can bring the highest medical evidence in London to show that I was reduced to a state of complete prostration. When I went to Scotland later I was quite useless, and never had a salmon rod or a gun in my hands the whole time I was there, and I was strongly urged either to apply for long sick leave or to leave the Home Office altogether.[21]

Erskine supported Campbell, pointing out the increase in work since 1876 when the staff had been reduced to the lowest possible level. He complained of both the work which derived from the many inspectorates supervised by the domestic department – mentioning in particular the 1875 explosives act and the 1876 cruelty to animals act – and the legislation which directly affected his department.[22]

Throughout the 1870s government departments continued to

undertake new responsibilities as life in England became increasingly subject to central control. For instance, Disraeli's Conservative government of 1874–80 produced 'the largest crop of social legislation yielded by any British administration before that of 1906'.[23] Space does not permit a list of all the acts of the 1870s which increased the responsibilities of the home secretary. But taking a couple of years at random it is possible to pick out acts which contributed to the work-load: in 1876 the wild fowl preservation, convict prison returns, winter assizes, cruelty to animals and merchant shipping acts; in 1879 the spring assizes, habitual drunkards (which led to the establishment of a new inspectorate), prosecution of offences, salmon fishery law amendment, petroleum, elementary education (industrial schools), and shipping casualties investigation acts. Some acts primarily affected the sub-departments, but all led to increased work for the domestic and criminal departments, even if only by creating a greater flow of paper. Between 1872 and 1880 the annual number of incoming papers was estimated to have grown by 48 per cent from 30,047 to 44,541.[24]

Harcourt, as home secretary, felt as oppressed as did his departmental clerks. In 1881, grumbling about the 'formidable growth in the number of inspectors', he argued:

> Nothing would be more satisfactory to the Secretary of State than to be able by any means to relieve his Department of these burthens ... by 'throwing details on local administration' but unfortunately of late the policy of Parliament has been exactly in the opposite direction ... relieving the local ratepayer by throwing at once the responsibility and the cost of sustaining it on the Central Administration.[25]

It was not merely that the office was having to deal with more papers but also that legislation was making new demands on officials:

> ... the tendency is for the work of the office to increase through the Acts of Parliament that are passed now not defining exactly what is to be done, but leaving a great deal of the detail to be worked out afterwards by the Secretary of State.[26]

Thus, while the prison act formulated the principle of central take-over and rationalization of local prisons, it was up to the Home Office to select the prisons which were to be discontinued and decide the basis on which settlements were to be made with prison authorities about the transfer or abolition of their prisons. For the significant new feature was delegated legislation whereby authorities, including government departments, were permitted by acts of parliament to make detailed regulations. The large consolidating industrial acts are good examples of this: the 1875 explosives act empowered the secretary of state to issue bye-laws governing the handling of explosives and to recommend orders in council extending the act to other explosives. Thus, although much of the additional work which the principal and senior clerks were complaining about might at first appear to have been temporary, lasting only as long as it took to put the legislation into operation, in fact many comprehensive pieces of legislation brought permanent extra work to the department.

In addition, heads of department – almost unnoticed – were acquiring increased responsibilities. Troup pointed out in 1885, during his temporary headship of the criminal department, that departmental officials were now making decisions and judgements of an unprecedented kind. He observed, for example that formerly nine-tenths of the metropolitan police expenditure was passed on the mere recommendation of the receiver of the metropolitan police without his even having to give particulars; now full details of all expenditure were carefully examined by criminal department officials. Police pensions had earlier been granted 'simply on the recommendation of the Commissioner'; now the medical reports and default sheets were sent in to be read and examined, and the papers had to be fully minuted. Discharges from reformatory and industrial schools were formerly granted 'without question on the recommendation of the Inspector'; but now all applications for discharge have to be minuted in the Department'.[27] All these additional responsibilities called for far more considered examination of incoming papers.

The department reacted to pressure by trying to have responsibilities removed from it wherever this was politically acceptable. Harcourt suggested to Gladstone in 1882 that a projected 'ministry of commerce' might include part of his department's work. He also put it that the regulation of mines, factories and workshops, and the supervision of freshwater fisheries belonged more properly to 'trade' than to the Home Office, 'which should be confined as much as possible to Law, Justice and Criminal Administration'.[28] In 1885, when a cemeteries bill was being discussed, he shared the alarm of one of his senior clerks at the possibility of more work being thrown upon the office and agreed that it would be better to transfer all burial work from the Home Office to the Local Government Board.[29] For the time being this proposal failed. However, two subsequent acts did remove some work from the department. In 1885 the secretary for Scotland act diverted some responsibilities – particularly those connected with police and prisons – to the new

Scottish Office. The following year the salmon and freshwater fisheries act transferred all responsibility for this subject (and therefore the inspectorate itself) to the Board of Trade.[30] These changes may have eased matters: certainly the number of incoming papers does not appear to have increased to the same extent during the next few years.[31]

The Home Office would dearly have liked to increase its upper division staff. Troup strongly urged the addition of an extra official in the criminal department in 1885; and this plea was echoed by Campbell for the domestic department.[32] Lushington himself, after becoming permanent under-secretary in 1885, thought an additional under-secretary might be necessary.[33] But none of these requests appear to have been formulated into applications to the Treasury despite Harcourt's scorn about its notion of civil service economy. ('All this economy talk is for the "gallery" and not real business,' he claimed. 'The real truth is that there has been much growth of work and little growth of expenditure in the Civil Service of late years.')[34] For the principle of maintaining the upper division at the lowest possible level while allowing lower division clerks responsibility for everything which could possibly be termed routine – a principle which had been put forward by the Playfair Commission in 1875 and was to be reiterated by the Ridley Commission in 1887 – continued to be pursued relentlessly by the Treasury. After the Ridley Commission had reported it circularized departments asking to what extent they could reduce their upper divison staff – a query to which the Home Office replied categorically in the negative.[35]

Since there was little opportunity either for transferring responsibilities from the department or for acquiring more staff, senior Home Office officials were forced to conform to Treasury wishes: to devolve responsibility at all levels in the upper division. Shortly after his promotion in 1885, Lushington sounded out his principal clerks about the problems of overwork which even he, the arch-glutton for work, was beginning to find a strain. They put forward suggestions for giving heads of department more responsibility in order to relieve pressure at the under-secretary level. Campbell suggested that the lithographed signature of the permanent under-secretary might be used on certain categories of routine letters with which he need not then be bothered. But hard-pressed as they felt, the two older heads of department, Campbell and Knyvett, remained hostile to the idea of juniors being allowed to minute papers. 'I cannot say that I hold with such a view, believing as I do, that some experience and training are necessary before a minute can be of any value to an Under-Secretary,' expostulated Knyvett.[36] It was Troup who, for the criminal department, analysed clearly the kind of work which heads of department might do. First, 'while all *decisions* must be approved by the Secretary of State or Under-Secretary, inquiries leading up to decisions, and results necessarily following from decisions may be dealt with by the Department. Secondly, whenever the department was working 'within well defined rules' ordinary cases could be settled without reference to the under-secretaries. Thirdly, 'mere requests for information not of special importance might be dealt with by the Department'.[37]

In his support for these proposals Lushington showed his awareness of the profound change which was gradually occurring in departmental administration. While the 'established rule of the Office' had always been that every paper coming in or going out went through the under-secretaries, who alone could make minutes equivalent to orders and sign letters, this was no longer going to be possible. Since the parliamentary under-secretary was frequently 'occupied with Deputations, Committees, attendance in Parliament etc.', the bulk of the work fell on the other two under-secretaries. He estimated that by this date (1886) an annual 47,000 letters came into the office which gave seventy-five a day to each of them. A single difficult case, let alone the absence of the other, made it difficult for an under-secretary to get through the day's work.

> It is not merely that the employment of the Under-Secretary in revising much of the formal work done by the clerks . . . is unnecessary and therefore a wasteful and expensive arrangement; but the multitude of those unimportant papers distracts the attention of the Under-Secretary from more serious work, hurries him, and prevents him from giving to it the proper time, and rendering to the Secretary of State such assistance as is rightly expected from him.[38]

The changes which were sanctioned at this time were, in retrospect, extremely moderate and probably did not go far enough. Lushington wanted 'to proceed by degrees and with caution'. However, they set in motion a process of devolution which affected all levels of the office. For the time being papers of any significance still went to the under-secretaries, but the minutes of the principal and senior clerks became more substantial so that the under-secretaries could often simply initial them rather than write out full draft replies. Murdoch claimed in 1888 that 'in a large number of cases the minutes of the Juniors do go forward as the recommendation of the Under-Secretary'.[39] This may have been over-optimistic. The same year L. N. Guillemard, in despair at ever being given responsibility in the Home Office, had left it for the Treasury – an experience he likened to 'coming out of a morgue and into a busy workshop'. But even he admitted that during his two years in the office the juniors had been 'relieved of the menial work of writing out letters for signature' and had been 'allowed to read and minute some of the less important papers on their arrival'.[40] What had happened, then, was that the under-secretaries had been divested of some of their responsibilities by the already over-burdened principal and senior clerks, all of who had been recruited before the days of open competition for less demanding work. Meanwhile, some of the abler juniors, although undertaking more responsibility than their predecessors, still felt that their talents were under-utilized.

The changing relationship between the Home Office and its sub-departments[41]

It might have been thought that the central officials' sense of being over-burdened would have led to the greater administrative independence of the sub-departments. Under-secretaries and heads of department, flustered by the great influx of paper, might have been tempted to rely increasingly on the decisions of the inspectors, the prison commissioners or the commissioner of metropolitan police without much additional consideration. In fact the very reverse was true. The role of the pricipal clerks as an important link between heads of sub-departments and the under-secretaries had hitherto been somewhat embryonic. But by the late 1870s at least one principal clerk was conscious of the importance of this function. The machinery for control had always been there. In both the criminal and domestic departments the system of passing all incoming papers through the departmental clerks and up to the under-secretaries, then back through the departmental clerks to the sub-departments, ensured that, even if they acted as little more than a post-box, at least the principal clerks saw all the important papers of the sub-departments with which they were concerned. And when various heads of sub-departments, yearning for greater autonomy and frustrated by this cumbersome method of dealing with papers, tried to by-pass the system, they were firmly put in their place by departmental officials.

It was Maconochie, head of the criminal department, who saw that such deviation had to be resisted. Shortly after the formation of the Prison Commission, in an attempt to ensure that the commissioners would not be too tied to the criminal department, Du Cane suggested expanding the categories of its papers which did not pass through the main Home Office.[42] Due to some mis-understanding about the acceptance of this plan, the Prison

Commission dealt with a certain matter itself rather than forwarding it to the criminal department. This led to an immediate outburst from Maconochie, who was well aware of the implications:

> Hitherto the Criminal Branch of the Home Office has been the channel through which all communications on convict or prison business addressed or emanating from the Secretary of State has passed. Every decision of the Secretary of State and every circular issued by him are recorded in the office books, and the Department is consequently in possession of complete information as to previous practice and precedents in every case in which opinions have been expressed or directions given by the Secretary of State.[43]

If the criminal department ceased to be fully involved in prisons work it would cease to be an effective sieve for the secretary of state and it could not develop a co-ordinating role. How, for example, could it even suggest answers to letters from the Scottish Prison Commission if it was not fully apprised of decisions made about English prisons? As a result of Maconochie's protest Du Cane was not granted the independence he wanted.[44]

The devolution of authority within the upper division had the effect of giving less senior officials greater authority over heads of sub-departments. In two areas this changing relationship led to public and therefore embarrassing conflicts. Severe disagreement came about not so much with the heads of the inspectorates – none of whom appears to have done serious battle with central officials – as with the heads of the two departments, subject to the home secretary's authority, which were somewhat more apart from their parent department: the chairman of the Prison Commission and the commissioner of metropolitan police. In both cases certain factors combined to cause the home secretary embarrassment: first during the 1880s there was increasing concern about crime and public unrest – particularly in the metropolis – which derived partly from the downturn of Britain's economic fortunes and the consequent rise in unemployment and which reached a peak in 1886; secondly, two of the key officials involved were military men of autocractic temperament who strongly disliked the changing nature of Home Office administration and found themselves up against an un-compromising permanent under-secretary.

Relations between Sir Edmund Du Cane and the Home Office
The 1877 prison act set up the Prison Commission to effect the transfer to the home secretary's authority, and subsequently to rationalize, the 113 local prisons, responsibility for which had been

vested in county and borough authorities. The new board consisted of three commissioners and a chairman, Sir Edmund Du Cane, who was the key figure in the new administration. He had had a military career in the Royal Engineers before being appointed in 1863 director of convict prisons and inspector of military prisons. By the time Cross appointed him chairman of the new Prison Commission Du Cane had also become chairman of the directors of convict prisons, surveyor-general of prisons and inspector-general of military prisons. He was thus at the centre of all aspects of prison administration in Britain. His previous experience, together with his considerable administrative talents and position, enabled him to carry out the feat of nearly halving the number of prisons, completely reorganizing the staff and buildings, and imposing the uniformity and financial saving which the legislature had demanded.

Du Cane was a man who could brook no challenge to his own authority and he managed to concentrate the control of prison administration in his own hands. Prison governors and staff were nominated by the home secretary who was closely advised on appointments by the chairman. The same was true of the prison inspectors who tended to be ex-governors and who, although intended to be independent of the commissioners and responsible directly to the home secretary, were in effect subservient to Du Cane.[45] The commissioners themselves were cowed by the chairman who summoned them to board meetings 'chiefly for the purpose of considering prison appointments' and not to discuss prison policy. He reprimanded the younger prison commissioners – Ruggles-Brise and Robert Anderson – when they showed signs of independent judgement and he 'completely sterilized' the 'large body of trained experts at his command'.[46] Even the visiting committees of justices, who were intended to promote local interest in the welfare of prisoners, were sapped of their independence when they seriously challenged the central authority.[47]

For eighteen years, from 1877 to 1895 when Du Cane retired, his relations with the Home Office were frequently strained by his unbending belief in the supreme importance of his own status and authority. He resented criticism from Cross, found Harcourt's tenure 'very tiring' because 'he was so evidently bent on being disagreeable and . . . bullying', and had a row with Henry Matthews when he felt that the home secretary was interfering in the appointment of prison chaplains (even though the patronage in fact lay with the home secretary).[48] Since he could not easily tolerate a challenge to his authority, even from the home secretary, it was hardly surprising that Du Cane's relations with Home Office officials were poor. He was simply unable to accept that, for the purposes of administrative authority, the secretary of state and his staff formed a unit, the intricacies of which were no one's business except that of the department itself. In October 1886 Troup apparently criticized a certain prison medical officer in a minute which evidently contributed to the sense of a subsequent letter from the permanent under-secretary to the Prison Commission. Reading through the papers Du Cane spotted Troup's minute and protested. Lushington reacted as though Du Cane had interfered as an outsider in a bit of private domestic house-keeping and dealt him a severe reprimand; he pointed out that the minutes had been sent over to the Prison Commission instead of an official letter simply in order to save effort and time, but that whatever process was involved in the creation of the final departmental minute was none of Du Cane's business. The chairman metaphorically drew himself up to a great height, regretted former days when it had been 'a very uncommon thing for the Home Office to originate reprimands' and grumbled that 'the office is full of new blood in its upper ranks'. Lushington won the last round by setting out the theory of Home Office administration:

> Our clerks... necessarily play a more important part than previously. Old Waddington never allowed anybody to minute a paper but himself: and on that Minute an official letter was always written ... but the day for that has long gone by, ... and now so great is the increase of work [that] every clerk, however junior, minutes ... The clerk writes for the Under-Secretary and ought to write what should help him form a judgement and settle his Minute. Especially should he point out any objection to an application or anything amiss which the Secretary of State ought to take notice [*sic*]. And he would cease to be useful if he shrank from doing this on account of the station or merits of the person he was criticizing.[49]

In 1889 Du Cane reacted bitterly to the way the department dealt with his proposals for the annual prison estimates, believing that for the first time he had been 'entirely shut out from any discussion' about the question and instead had merely received a formal letter from the secretary of state making certain alterations to his submission. This became a running sore with him. He simply could not understand how recommendations of mere clerks, 'countersigned without perhaps much consideration by an Under-Secretary', could weigh more heavily with the home secretary than 'the experience of the prison department'.[50] In 1893 he wrote a rather pathetic letter to his erstwhile chief, Harcourt, in an attempt to enlist his support against the way Lushington conducted business so as 'to create a sort of screen between me and the Secretary of State'.[51]

Yet the Home Office does not appear to have imposed ideas about the running of prisons on Du Cane, and the way in which he had emasculated the administrative machine he headed meant that it was virtually impossible to introduce changes in administration or policy unless he himself approved them. Although he was effective at carrying out the intention of the 1877 act he was out of tune with new ideas which were being discussed in the early 1890s. Certain prison reformers questioned the stress on punishment, deterrence and uniformity, believing that more attention should be paid to prisoners' welfare and that there should be greater classification according to offences committed. Du Cane continued to concentrate on rigid discipline and on the maintenance and construction of buildings rather than on reform of the inmates and training of the staff. Eventually, serious criticism in the press – probably inspired by W. D. Morrison, chaplain of Wandsworth prison – impelled the home secretary, H. H. Asquith, to set up a departmental committee of inquiry into the prison system.[52] Its report, issued in 1895, recommended far-reaching changes in the treatment of prisoners, the training of prison officers and in the roles of visiting committees and prison commissioners. Du Cane himself was exonerated from blame for faults in the prison system and he retired as chairman of the Prison Commission in 1895 at the age of sixty-five. To his successor, Ruggles-Brise – ironically, part of the Home Office's new blood which had so irked Du Cane – fell the task of implementing the proposed reforms.

It is difficult to ascertain the extent to which Du Cane's uneasy relations with the Home Office aggravated a situation which eventually led to public criticism of him. Home Office officials do not seem to have tried to recommend to the Prison Commission the kind of reforms advocated by Asquith's departmental committee until public attention was focused on the subject. Lushington later argued that such changes should result from the exercise of public opinion on the secretary of state or through a parliamentary committee.[53] Even so, over day-to-day administrative matters, dealings with prison staff and relations with visiting committees, the home secretary's path would have been smoother had there been better communication between Du Cane and departmental officials. It is perhaps a criticism of the latter that they did not sufficiently draw their chief's attention to the fact that Du Cane's personal administration was actually distorting the original intention of the legislature by minimizing the independence of the inspectors and the visiting committees. But had they done so, and had successive home secretaries tried to take a tough line with Du Cane over these matters, his personality and his entrenched position of power might well have prevented reform or led to the public embarrassment of his resignation.

Relations between Sir Charles Warren and the Home Office

Relations between the metropolitan police and the Home Office were chronically difficult partly because of ambiguity about the commissioner's ultimate authority. In the 1880s this difficulty was exacerbated by other factors which related to internal Home Office changes. In 1886 Major-General Sir Charles Warren was hastily summoned from a campaign in Egypt to restore morale, order and public confidence in the metropolitan police. This followed the resignation of the previous commissioner, Sir Edmund Henderson, after his censure by a committee set up by the home secretary, H. C. E. Childers, to investigate the administration and organization of the police. Its report had been prompted by the events of 18 February when, following a meeting of the Social Democratic Federation in Trafalgar Square, a mob got out of hand and attacked clubs and shops in the West End. The committee had blamed the police for the lack of a proper command structure, a badly organized system of communications and sheer misunderstanding within the force.[54] The metropolitan police was familiar with a military chief but the new commissioner sought to impose on it an unprecedented military order and outlook. Almost immediately after his appointment, he sat on a committee which re-examined its structure and recommended the creation of new posts at a senior level to which military men were appointed.[55] He placed far less emphasis on the detection of crime and more on the direct maintenance of public order through the uniformed branches than had his predecessors.

Accustomed to having the authority of a general in action, Warren had firm ideas about his own power and status which did not coincide with those of the Home Office. Determined to be master in his own domain, he was soon irked by the position of the receiver of the metropolitan police, whose office was deliberately designed to constitute a check on the commissioner. The receiver was bound on the one hand effectively to provision and support the force, and on the other was responsible directly to the home secretary for restraining police spending.[56] The post was held by A. R. Pennefather (previously the Home Office accountant) and a running conflict soon developed between him and Warren who wanted the receiver to act as little more than an accountant. Pennefather found it increasingly difficult to do his work and was bound to defend himself when the commissioner unjustly complained about him to the Home Office. Horrified at Warren's 'unfounded pretensions' Lushington wrote firmly to Matthews, the home-secretary:

> The Secretary of State will observe that the Commissioner not only makes to him pertinacious proposals for the transfer to himself of the statutory functions of the Receiver: he takes the law into his own hands, and appropriates some of the functions regardless both of the statute and of the regulations of the Secretary of State . . . This state of things seems to me intolerable, and in my opinion it is the duty of the Secretary of State to uphold his Financial Officer and I may add his own authority.[57]

Eventually Matthews was forced to set up a committee to report on relations between the two officers. However, it never reported because of Warren's subsequent resignation in 1888 and the receiver's position was left undisturbed.

Warren had equally bad relations with the criminal investigation department which, from 1884, had been under the control of an assistant commissioner, James Monro. Warren distrusted Monro's specialist, non-uniformed branch which performed 'secret agent' work and which inevitably had operational independence from the rest of the force. The Home Office was inevitably brought into the quarrels of the two men as Warren complained about Monro's insubordination, thereby making his position virtually untenable. In August 1888 Monro handed in his resignation with a list of their differences which included Warren's apparent lack of interest in the CID and his imposition of restrictions on it, including its communication with the Home Office. Lushington tended to support Monro but in the end the home secretary, Matthews, took the line of least resistance and accepted Monro's resignation.[58] Even so, he had publicly to admit these embarrassing differences within the metropolitan police to a critical House of Commons.

Warren had no more truck with Home Office officials than had Du Cane. Lushington complained that he would

> . . . not treat with common civility suggestions on Police Matters proceeding from others though they are forwarded to him by the Secretary of State for consideration: he recently disputed the sufficiency of the Under-Secretary's signature as authenticating official instructions . . .[59]

Warren consistently maintained that 'neither he nor the Metropolitan Police have anything to do with the Home Office' (meaning its officials), a statement which Lushington disposed of with his usual vigour, pointing out that it was impossible to distinguish the Home Office from the secretary of state since it had no existence except as his office. Further, he argued that the metropolitan police, although not technically part of the imperial civil service, was effectively simply another sub-department of the Home Office:

> ... for practical every day purposes the test of a Department being attached to the Home Office is whether it is subordinate to the Secretary of State. It is in this sense that the Commissioner denies that the Metropolitan Police is a department of the Home Office and it is in this sense that I maintain it is, just as much as the Prisons Department for instance.[60]

The serious and obvious lack of co-operation between the Home Office and Warren aggravated the difficulties facing both in coping with public unrest. The legal relationship between the commissioner of police and the home secretary over the maintenance of public order was not clear. The committee of inquiry into the metropolitan police in 1886 had maintained that primary responsibility rested with the commissioner who should inform the Home Office about any disturbing circumstances. Yet the secretary of state was the minister responsible to parliament for the metropolitan police and for the preservation of public order in London. Unemployment had swelled the numbers involved in constant demonstrations mounted by the SDF and socialist groups in the autumn of 1887. At the same time Trafalgar Square, the Mecca of demonstrators, was providing a base for large numbers of homeless outcasts who were potential rabble. Warren's policy of maintaining public order – considered by some as one of military repression – was that of strenuously opposing the holding of public demonstrations. To Lushington's fury, without debating with Home Office officials the wider, extremely controversial and legally complicated issue of the right to hold public meetings, he instructed the Office of Works, in the event of disorder, to close Trafalgar Square.[61] On 1 November Warren issued a police notice – again without Home Office sanction – that disorderly crowds would be dispersed. It was in defiance of this, and a similarly doubtful legal prohibition of public meetings made on 8 November,[62] that the Metropolitan Radical Association, on 13 November 1887, held its subsequently famous 'Bloody Sunday' meeting which ended in a battle between the police and the crowd who were ultimately dispersed by Foot Guards and Life Guards. Warren was publicly vilified by liberals and supported by those fearful of disorder; once again Matthews faced parliamentary attack during a long debate on public meetings in the metropolis.[63] The stand he took only reinforced Warren's view that the home secretary did not firmly back the commissioner and his force who were doing their best to maintain order under trying circumstances.

The Home Office and Warren were also in conflict over a long-running public order problem, the control of prostitution. The 1885 criminal law amendment act set out one aspect of the public attitude to prostitution: it forbade both street solicitation and brothel-keeping and imposed on constables the duty of apprehending prostitutes loitering or soliciting. Yet clearly there was plently of custom for prostitutes; moreover, many people were opposed to police officiousness. This ambivalence was reflected among magistrates who followed no consistent line in police cases. It led to a difficult situation for the police who were frequently harassed by charges of blackmail. Constables badly needed direction – which they did not get from the home secretary – and Warren tried to provide this in July 1887 by issuing a police order without consulting the Home Office. The order set out a 'laissez-faire' policy, discouraging constables from taking action against prostitutes and brothel-keepers.[64] It led to an outcry from the clean-up-the-streets faction and once again Matthews was questioned in the Commons where he had to admit that he had known nothing about the order before it appeared.[65] Lushington attacked the commissioner for abusing his position by not consulting the home secretary and for issuing an order which was illegal.[66] But the order was not cancelled and its existence led to strong protestations from London vestries who found they could no longer secure police co-operation in watching suspected brothels. Warren categorically refused to allow the police to exercise 'espionage' over private houses; and Matthews found it virtually impossible to mediate between him and the vestries.[67]

These problems arose at a time when the increased amount and complexity of Home Office work had changed the system whereby the secretary of state could make day to day decisions himself. The new way of operating did not suit the autocratic Du Cane and Warren who were both irked at having their memoranda read and being given instructions by officials. Part of the reason for this friction must have been their military training and discipline: they were used to a more straightforward command structure. But, after all, army officers could make successful government servants as other commissioners of the metropolitan police demonstrated. The problems also derived from the uncompromising personalities of these men who needed careful treatment.

This they did not receive from the Home Office. Lushington was not noted for his tact: precise and legally minded, he was hostile to anyone who stepped out of constitutional line; and this was the attitude he imparted to his junior officials. His schoolmasterly reaction to Du Cane's and Warren's behaviour was to draft firm memoranda, setting out the limits of their authority. This was hardly calculated to mollify, and no doubt Anderson's quip about Lushington, that 'where a plaister is needed the effect of a blister is intolerable', had a good deal of truth in it.[68] Lushington did sometimes appear lacking in sympathy towards, for example, the very real problems of the police. Nor were the home secretaries more successful at dealing with these men. Du Cane was apparently annoyed by Cross, Harcourt and Matthews. Certainly Matthews did not handle Warren well. He neither followed the tough line recommended by Lushington, nor had his own positive or consistent policy. Nor did he have any personal 'rapport' with the commissioner. Altogether there is no sign that these men even tried to sit down together to sort out their differences and work out a means of tackling the police or prisons problems they faced.

It is perhaps not suprising that these difficulties arose in an acute form with the two subordinate departments which had the greatest status. Lushington may have argued that the metropolitan police barely differed from another sub-department, but the fact was that the commissioner was in charge of more than eight thousand men over whose operational activities he was in sole control. As Warren pointed out, various statutes imposed duties on him without reference to the secretary of state, a situation which did not apply to inspectors. The chairman of the Prison Commission was more clearly subject to the authority of the secretary of state who appointed all the commissioners, determined their number and sanctioned the prison regulations they made and many of their activities. But even Lushington admitted that they were superior to their inspectors. Moreover, the size of their parish too was comparatively large: the Prison Commission's own office numbered some thirty-five in 1885; and among the sixty or so prisons there were twenty-one different grades of prison officials. By comparison the largest inspectorate, the factory inspectorate, numbered fifty-six in 1885. Not only did size give the head of an organization a certain standing, but the occupants of these two posts commanded more public attention than did any inspector. Their standing was reflected in their salaries. While the inspectors' salaries were all less than those of either of the under-secretaries (£2,000 and £1,200–£1,500), those of the chairman of the Prison Commission and of directors of convict prisons (£2,000) and that of the commissioner of metropolitan police (£1,500) equated these officials with the under-secretaries.

The new recruits and statistical reform

By 1890 several able young men had been recruited to the Home Office: Troup, Ruggles-Brise, Simpson, W. P. Byrne and J. G. Legge. Among these Troup stands out: he was the first and probably the most capable. Lushington put Troup's talent to good use in 1887 when he rationalized the parliamentary work. Hitherto the different types of parliamentary bills had been dealt with in a haphazard way by various parts of the office. Lack of co-ordination meant that it was possible for the department to fail to notice bills originating in other departments which affected its interests; moreover, there was no systematic way of dealing with private bills. Although in 1885 Lushington had committed the problem to the examination of C. Deffell, a senior clerk, who had recommended creating a new co-ordinating branch, nothing had been done. Then in June 1887 Matthews complained:

> The Parliamentary work of the Home Office is always badly done, or not done at all . . . There are many bills brought in by private members on Home Office subjects – all of which, I feel, ought to be examined and reported on in the office, for purposes of debate in both Houses: but I have not found any part of the staff accustomed or able to do that kind of work.[69]

So the following November Lushington instructed Troup to spend part of his time in a new parliamentary branch within the general department.[70] From then on Troup appears to have worked on most bills. He dealt with private members' bills, bye-laws and provisional order bills. He took over the work, hitherto done by a Local Government Board representative, of monitoring for the Police and Sanitary Committee all local authority private bills relating to police and sanitary matters which affected Home Office interests.[71] He watched government bills emanating from other departments and helped Lushington with Home Office bills. From this date Troup's comprehensive memoranda, setting out the past history, aims advantages and disadvantages of draft legislation, become a regular feature of Home Office records.

It was not only that Troup was efficient and intellectually capable. He also had a different attitude from that of the older clerks towards the role of the Home Office. He deplored the tendency of wanting the department to shed its load wherever possible in order to ease the work burden. In 1890 he wrote a memorandum on a private member's burial bill which proposed to transfer all burials work from the Home Office to the Local Government Board.

> The proposal to make the Local Government Board the central authority is open to serious objection and should be opposed. From the point of view of the Home Office it would appear that the process of devolution upon other authorities of important powers and duties of the Secretary of State has already gone far enough.[72]

He even suggested that work should be transferred from the Local Government Board to the Home Office. Similarly in 1892 he opposed a Board of Agriculture suggestion that all bills about commons enclosure should be sent directly to the board rather than through the Home Office, being particularly concerned to maintain the department's special interest in certain aspects of enclosure which involved public amenities. In the event Matthews decided that the Board of Agriculture should assume most of the Home Office functions but not those about which Troup (and Lushington) were particularly concerned.[73]

Both Troup and Simpson played an important part in the reform of departmental statistics in the early 1890s. One group of these was the judicial statistics, divided into two parts – criminal and civil – and since 1856 compiled annually from returns submitted by the police, justices' clerks, prisons inspectors and civil court officials. Since 1876 the collation of these statistics was done in a small branch of the general department by the clerk for statistical returns, a supplementary clerk called George Grosvenor. He may also have drafted the introduction in which an attempt was made to draw conclusions about matters such as the changes in the proportion of police officers to population, whether judicial commitments were increasing, and so on. The head of the general department, Knyvett, actually signed the introduction and was the senior clerk responsible for the production of these statistics.

They had long needed overhauling. Little original thought was given to their production. Each year's statistics was simply an up-dated version of the previous year's tables. Returns were not checked to ensure accuracy or to discover whether the various contributing authorities were forwarding the same type of information under each heading. In truth the statistics branch had become the Cinderella branch of the office. Statistical developments apparently did not interest senior Home Office officials as they did officials in certain other government departments.[74] In 1876 Robert Giffen, head of the

Board of Trade statistical department, wrote a memorandum on the 'Compilation and Printing of the Statistics of the United Kingdom' in which he singled out the Home Office judicial statistics for containing 'superfluous matter' and presenting an ambiguous picture because no account was taken of the different legal systems and methods of submitting returns in different parts of the United Kingdom. The Treasury then set up an Official Statistics Committee, one of whose recommendations was that 'statistically important departments' should each appoint a competent officer to supervise the presentation of statistics to parliament.[75] The Home Office apparently ignored the suggestion, even though it received a request from the committee for details about its statistics and the statistical staff.[76] Instead the judicial statistics went on being produced the same way year after year. Moreover, important statements about crime were deduced from them. In 1885, for example, Harcourt proudly informed Gladstone that over the past four years there had been a 'remarkable diminution in crime', a conclusion he mistakenly drew from information that the prison population was declining.[77]

A later head of the statistics branch blamed Grosvenor for the problem. But the fault lay as much with his superiors' lack of interest in his work as with Grosvenor's inability to correct the statistical fallacies. He did at least point out one of the gross deficiencies – the fact that different contributors submitted information for different annual periods (that is, not starting at the same date of the year) which made comparison difficult and delayed publication. Knyvett, his superior, agreed that this was a defect but was nevertheless reluctant to alter the system. Lushington showed no real interest in Grosvenor's suggestion.[78]

In November 1890 the head constable of Liverpool complained in his annual report that an incorrect impression was given by the Home Office in its crime tables. Meanwhile Simpson, then a junior clerk in the criminal department, had written a long memorandum pointing out the inadequacies of the criminal judicial statistics. He reiterated Grosvenor's point. He showed how many subjects presented were of little interest while certain important categories such as 'police' and 'prisons' did not contain the exhaustive summary of information implied in the headings. The data presented were often dubious because the various headings under which the police and others submitted information could be variously interpreted. The returns also contained straightforward errors. Troup, Simpson's immediate superior, fully concurred. Lushington agreed that the judicial statistics were inadequate and should be reconsidered but apparently saw no urgency about the matter and minuted 'put up for the present'.[79]

Criticism of the judicial statistics became more public and was bound up with the whole debate about prisons administration. Discussion centred around the vexed question of whether or not crime was decreasing. Two of the principal protagonists were Du Cane and Morrison. The latter, using these statistics as his source, wrote an article in *Nineteenth Century* in June 1892 showing how crime had recently increased. The following month Du Cane reposted in his fifteenth annual report that, on the contrary, crime was decreasing.[80] Clearly there was something wrong with statistics which could produce two such totally different conclusions. Troup tried to unravel the conflicting threads of these arguments. He pointed out two important factors of which neither the statistics branch nor the Prison Commission had taken account. First, there had been a general reduction in the length of sentences over the period. Secondly, there had been important changes in legal procedure – particularly as a result of the 1879 summary jurisdiction act – which had the effect in certain of the statistical tables of artificially inflating some categories of crime while reducing others. On this basis Troup distrusted the arguments of both Morrison and Du Cane and also suspected the judicial statistics as a source.[81]

These factors forced the Home Office to form a departmental committee to examine the criminal judicial statistics. It is not certain whether this was appointed under Matthews or after Asquith had taken office in December 1892. But its final report, signed by E. L. Pemberton (assistant under-secretary), Troup, Simpson and Byrne, was published in 1895 and presented to parliament. The committee took evidence from a wide variety of outside witnesses involved in the production and use of these statistics; it looked at continental methods of the statistical examination of crime. The report presented a detailed plan for complete revision and included the criminal judicial statistics for 1893 as a prototype. The basis of rationalization was accuracy and uniformity: ambiguous terminology was abolished and a code of instructions prepared for those submitting information to the Home Office; irrelevant information was omitted; headings were grouped so as to focus the reader's attention on the subject he sought; all tables ran from 1 January to 31 December.[82]

The introduction was recognized as the key to interpretation, and in his special introduction for 1893 Troup discussed the general bearing of available statistics on a few issues of particular and controversial interest. One of these was the question debated by Du Cane and Morrison. Troup showed how misleadingly compiled statistics had so far muddled attempts to deduce whether or not crime was decreasing. On the basis of the only set of statistics which he felt formed a reliable guide (figures for certain specified indictable crimes), he concluded that on the whole 'the decrease in crime, though not so great as it has often been represented, though by no means comparable, for instance, to the decrease in prison population, is nevertheless real and substantial'.[83] It was the first time that this important issue had been effectively analysed in the Home Office and by an official as high ranking as a first divison clerk, with a legal training and the ability to comprehend how to use statistics.

This started a whole process of Home Office statistical reform. In 1894 the lord chancellor set up a separate committee to investigate the civil judicial statistics. This committee discovered comparable defects to those found in the criminal statistics and its recommendations for reform were based on comparable principles.[84] Henceforth the civil statistics were produced separately and although they were still compiled by the clerk for statistical returns at the Home Office the introduction was written by the master of the supreme court. Meanwhile Asquith had instigated a major reform of the factory inspectorate which included reform of the factory statistics. Simpson, as Asquith's private secretary, wrote a memorandum suggesting alterations in the statistical appendices of the annual report of the chief inspector of factories.[85] This prompted Asquith to appoint an investigatory committee whose proposals led to the clarification of terminology, the addition of maps and diagrams and the rationalization of tables.[86] In December 1893 Asquith also appointed a committee on mining and mineral statistics which was partly the outcome of criticism by the Royal Commission on Mining Royalties. This committee made recommendations along the lines of the other statistics committees and thus led to the more effective production of statistics in this field as well.[87]

The initial impetus for all these reforms came largely from outside the department. Home Office officials of the 1870s and 1880s were apparently not concerned in either official or non-official discussion about improving the collection and application of government statistics, nor did they take the hint that all was not well in their own statistical domain. It was only in the early 1890s, when the department was publicly attacked for its inadequate judicial statistics and bad administration of industrial subjects that it began in earnest to investigate. Criticism about industrial matters in particular galvanized Asquith into action. But in terms of response to outside criticism of the judicial statistics and in the application of intelligent analysis to all Home Office statistics, the younger officials played the important role. It was not Knyvett, head of the general department and therefore responsible for the criminal statistics, but Simpson who first pointed out the need for their reform. Troup supported him, chaired the reforming committee and wrote the introduction for the next few years. Again, the first effective official minute analysing the weakness of factory statistics and proposing their investigation came not from the chief inspector of factories or head of the domestic department but from Simpson. When the factory statistics commitee had reported it was Troup who urged that its recommendations be carried through as soon as possible.[88]

Breakthrough of the open competition officials

When Asquith and Herbert Gladstone became secretary of state and parliamentary under-secretary respectively in August 1892, the weakness of factory and mining statistics was only one element of what amounted almost to a crises at the Home Office over the administration of industrial inspection. Apart from problems within the inspectorate, the secretary of state was hampered by the weakness of the Home Office domestic department where officials were simply not able to provide intelligent guidance on industrial problems. One factor was that the status of criminal work had risen so much under Everest and then Maconochie that by the 1880s the criminal department was clearly the superior department of the office. Once, when Lushington reallocated some work hitherto done in the criminal department to the domestic department, an aggrieved E. J. Stapleton complained:

> I cannot but feel that it is a transfer of dry and uninteresting work to a Department which has already the reputation of having charge of the least interesting work in an uninteresting Department of State, all the 'interesting' work having been gradually gathered into the Criminal Department . . .[89]

Whether the status of a department was the result or cause of the quality of its staff is hard to ascertain. But certainly there was a clear contrast in ability between the staffs of these two departments from 1886 until 1894. The criminal department was headed by the ablest of the older generation, who was Murdoch (Maconochie having died in 1884), whose second-in-command was Troup; while the domestic department was in charge of the rather ineffective Stapleton whose senior clerk was F. M'Clintock for whom at one time special leave arrangements had had to be made to ensure that too much responsibility was not left in his hands.[90]

There was talk at this time of removing the industrial work from the Home Office. But after Asquith's arrival it became clear that the department would not relinquish it. There were external reasons for this. But also the Home Office line hardened. Not only did the new secretary of state believe in the importance of its industrial work but also at least one of the younger officials, Troup, was against the removal of part of the department's responsibilities: 'It is . . . much to be desired,' he wrote, 'that the labour department should not be an entirely distinct department but a branch of the Home Office.'[91] While the factory inspectorate was being reformed Gladstone turned his attention to the organization of the work within the office. Earlier in 1893, on the grounds of increasing pressure, the Home Office had requested the Treasury for the permanent addition to the first division staff of a temporary recruit, G. A. Aitken. The Treasury agreed to this flouting of the Ridley recommendations but not without a flurry of internal minutes critical of the way the Home Office conducted its business. Francis Mowatt (permanent secretary) made two points. First, much less of the routine work ought to be done by the first divison (as the upper division was called since 1890). Lushington justified existing practice on the basis that criminal matters at the Home Office were

> . . . subject to such keen criticism and . . . beat upon by such a fierce light that it is not possible to entrust any but a very small part to clerks who have not been educated at a university and are not fully competent to conduct correspondence with local authorities and the Public, subject only to general and occasional supervision.[92]

Mowatt's second point was that there was an imbalance both of the volume of work and of talent in the three departments: the work of both the domestic and general departments was 'of a routine character and could well be managed by one principal clerk'; 'the officers in the[se] Divisions are not very capable' otherwise they could have eased the burden on other parts of the office – in the criminal department, parliamentary branch or at under-secretary level.

In July 1893 Gladstone submitted to his chief detailed proposals for a complete redistribution of work within the office. Most significant was the proposed formation of a new and separate industrial department under Troup to administer work connected with factories, workshops, mines and explosives. This would have its own special branch to deal with industrial statistics in order to relieve the chief inspector of factories who Gladstone felt was responsible for much work which ought to have been done in the domestic department.[93] For some unknown reason the plan was unfortunately shelved and early in 1894 there arose some kind of serious crisis in the domestic department. Asquith wrote to Gladstone:

> Lushington was bound to do all the whitewashing he could, as he cannot but feel that each fresh proof of the inefficiency of the Domestic Department is, at least indirectly, a reflection upon himself.
> ... We shall never get the thing right, until we have two or three men at headquarters with the same kind of expert knowledge and ability in industrial matters, which clerks in the Criminal Department have in regard to their special work.[94]

Even this did not yet lead to reorganization but at least the unfortunate M'Clintock was asked to resign and the inexorable rule of promotion by seniority was broken for the first time in the first division in order to allow Simpson to be promoted to the vacant senior clerkship.

In the autumn of 1894 a personnel problem of a different kind was triggered off by the proposed retirement of Lushington. This bombshell fell shortly after Pemberton's replacement as legal assistant under-secretary by Henry H. Cunynghame. The vacancy was intended to be filled in the customary way by an outside appointee. Now at this stage Troup and Simpson, aged thirty-seven and thirty-three respectively, were senior clerks. Both had a legal training in addition to good university degrees and had proved themselves able officials. Below them were some good juniors: Byrne, Legge and M. Delevigne. Even though in some ways the juniors were not given sufficient responsibility for them to utilize their full talents, they had a considerably wider experience of Home Office and civil service work than they would have had in, say, the 1870s. By 1894 they were drafting full and valuable minutes and memoranda which formed the basis for decisions. They also acted competently as secretaries and members of both departmental and inter-departmental committees. The best of them acted at some point as private secretaries to the secretary of state, the parliamentary under-secretary or the permanent under-secretary. Yet as things stood, the highest point to which these officials could aspire was a principal clerkship, only the next rung up the ladder for Troup and Simpson. This might have been reward enough for Home Office clerks of the past but it was not going to be sufficient for able men recruited through open competition and on the basis that the civil service offered a good professional career.

At the announcement of Lushington's imminent retirement, Troup and Simpson seized the opportunity to lead an assault on the ranks of their superiors. On 30 November 1894 Lushington was presented directly with a memorandum signed by Troup, Simpson, Byrne, Legge and Dryhurst who were worried that a new permanent under-secretary and a comparatively new assistant under-secretary would simply not be able to supervise the enormous work-load of the office. At present it was only managed effectively as a result of the amazing hours of work put in by Lushington who had always liked to do as much of the work as possible himself. They proposed the creation of an additional under-secretary, selected from the first division and their candidate for this post was Murdoch. As grist to their mill they cited several comparable appointments of career officials at the Colonial Office, Foreign Office and Treasury.[95]

Lushington was taken aback at the unorthodox approach of the young clerks. He was not altogether averse to the idea of an additional assistant under-secretary – inded he had mooted it himself in 1885 – and he admitted that if his successor were burdened by 'literary or social or other pursuits . . . they would undoubtedly tend to make it more difficult for him to get through the routine work'.[96] But he felt that such an appointment, made at that particular moment, might look like a slur on the efficiency of his successor. Moreover, he was dubious about the unprecedented idea of promoting a first division clerk. With the caution which derived from his legal training, age and long service at the Home Office, he urged that it was important to have as senior officials men who were not merely legally qualified but who also had legal experience because of the quasi-judicial functions of the home secretary. Asquith agreed with most of this; and there, for the time being, matters rested. Early in January 1895 Lushington was succeeded by Sir Kenelm Digby.

Before the year was out the new, over-burdened permanent under-secretary was urging the creation of an additional assistant under-secretary. As things stood the permanent under-secretary and assistant under-secretary – still the only officials who could sign letters with the authority of the home secretary – simply shared out in a rather haphazard way the work which came up from heads of department. With Digby's plan, each of two assistant under-secretaries would be responsible for defined areas of work and pass on anything needing a more senior decision to the permanent under-secretary who would thereby be able to supervise the work of the office overall. As far as the reorganization of office work was concerned he wanted to retain three departments but with a redistribution of the subject-matter.

The home secretary, by then the Conservative Matthew White

Ridley, convinced the chancellor of the exchequer, Sir Michael Hicks Beach, of the importance of Digby's request. At official level Mowatt upset Digby with his implication of blackmail: that if the Home Office would reorganize its work and get rid of certain officials the Treasury would consider granting an additional under-secretary. But the Ridley-Hicks Beach discussion evidently clinched matters: in January 1896 the Treasury formally consented to the creation of an additional assistant under-secretaryship, at which the Home Office agreed to go ahead with the redistribution of its work into three reconstituted departments and also conceded that the number of junior clerkships should be reduced to the pre-1893 level of seven.[97] Murdoch was appointed to fill the new post as the memorialists had originally requested. His appointment again broke the rule of promotion by seniority, for the ageing Knyvett had entered the office earlier and had been a principal clerk for longer. He was compensated for this indignity with a KCB and retired within two years. For the younger clerks these events had at last opened up the highest positions in the office to career officials and meant that they had successfully challenged the unwritten Home Office rule that senior positions were filled only by barristers. Now the career of a first division official could run from a junior clerkship to an assistant under-secretaryship, with the obvious implication that the very top post would eventually be open to him.

New departmental arrangements followed Digby's proposals which were largely based on Gladstone's earlier plan. A new industrial and parliamentary department – with Troup as principal and Byrne as senior clerk – was to administer the factories and workshops, and mines and quarries acts and was to be backed up by a sizeable statistics sub-branch of its own; it was also to deal with parliamentary returns and all bill work. The new domestic department – under Knyvett – was to take over the work of the old general department: the formal business of warrants and appointments and the grant of licences, personnel matters, and the supervision of accounts and registry work. The criminal department – headed by Simpson, with Dryhurst as the senior clerk — kept its old administrative responsibilities, having its own statistical branch which produced the judicial statistics. These changes redistributed the work-load more evenly and at last gave the industrial aspect of the work increased status by placing it in a distinct department.

The pattern of senior officials and first divison staff after the changes was as shown in Table 4. There was no increase in the total number of staff since the changes had given the office an additional under-secretary at the expense of a junior clerk. Despite the meagre

Table 4   Senior officials and first division staff after the changes of 1896

Office	Salary (£)
1 permanent under-secretary	2,000
1 assistant under-secretary (legal)	1,200 – 1,500*
1 assistant under-secretary	1,000 × 50 – 1,200
3 principal clerks	900 × 50 – 1,000
3 senior clerks	700 × 25 – 800
7 junior clerks	200 × 20 – 500

*Subject to reconsideration on a vacancy.

cost of this reform, cheese-paring Treasury officials could congratulate themselves that since the last major reorganization of the Home Office in 1876 the increase in cost of its first division (including under-secretaries) had been minimal: it had risen from £11,236 to £11,948.[98]

The sixteen years since Troup had entered the department in 1880 had been difficult ones for it, not only because of the personnel problems created by the arrival of a new 'caste'. The 1876 reforms had reduced the staff to what senior officials considered the bare minimum for the current work-load. Yet this load increased substantially from the late 1870s. The almost automatic Treasury hostility towards departmental requests for more upper division staff, reinforced by the Ridley report, had the effect of forcing staff at all levels to devolve work downwards as the Treasury had long been advocating. This had the side-effect that senior first division officials were gaining greater authority over out-departments subject to the authority of the home secretary which, in the case of the Prison Commission and metropolitan police led not merely to friction but also to embarrassing public consequences. Meanwhile, some of the older upper division clerks were finding it difficult to cope with the new pace of work which led to an awkward situation especially in the domestic department whose inability to cope with its industrial responsibilities became the focus of attention in the early 1890s.

By this time the open competition entrants were demonstrating their ability not merely to minute effectively, participate in committee work and act as competent private secretaries but also to spot a major weakness in the departmental organization of statistics and effectively to suggest remedies. In addition they showed signs of being aggressive about the areas of Home Office responsibility. After Lushington's retirement the permanent head of the office was

no longer an official who believed in the nineteenth-century departmental virtue of dealing personally with as much work as possible
which gave authority and status to the under-secretaries and
principal clerks. From 1898, after Knyvett had retired, the new men
occupied all the first division posts except one senior clerkship. The
question which naturally poses itself is: what was this new breed of
official, now in a position of authority, going to make of the peculiar
problems which faced the Home Office? One characteristic in
particular strikes the historian of the late nineteenth-century Home
Office: its frequent inability to bring about desirable change – in
prison administration, factory inspection, the management of
statistics – without the impetus of public criticism. Was this due to its
hard-pressed, sometimes incompetent officials at the upper division
level? Was it an inherent aspect of a naturally conservative
department? Or was it an inevitable feature of bureaucracy?

4 The growth of bureaucracy and the role of the pre-war civil servant: 1896–1914

New departmental arrangements 1896–1906

Legislation increasingly provided Home Office officials with activity, the focal point of which was the parliamentary session. Prior to a political decision to legislate, officials may have participated in a departmental inquiry. Before and during the early stages of the session they were involved with the preparation of government bills:[1] they considered the government's requirements and also those of other pressure groups, weighing up the potential legal and administrative consequences of the changing clauses. While government bills were going through parliament, officials supported their ministers with information and advice. Subsequently, for those which became law, they had to notify and guide authorities about implementation. Increasingly they were being delegated by parliament the power to formulate regulations according to the basic principles of the acts and this work took up a good deal of time. Besides, they were occupied with continual parliamentary questions; regular inquiries from outside correspondents; visits from representatives of associations concerned about aspects of Home Office work; frequent communications from officials in sub-departments; and, inevitably, the occasional emergency which brought the home secretary into the limelight and took up the time of scurrying officials. In short, the promotion of the open competition clerks in 1896 to the principal and senior clerkships in no way altered the familiar pattern of officials at all levels feeling constantly stretched by their work.

Between 1899 (the first year of a 'properly corrected return') and 1906 the annual total number of incoming papers had risen from 50,224 to 62,624.[2] The sheer physical problem of coping with the influx of paper became chronic. Batches of old papers were continually being sent to the Public Record Office. The Office of Works was besieged with requests for more bookcases, more accommodation. The Local Government Board, next door – itself in the same trouble and therefore partly moving to new premises – was jostled into making room for some Home Office overspill. It was also annoyed to find its light and ventilation seriously threatened by a temporary 'iron building' which was actually constructed in the central quadrangle between it and the Home Office in order to house the Home Office factory inspectorate and mining statistics branch.[3]

Between 1896 and 1904 the office heads of business were distributed between the criminal, domestic, and parliamentary and industrial departments – each headed by a principal clerk.[4] By 1904 the existing first division staff (increased since 1896 by a senior and a junior clerk) was felt to be insufficient. In a letter to the Treasury, Sir Mackenzie Chalmers, who had become permanent under-secretary in September 1903, justified his department's request for extra staff with the familiar argument that the work had increased in quantity and complexity.[5] The additional work which he singled out was that created by the 1903 employment of children act which, through the agency of local authorities, imposed restrictions on the employment of young children and which involved the Home Office initially in explaining to, and subsequently in cajoling, these authorities about their duties under the act. There was the imminent prospect of a shop hours bill and a licensing bill; and a projected aliens bill and workmen's compensation bill, to be prepared for the next session, would also create more permanent work. The upshot was the creation, in August 1904, of a new, small department intended to deal with the employment of children act, the 1904 licensing act and the proposed aliens legislation.[6] It was to consist of an acting principal clerk, J. Pedder, a junior clerk and clerical assistants. The new department was called the 'special subjects' department or division (as departments were coming to be called) S. The arrangement was ostensibly provisional but inevitably became permanent.

The Treasury appears to have agreed with equal ease, a year and a half later, to a Home Office request for an additional senior clerk to ease the strain in the industrial and parliamentary division – division I.[7] The Home Office's long justification of this request shows how industrial legislation had significantly increased the work of the office. Since this department had been formed in 1896 its first division staff had remained the same – one principal, one senior and one junior clerk. Yet its work had 'materially increased in every direction'. This was less true of the parliamentary aspect of the work than of the industrial aspect which by 1906 fell into five categories: factories and workshops; mines and quarries; truck; workmen's compensation; and the employment of children. In the first of these the work had more than doubled since 1895 as a result of the 1895 and 1901 factory and workshop acts:

... the new work consists largely of the drafting of statutory rules and orders, the settlement of legal difficulties, and advice on questions of public or parliamentary policy for which the qualities required are somewhat different from those to be found among even the ablest members of the Factory Inspection staff.[8]

Coal mines inspection had greatly increased as a result of the 1896 coal mines regulation act:

... which, among other changes, brought the Explosives used in Coal Mines under Home Office regulation – a subject full of difficulty which has involved the appointment of several committees, the establishment of a permanent testing station and a long succession of Home Office orders.[9]

The last three categories of work had been imposed on the department virtually over the previous ten years. The 1896 truck act, which set out circumstances under which an employer could pay his employees other than in cash, imposed on the home secretary the duty of inspecting such arrangements in factories and mines and gave him the power to exempt employers, in certain circumstances, from the provisions of the act. The 1897 workmen's compensation act, which obliged employers to compensate seriously injured workmen in certain work categories, required the secretary of state to appoint doctors to examine injured workmen in cases which went to arbitration. And the workmen's compensation bill, then going through parliament, would involve the department in 'numerous regulations, orders and provisional orders'.[10] Work on children's employment had started with the 1903 children's employment act which again gave the Home Office powers to issue orders and also authority to approve local bye-laws. In nearly each case the story was the same: the bulk of the work increase resulted from the powers delegated to the secretary of state by parliament.

The addition of staff granted by the Treasury on these two occasions illustrates a new promotion phenomenon. After the creation of division S, Pedder – as its head – although actually a senior clerk, became an 'acting' principal clerk while he received an 'acting' allowance of £200. The senior clerk in divison I also, for the time being, remained a junior, 'acting' as a senior. This increasingly common practice of effectively promoting clerks before there were vacancies in the grade above was a means of compensating juniors for doing more responsible work than their status was supposed to merit without overtly increasing the establishment at senior and principal level.

The Beck case

In 1904 there occurred an incident which was to cause a major staff change at a senior level and which focused the spotlight of public attention upon Home Office officials in an unprecedented way. It arose out of an aspect of the criminal side of the work which was always potentially sensitive: the scrutiny of prisoners' petitions. This was an ancient and non-legislative function of the office which derived from the secretary of state's responsibility for seeing that justice was done and exercising the crown's prerogative of mercy.

The origins of the case went back to 1877 when a man who called himself John Smith was sentenced to five years' penal servitude for defrauding prostitutes. In 1894 the police received complaints of a man of a similar description, using the same methods including passing cheques in apparently similar handwriting. Their efforts to locate the culprit were unsuccessful. But in December 1895 a woman who had been thus defrauded happened to meet Adolph Beck. She accosted him as the man who had defrauded her and, when he hotly denied the charge, they both appealed to the police. The police found that they had a case on their hands when several of the previously wronged women identified Beck as the man who had defrauded them; also, the police constable who had originally arrested Smith identified Beck as the ex-convict.

The case came before Sir Forrest Fulton, the common serjeant, in March 1896. Beck was convicted and sentenced to seven years' penal servitude both on the evidence of his personal identification and on allegation of an 'expert' that his handwriting was identical with that on Smith's earlier cheques. His defence was that the real culprit was the man who had been convicted in 1877 and that he was not that man. His defence counsel had wanted to call witnesses at the trial to provide an alibi for Beck during the time Smith was alleged to have committed the earlier crimes. But the judge had ruled that this was inadmissible evidence. In prison Beck was labelled as the man who had been previously convicted. Beck immediately presented several petitions to the Home Office on the grounds that his case was one of mistaken identity. He received no response until an appeal by his solicitor in May 1898 caused the Home Office to make inquiries to the prison authorities who informed the department that while Smith had been circumcised, Beck had not. The two men were therefore clearly revealed as not identical. At this point the Home Office consulted the judge who decided that there should be no interference with Beck's sentence beyond his having his previous conviction struck out. The Home Office accepted the judge's decision without protest and it did not inform the police or the public prosecutor of the discovery. In July 1901 Beck was released on licence. Then, in April 1904, he was again arrested on a similar charge to his previous one and again convicted. However, the judge at his trial felt misgivings about the case and postponed sentence. At that moment Smith himself was arrested on similar charges, based on acts committed while Beck was in custody. This led to further police investigation and Beck's consequent release and pardon.[11]

Beck's cause was taken up by the press. *The Times* argued that the case had caused a lack of confidence in the public mind and applauded the decision to appoint an official inquiry committee – a decision which Chalmers later admitted was the indirect result of a *Daily Mail* article.[12] The committee consisted of the master of the rolls, a retired civil servant and a member of the Council of India. Chalmers was worried about public revelation of the evidence, believing that 'many points of Home Office practice and the confidential relations with judges had much better not be discussed in public'.[13] But as the result of 'strong representation of the Master of the Rolls' the home secretary, Aretas Akers-Douglas, gave way on this: the hearing was conducted publicly and all the evidence was published with the report.[14] The latter came out in November 1904.

Digby, Murdoch, Chalmers and Troup were examined by the committee. In a separate paper on the Home Office practice of dealing with criminal petitions Digby pointed out the large number of petitions (some five thousand) – many of which were long and complex – which the department received annually from or on behalf of prisoners. In non-capital cases the official concerned usually read the central criminal court sessions papers and a good newspaper report of the trial, as had been the case during the Beck appeals. On this basis a minute was written recommending whether or not action should be taken. Since the Home Office was not a court of appeal and since good relations with judges were important for the legal aspects of its work,'very strong grounds indeed' were required to induce it to take action where no new material evidence was offered. When new light was shed on a case the department normally referred the new facts back to the judge concerned and followed his opinion as to guilt or innocence.[15]

The Home Office came out of the report badly. Its officials were not regarded as the only sinners: the judge, Forrest Fulton, was felt to have committed a 'cardinal error' in not allowing the evidence of Beck's counsel to be heard at the 1896 trial. But the department had failed in its role as 'the reviewing authority to detect the flaw and redress the wrong'.[16] The committee urged that the officials concerned should have realized, when the vital fact about the circumcision had been revealed, that there had been a grave miscarriage of justice and have pressed the judge on this account. It went into the question of the chain of responsibility within the office. At the critical moment in 1898 Digby was the permanent under-secretary. The immediate subordinate concerned was the assistant under-secretary, Murdoch, to whom the head of the criminal department, Simpson, had submitted the minutes which had apparently been seen and initialled by Digby who had taken no further action. These minutes clearly showed, argued the committee, that Murdoch and Simpson had failed to appreciate the significance of the new information and 'to look at the matter as *res integra* and form an independent judgement upon it'.[17] In other words, Digby had been misled by the judgement of his subordinates. The report also stressed that there was far too little criminal experience in the Home Office and recommended that at least the criminal department be staffed by trained lawyers. A po.nt the committee seems to have missed was that Simpson (like Troup and Byrne) had in fact been called to the bar and was regarded within the office as 'a great authority on criminal law'.[18] But it was true that Murdoch had no legal training – indeed, that had been one of Lushington's objections to his promotion in 1894.[19]

After publication of the report Akers-Douglas leapt to the defence of his department in a cabinet paper. He argued that 'in their (very proper) desire to shield the Judge' of the 1896 trial, the committee had 'cast an undue proportion of blame on the Home Office'. On the issue of recruiting lawyers as Home Office officials he felt it would be unwise and unnecessary; the home secretary had ample legal backing from his own legal assistant under-secretary, from the law officers of the crown and, if necessary, from the lord chancellor himself.[20] This was stated to the House of Commons where he stoutly supported his staff and was backed by Asquith among others.[21] But despite these parliamentary plaudits, within the Home Office itself there was inevitably much heart-searching and it was later felt that Simpson had taken much of the blame: ' . . . the feeling that he had been made a scapegoat had tended over the years to sour him and to accentuate his eccentricities'.[22]

The home secretary was not averse to the prospect of an addition to the senior members of his staff – especially as he considered the criminal department overworked. Therefore, after consultation with Chalmers and Troup, he proposed two new appointments: an additional assistant under-secretary, a good barrister, who would relieve Troup and strengthen the criminal department by assuming a particular responsibility for deciding doubtful criminal petitions;

and an additional junior clerk in the same department. The Treasury evidently put up some kind of a fight because, while it immediately agreed to the additional junior, it took five months and 'an unofficial communication ... between the Chancellor of the Exchequer and the Secretary of State' to achieve agreement about the new senior appointment.[23] However, in May 1906 Ernley R. H. Blackwell was appointed to the new post at a salary of £1,000 a year. He was a Scot, aged thirty-eight, who had been called to the (English) bar in 1892.

The Beck case had a wider consequence. Although it had been generally accepted that this was a highly unusual case which was unlikely to recur (partly because of the subsequent discovery and use of the fingerprint system for checking identity)[24] it renewed earlier discussion about the need for an English court of criminal appeal. This had not been recommended by the Beck committee but it was fairly widely accepted by legal opinion[25] and a bill to establish such a court was introduced in the session in which the Beck case was debated. But it was two years before an effective bill was passed. Meanwhile the home secretary – then Herbert Gladstone – had been troubled by publicity generated by the George Edalji case in which a strong lobby believed that this man had been wrongly convicted and forced the holding of a special inquiry. This put Gladstone in the awkward position of having to pardon the accused without being certain of his innocence.[26] It was therefore a relief to the Home Office when the criminal appeal act of 1907 set up the criminal appeal court to be accessible to those tried on indictment and convicted. This did not affect the prerogative of mercy exercised by the home secretary and enabled him to refer cases, if necessary for retrial, to the new court.

The Beck case raised fundamental questions: was it right to have legal recommendations made in the office by non-lawyers? Had the process of devolution gone too far in certain areas? Through the classic façade of responsible ministers defending their officials in parliament, it can clearly be seen that these ministers had faith in their first divison officials. To prevent a recurrence of such a case various improvements were wrought: all miscellaneous work, that is work which did not relate to 'crime in the strict sense' or to 'the machinery of justice', was removed from the criminal department, division C; and there was to be greater liaison with outside authorities such as the prison staff and police over such matters.[27] But there was no reversing of the process of recruiting able generalists rather than lawyers or even graduates with law degrees;[28] nor did the incident in any way halt the devolution of responsibility.

Troup becomes permanent under-secretary: 1908

In March 1908 an event occurred which put the seal on the triumph of the open competition generation of Home Office clerks: the first promotion of one of them to the most senior permanent post of a career official. In March 1907 Chalmers had written to Gladstone, 'The work at the Home Office has increased, is increasing and will increase and I think you will find you will want a younger man to keep pace with it efficiently.'[29] Chalmers did not actually retire until early the following year, so his chief had several months in which to consider a successor. By the end of August Gladstone had fairly firmly decided to offer the appointment to Troup who, apart from Cunynghame, was the most senior permanent official. Troup had had wide experience of the office's work: he had first entered the criminal department; was given additional responsibility for parliamentary business in 1887; became head of the new parliamentary and industrial department in 1896; and in 1903 was made under-secretary in charge of police and criminal work. He was outstanding among able colleagues. Gladstone apparently secured the permission of the prime minister (Campbell-Bannerman) without great difficulty. There may, however, have been slight doubt about the appointment for, although Gladstone gave his private secretary (M. L. Waller) permission to intimate his decision to Troup, Waller felt constrained to add in the letter that nothing human was certain until it had happened. 'Troup', Waller told Gladstone, 'will understand just the tinge of caution conveyed in that.'[30] Troup's appointment was finally announced in the middle of December. He himself was clearly delighted. He admired Gladstone whom he regarded with affection and it was with evident feeling that he added in his letter of acceptance: 'It adds much to the value of the promotion that it is from you I receive it ... Please accept the thanks which I feel much more strongly than I can express.'[31] He became permanent under-secretary on 1 February 1908.

The one official who clearly resented the decision was Troup's senior in terms of age and seniority. Cunynghame had been appointed in 1894 from outside the office to succeed Pemberton and from 1903, when Troup had been promoted to take Murdoch's place, the two had worked side by side as assistant under-secretaries, Cunynghame in charge of industrial work. Now he felt he had been passed over. In a petulant letter to Asquith – as the politician who had originally appointed him – he directed his bitterness not so much at Gladstone as at his fellow officials, and his implication that somehow he had been by-passed in the office system rings a little of the earlier complaints of Du Cane and Warren:

After you left and for years I found the want of organisation in the Office very detrimental to my work. By the system then in vogue I rarely saw a paper after I had minuted it, my minute was usually discussed by Digby with some clerk who was under me, and then acted on without my further knowledge. If any inquirer called he was interviewed by a clerk.[32]

This 'rubicund', slightly pompous man was an interesting eccentric who certainly added colour to the routine of the department. His great passion was science and invention. He had a laboratory at home and he derived his ideas for his inventions from his office responsibilities. On one occasion, when the disease 'phossy-jaw', contracted in the manufacture of matches, was of concern to the department, he announced that he had invented a non-phosphoric safety match. 'A meeting in the Home Secretary's room was accordingly arranged for the testing of this invention, but the future prospects of the Cunynghame match went up in the smoke of the explosion that ensued.'[33] The author of his obituary in *The Times* felt that 'with his wide learning and practical knowledge of many departments of life' he might 'if he had concentrated more, have been one of the great departmental heads of his generation'.[34] But, in fact, he was not in the mould of the new type of civil servant. He felt very different from his colleagues whom he regarded as a deskbound, bureaucratic élite with no experience of the world beyond Whitehall.[35] Gladstone felt sorry for him and urged that he be consoled with a knighthood.[36] The award of a KCB in 1908 evidently checked his initial impulse to retire early and he remained as assistant under-secretary until 1913.

Troup was also knighted in 1908. He was then fifty-one, two years younger than Lushington had been on his promotion to the post. In many ways Lushington's protégé, Troup resembled him more than any other Home Office permanent under-secretary of the period. Each had had previous working experience within and therefore loyalty towards the office; each worked extremely conscientiously and demanded high standards; and each left his particular stamp on the office. Troup's personality is less easy for the historian to grasp.[37] Described by one contemporary as 'a rather silent, heavy Scot, with little sense of humour',[38] he was evidently rather shy. Official documents show that he had a definite sense of history and that he was less legalistic in his approach than Lushington. The most obvious apparent difference between the leadership of the two men derived from the different pressures and demands of the two periods: Troup was more in contact with the office as a whole; he delegated work and generally utilized his staff to the maximum.

Before the war the office was still small enough for its permanent head to run it personally and Troup evidently possessed good management techniques, as one of his junior officials explained:

> Soon after my arrival Sir Edward found an excuse to summon me and to talk over my work. It was his custom to seek such interviews with his junior staff at fairly frequent intervals, and there can be no doubt as to their stimulating effect. However busy he might be – and he was a tremendous worker – he always found time to maintain touch with his men and to keep them up to the mark.[39]

Although Troup does not seem to have had a charismatic personality, his reputation long illuminated the department. 'What the Home Office is today Sir Edward Troup has made it', said Blackwell on Troup's retirement in 1922. Nearly forty years later an ex-under-secretary of the Home Office echoed this view.[40]

The office of private secretary

There is one particular function of first division clerks which has not been described: the work of the private secretary. This is easy to omit because the work involved simply being the 'right hand man' of the minister or under-secretary and had no special place in the departmental hierarchy. But it is worth describing because it was a coveted job and seems often to have marked a man out for a successful career, although Troup's career shows that it was not a *sine qua non* for success since he only spent a few months as private secretary.

The secretary of state had had a personally-appointed private secretary since the late eighteenth century; but it was only in 1870 that he was granted an official allowance for a junior clerk to act as such alongside his political nominee.[41] The parliamentary under-secretary had first been granted a similar allowance in the 1860s and had invariably been served by a junior clerk.[42] Lushington had been granted an allowance by the Treasury for secretarial help when he was first appointed legal adviser, and then when his personally-appointed clerk died in 1890 it became the norm for the permanent under-secretary too to have a junior clerk as private secretary.[43] The home secretary's private secretaryship was regarded as the 'plum' post for it carried with it an allowance of £300 as compared with £150 for the other two. Some remained in that post (although not necessarily serving one master) for several years: Ruggles-Brise broke all records by working for four home secretaries over a period of eight years; Pedder worked for three over a period of six; and Waller served Gladstone for his whole four years' period in office. A private secretaryship was very often a stepping-stone to promotion. This was usually to a senior clerkship although Pedder and Waller were actually promoted while acting as private secretaries. Some subsequently left the first division on promotion: Legge became inspector of reformatory and industrial schools after working for Gladstone when he was parliamentary under-secretary; and between 1873 and 1913 four of the thirteen private secretaries to the home secretaries became prison commissioners.[44]

At least one of these – Ruggles-Brise – admitted that after the excitement of having been a private secretary he did not want to return to the humdrum life of a senior clerk.[45] Harcourt had once described the world into which a new private secretary stepped as that of the 'inner circle'.[46] Guillemard, who served Harcourt and then Sir Michael Hicks Beach at the Treasury in this role during the 1890s, called it 'a freer and fuller life':

> The years which I spent as his [Harcourt's] private secretary count amongst the happiest in my life: they were certainly some of the fullest. The work was absorbing and varied: one saw the inner working of Government and knew the secrets and the gossip of the Cabinet; one met all the most interesting people, and heard the best of talk.[47]

Private secretaries could become close to their chiefs in a way that other officials never did. They had a close day-by-day working alliance which inevitably involved knowing a good deal about the private life of their chief. Waller was obviously fond of Gladstone whom he regaled with his hunting and shooting experiences and by whom he was sent pheasants and even invited to join house parties.[48]

Part of their work consisted of the purely secretarial business of making appointments and forwarding despatch boxes. During the parliamentary session a private secretary also helped his minister with legislation – not merely chasing up papers from Home Office departments but actually writing briefs. He had to deal diplomatically with a wide variety of people. He might have to smooth a minister's way by discreetly indicating his views, or even by direct negotiation: Legge, on Gladstone's behalf, once spent three hours with H. W. Massingham, editor of the *Daily Chronicle*, pointing out the damage he was doing by bitterly attacking the prison system, and thereby got him to 'climb down'.[49] The home secretary's private secretary acted as patronage secretary. With the parliamentary under-secretary and chief inspector of factories, he formed a committee which nominated candidates for factory inspectorships;[50] and he participated in a similar committee for inspectors of mines. He could be involved in appointments to departmental committees: Waller urged Gladstone to appoint a senior factory inspector to the committee on factory accidents in 1908.[51] He was often 'in the know' about senior office appointments: we have observed that it was Waller who informed Troup about his probable appointment as permanent under-secretary. Yet this very variation of work could ultimately be wearisome. When it was announced that Gladstone was to leave the Home Office and he proposed a prison commissionership for his loyal private secretary, Waller wrote to him:

> And though all our subjects are interesting, and there is a certain regret at dropping any of them, I begin to feel that I should be glad to *specialize* some time fairly soon and not prolong indefinitely the species of mental dissipation known as private secretarying![52]

By this time it was common practice for career officials to fill the principal private secretary post although ministers sometimes brought in additional political secretaries. However, the unorthodox Winston Churchill, Gladstone's successor, brought his own principal private secretary, Eddie Marsh, to the Home Office. When he left, the department persuaded the Treasury to allow his successor, Reginald McKenna, to have two full-time private secretaries: a senior clerk and a junior clerk with respective allowances of £300 and £100. The increase was pressed for by the Home Office on the grounds that the secretary of state needed more time from a private secretary particularly in the Commons and also for the work of nominating factory and mines inspectors.[53] Thus by 1914 three of the sixteen juniors and one of the six seniors were permanently employed on private secretary duties and thus removed from ordinary departmental work.

Further departmental growth and specialization: 1906–14
First division officials were chronically harassed by their work-load and during the period 1908–10, when Liberal social reform forcibly struck the department, they were particularly weighed down with increased paper work – see Table 5. Yet the number of officials to cope with those papers had also risen: in 1899 seventeen first division and twenty-nine second divison clerks had processed 50,224 registered incoming papers; in 1909 twenty-four first divison and thirty-six second division clerks had processed 71,153 such papers.[54] This would have made a straight overall average increase of 8.6 per cent per clerk which does not, on the face of it, seem excessive. But, argued Troup, 'the work of the Office tends to increase in an even greater ratio than is indicated by the mere number of official papers'; and Pedder gave the example of cases involving the ex-

Table 5   *The increasing number of registered papers dealt with by the Home Office 1906–9*

Division	1906	1907	1908	1909
Criminal (C)	20,648	20,757	22,014	23,593
Domestic (D)	21,507	21,884	22,683	23,641
Industrial (I)	7,491	9,601	11,349	7,745*
Special Subjects (S)	12,528	11,942	14,165	16,174
Total	62,624[†]	64,184	70,211	71,153

*This sudden drop may be accounted for by the transfer of the parliamentary side of the division's work to division S.
[†]This total does not appear correct, but it is quoted in official papers as the annual figure.[4]

pulsion of aliens where an enormous amount of work could be incurred by just a few papers.[56] Also, the output of papers generated within the office – circulars, for example – was steadily increasing. In January 1908 Chalmers was dramatic about the work situation:

> Our hours of work have considerably increased since I came to the Office, and Saturday, in particular instead of bringing an early day, is now often a late day for many of the higher division men. Certainly of late we have had more men on sick leave, and I am inclined to attribute this to overstrain. I think soon it will be requisite to overhaul the whole machinery of the HO otherwise a serious breakdown may occur . . .[57]

A year later three divisional heads – Pedder of division S, Delevigne of division I and Aitken of division D – complained about their heavy and growing load. Byrne, the assistant under-secretary, commented on the 'remarkable' growth of parliamentary questions (from 847 in 1906 to 1,028 in 1908), which Troup attributed to the regular holding of an autumn parliamentary session.[58] In addition, MPs were demanding much more detailed information than formerly.[59] By January 1910 a note of desperation had crept into the work reports. Pedder noted an increase of 28 per cent in his division's papers and reported that the strain on the staff (who were always harassed by a deadline on naturalization cases) had been 'very severe throughout the year'; Delevigne argued that it had been difficult to cope with the work satisfactorily and would have been impossible without further aid had certain bills which were contemplated actually made progress.[60] Gladstone admitted the 'very severe' strain 'borne by a continuous and self-sacrificing effort', adding: 'With a rather guilty conscience I must record my opinion that it has been too great. There has been a constant risk of breakdown. Unless there is a marked decrease in the volume and intensity of the work some relief must be sought.'[61] He took no positive action – his own appointment as governor of South Africa had already been announced – but he drew his successor's attention to the problem.

Gladstone himself was well aware of the increase in work, being proud of the Liberals' contribution towards social improvement. His private papers contain handwritten notes setting out the achievements of the Home Office between 1906 and 1909. He found that his department had been involved in the passage of forty-two bills (twenty-three of which were major government bills). He divided these into 'industrial law and administration' and others. In the former category he picked out as especially important the 1906 workmen's compensation act, the 1906 notice of accidents act and the 1907 factory and workshops act. In the latter category he drew attention to the 1907 probation of offenders act, the 1908 prevention of crime act and the 1908 children act. He drew up a little chart which showed that the Home Office had been involved in three royal commissions, ten select committees, twenty-one departmental committees and three special commissions of which respectively two, seven, nine and two had been 'acted upon, by legislation, or administration, or by preparations for them'.[62] Each major piece of legislation – with the exception of the 1907 criminal appeal act which removed some responsibility from the Home Office – immediately involved greater burdens on the office since there was no automatic increase in staff.

Yet all the 'strain' and 'breakdown' talk revealed in the official papers contrasts strangely with memoirs of the period. H. R. Scott, who began as a Home Office junior clerk in 1911, later commented on the 'grace, circumstance and leisure' surrounding the working life of that era when first division men still had time to don grey toppers and field-glasses during Ascot week and keen cricketers to attend Lords during the season – which, after all, was during the parliamentary session.[63] H. B. Butler, an entrant of 1908, hardly depicted his early days in the department as ones of strain and stress. This may partly have been because junior clerks had to mark time to a certain extent while they learned the rudiments. But one of his episodes shows that life at under-secretary level could also be relaxed. In 1911 Byrne, in charge of the novel subject, air matters, was sent to the Lake District for a fortnight to investigate the appearance of some 'hydro-aeroplanes' which were upsetting the locality:

> He heard all the parties concerned with exemplary patience and returned greatly refreshed by this agreeable interlude. Weeks

passed, but no report appeared... Months passed, and finally years, but no report was ever committed to paper. Sir William had correctly foreseen that the fire would die down, if he abstained from feeding it by issuing a report, which must have rekindled everybody's passions. So he sipped his half-bottle of Medoc every day at lunch, and smoked his cigar after it, and allowed time to do its work.[64]

Of course these are old men's memories of what they may partly have imagined were halcyon days compared with those of post-war government departments. Nevertheless, when one looks at the actual number of hours worked per day the officials do not, by modern standards, appear to have been unduly overworked. In 1910 Aitken submitted a statement showing the number of hours worked by each of his first division clerks over a period of three months. Excluding Saturdays the maximum average recorded per day was only 7.7 hours and the minimum 6.98 although it is true that a gloomier picture emerges from the estimated number of hours worked outside office hours: four hours a week in Aitken's case and ten in the case of Moylan (a junior clerk) who spent over half of this on committee work.[65]

One is forced to the conclusion that since there was no regular annual departmental or Treasury review of staff the only way in which divisions could acquire the increases they undoubtedly needed to cope with extra work was through pressure of complaint. Thus grumblings about overstrain may not in themselves have been significant unless either breakdown occurred – which it never did – or unless it actually prevented officials from performing their functions adequately. Some light is thrown on the latter point in mid-1910 when both Aitken and Pedder submitted renewed pleas for more staff.[66] Both divisions were in arrears with their papers and letters were being answered in a perfunctory manner. More interesting was the fact that – at least in Aitken's case – principal clerks were unable to read and consider reports, for example, of inspectors. In other words they were merely helping other clerks in their divisions to get through the daily grind of business. As Byrne put it:

> ...the existence of these heavy arrears indicates that the Higher Staff find it almost impossible to inform themselves by visits and conferences with the Subordinate Departments and the Heads of Institutions regulated and controlled by the Home Office of many things which they should know: the 'thinking' functions are almost suppressed by the pressure of urgent daily work.[67]

This was important because of the way in which heads of sub-departments had to pass their reports and papers through the central division before they went to the under-secretaries. If the head of a division had no time to read, consider and make recommendations on the reports of the inspectors for whom his division was responsible, there was every likelihood that these would get forgotten or ignored since the under-secretaries themselves had still less time to do this. This seriously hampered, for example, the reformatory and industrial schools inspectorate.[68]. There is less evidence that this fault lay with Delevigne and division I; but then Delevigne was an exceptionally capable official and was the head of a more specialist division which may have contributed to his being effective.

In 1910 Troup secured Churchill's support for a joint Treasury-Home Office inquiry, and a report was produced by Byrne and J. W. Cawston of the Treasury. They agreed that the formation of a new division might soon be necessary but that meanwhile what was required was the addition of three senior clerks who could make final decisions in a large number of cases 'in order that the principal clerks of the various divisions may be in a position to devote themselves to their proper work'.[69] The method of acquiring the new seniors was by now familiar: while one was to be a new appointment, the other two were to be juniors 'acting' as seniors for which they were to receive £150 on top of their ordinary salaries. These changes gave two instead of one senior clerk to divisions I, D and S.[70]

Within two years the projected creation of a fifth division had become essential and there was further reorganization. In view of the large number of miscellaneous subjects dealt with by the Home Office a totally logical rationale for their distribution into divisions was difficult. Since 1896 there had been increasing specialization. The first division to have become a specialist department was division C which had all the work which was not specifically to do with crime and the machinery of justice removed from it after the Beck case rumpus.[71] Division I, the old industrial and parliamentary department, had had the non-industrial side of its work (bills and bye-laws) removed from it following the recommendation of a departmental committee on the factory inspectorate in 1907. Bills and bye-laws then went to division S (whose title was altered in 1912 to division B) which, although it was hardly a specialist division, nevertheless had some kind of form dealing with licensing, naturalization, nationality and aliens, together with parliamentary work. Division D was the 'rag-bag' division: its subjects veered from children, to obscene publications, to Home Office establishment matters, to street traffic and others. The new division was created simply by hiving off some of these subjects to a new division E.[72]

This remained the position for less than a year. The case for giving the administration of legislation concerning children greater attention was forcibly put by the 1913 departmental committee on reformatory and industrial schools. As a result, division D was divested of most of its other responsibilities.[73] This left division E and a newly created division F to cope with the remainder of miscellaneous subjects. Meanwhile division I became 'division A' so that the six divisions were neatly labelled from A to F.[74]

By mid-1913 the first division staff consisted of four under-secretaries including the permanent under-secretary, five principal clerks, six senior clerks, and thirteen junior clerks two of whom were 'acting' seniors. It was a situation which the Treasury disliked for being top-heavy in terms of under-secretaries and therefore Troup obligingly offered to abolish one assistant under-secretaryship on Cunynghame's retirement, which was imminent, in return for the creation of an additional principal clerkship and a rise in salary for three divisional heads – Delevigne, Simpson and Pedder – on the grounds that they would incur greater responsibility. He also requested another junior clerk for the new division.[75] The Treasury was amenable, though added a caveat that a second post of assistant under-secretary be reconsidered on a vacancy. It also agreed that Delevigne be given a special title, 'Director of the Industrial Division of the Home Office', although it wanted him to retain the rank of principal clerk in order to prevent the Home Office regarding this as a new senior post.[76]

In its relations with the Treasury over establishment changes the Home Office managed during this period to get what it wanted with relatively little difficulty, no doubt because of the minimal expense involved.[77] Treasury officials occasionally found it difficult to resist a little homily: 'we do not expect persons in the position of Seniors or Principals to be sticklers for the bare minimum [number of working hours]' Cawston once reminded Byrne.[78] But the Home Office only occasionally felt the need to bring out its big gun as when Byrne threatened Cawston with 'all' Churchill's power during discussion of the 1910 changes and when in late 1913 McKenna evidently intervened in a minor altercation.

From the latter the Home Office emerged the clear victor with a somewhat changed first division structure. Byrne had vacated his under-secretaryship on being appointed chairman of the Board of Control under the 1913 mental deficiency act. Ignoring the Treasury's earlier stipulation that this post was to be reconsidered on a vacancy, Troup immediately proposed the promotion of Delevigne and thus provoked a snort from the Treasury which also objected to the situation whereby Home Office under-secretaries were controlling principal clerks who in some cases were earning roughly the same salary.[79] After McKenna's intervention the Home Office agreed that on the *next* occurrence of a vacancy it would reconsider Blackwell's post of legal assistant under-secretary (which, as the Treasury gloomily predicted, meant putting it off almost until the Greek calends since Blackwell did not in fact retire until 1933). In return for this 'concession' the title of the six principal clerks – all of whom were now placed on the higher salary scale – was changed to 'assistant secretary' while the senior clerks were promised a rise when the under-secretaryship was abolished.[80] The point of the changes, expressed in a memorandum by McKenna, was

> to increase the responsibility and improve the position of the six Heads of Division . . . I expect the Assistant Secretaries gradually to assume a greater responsibility in their respective Divisions, and the way to be prepared for the final form of organization in which only the Under Secretary of State and his Deputy will come between them and the Secretary of State. When this ultimate development is attained the status of the Senior Clerks will also be raised . . . In this form the Office will be in exactly the same position as the Treasury.[81]

Thus the first division establishment at the beginning of 1914 was as shown in Table 6. Since 1896 its size had increased from sixteen to thirty-two and its annual cost from £11,948 to £20,133.[82]

Table 6   *First division establishment at the beginning of 1914*

Office	Salary (£)
1 permanent under-secretary	2,000
1 legal assistant under-secretary (to be abolished)	1,200 – 1,500
1 assistant under-secretary	1,200 – 1,500
6 assistant secretaries	1,000 × 50 – 1,200
6 senior clerks	700 × 25 – 900
17 junior clerks	200 × 20 – 500

The 'crisis' aspect of Home Office work

There was one characteristic aspect of Home Office work which at times considerably added to the normal work-load. This was the 'crisis' aspect. Every so often some case would arise or some decision be taken which brought the secretary of state into the glare of publicity and forced officials to worry and scurry. Strong public feeling inevitably arose out of the nature of Home Office responsibilities: every other citizen had his opinion about his right to attend a public meeting in Trafalgar Square, about whether or not the death sentence should be passed on this or that criminal, about the way prisoners should be treated, about whether or not troops should be used to dispel riotous behaviour. Herbert Gladstone rightly said, 'the Home Secretary, of all administrators, stands closest to the lives of the multitude.'[83] Moreover, opinions diverge to such an extent that whatever action the home secretary took he was bound to be attacked from some quarter. Home secretaries are politicians and controversy is the stuff of politics but the responsibilities attached to this post have often made it an unpopular one among ministers. Gladstone would rather not have gone back to the Home Office in 1905 because 'the sense of responsibility weighed rather heavily upon him'.[84] Churchill is said to have been 'more glad to leave the Home Office than any of the numerous offices he had held'.[85]

Civil servants were even less fond of turbulence. In the first place there was no extra staff to cope with emergencies. A controversial event could arise like a squall and while it lasted dominate the working – and sometimes non-working – lives of the officials concerned who simply had to await calmer waters while they fended off parliamentary questions and importunate correspondents while trying to sort out the actual crisis. The humblest case could lead to trouble: who was to know, for instance, what prominent person might not take up the case of an alien excluded by the Home Office, or what MP might not try to make political capital out of the case of a factory inspector dismissed for incompetency? The Beck case had shown how lack of care over a prisoner's petition could lead to disaster. This whole aspect of departmental work had the effect of making officials cautious and conservative.

The period from Troup's accession as permanent under-secretary until the outbreak of war brought law and order problems of a greater scale and intensity than anything the office had hitherto known. Troup had good cause to remember this aspect of his work:

> ... during a widespread industrial disturbance, attended by actual or possible outbreaks of violence and the paralysis of the ordinary means of communications and transport, the staff of the department experience fully 'the joy of eventful life' and the office hours cover night as well as day.[86]

The extensive industrial unrest which included, under Churchill's home secretaryship, the Rhondda valley strike of coal miners, the seamen's and dockers' strike and the national railway strike, and under McKenna's the miners' strike and the London dock strike, caused constant extra strain on officials. The novelty of the disruption lay in the fact that it was prolonged and involved organized strikes of large numbers of workmen all over the country. This created widespread fear on the part of local authorities which felt they could not cope. The Home Office was the central point for receiving requests for help in quelling rioters or looters from local chief constables or mayors and for organizing the despatch of such help in the form of additional policemen or even soldiers. The 1911 railway strike posed the additional problem of how to ensure the maintenance of essential supplies to areas which complained of food shortages. Even after the strike Troup was preoccupied in trying to defend Churchill against charges of unlawfully having sent troops to aid the civil power and against criticism for the scheme to establish 'special constables' for use in an emergency.[87]

A further law and order problem was posed by the activities of the suffragettes whose actual cause was one for government decision but whose targets of attack gave the Home Office continual headaches. Not only were the militants successful in their attempts to disturb the peace by attacking prominent individuals and public property which created problems for the police, but their refusal to eat in prison achieved their aim of disturbing the prison authorities and creating at times difficult dilemmas for the home secretaries involved (Gladstone, Churchill and McKenna) as to how to treat this new form of non-criminal prisoner.

These problems are well documented and fully related in many sources. But in order to look more closely at the kind of work and tension generated within the office it is worth examining in detail the events surrounding one particular crisis which arose over the holding of a Roman Catholic procession (a subject which, more than once, caused problems for the Home Office).[88] The procession in question occurred on 13 September 1908 and led to accusations of administrative incompetence by the home secretary, Gladstone, which may have damaged his career.[89]

The proposed procession – part of a eucharistic congress in which the host was to be carried and elaborate vestments worn – had been announced by the cardinal archbishop of Westminster to the commissioner of metropolitan police, Sir Edward Henry, in July. Such a procession was undoubtedly illegal under the 1829 Roman Catholic emancipation act which forbade the exercise of Catholic rites and the wearing of Catholic religious dress except in church or in private houses. However, such stringency had long been waived and certain processions – although not on such a grand scale – had been allowed by the authorities without interference.[90] The commissioner's responsibility lay not with the illegality of the project but with the extent to which it would cause public disruption. At the time he was evidently unconcerned about this aspect and did not refer to the Home Office until early September. Meanwhile fierce opposition to the procession had arisen from militant Protestants, some of whom approached the king who took their protests seriously. At this time the prime minister, Asquith, was in Aberdeenshire and Gladstone was at Archerfield, near North Berwick; Troup was on holiday in Switzerland and had not returned to the office by 2 September when officials first became aware of the storm of protest.

It was not until 8 September that Troup – then back in harness – sent Gladstone the papers about the proposed procession.[91] By this time Gladstone was aware of the strong Protestant petition to the king who wanted the procession banned. It was a tricky situation involving the old chestnut, a potentially explosive public demonstration, spiced with sectarian controversy, an obsolete law and royal concern. It was not eased by Gladstone's unbroken sojourn in the north which meant that he had to rely on Troup's ciphered bulletins for on-the-ground information and was not in a position to have personal meetings with those involved. At first Troup was against interference (although the procession was technically illegal) on grounds of 'precedents' and 'policy'.[92] He felt that if it were to be stopped this was up to the attorney-general. He did not suggest that there might be a public order problem.

The following day (9 September) Troup set out for Gladstone the government's dilemma: the Home Office, through the metropolitan police, was bound to try to maintain order, yet the very fact of doing this would give the procession a semblance of official co-operation which he was most anxious to avoid. He suggested two possible courses of action, both of which differed from his previous day's advice. First, at least the police should make it clear to the organizers of the procession that they were not sanctioning illegal proceedings, that they would do their best to maintain order but that this might be difficult. Secondly, he felt that Gladstone might want to induce the Roman Catholic authorities to abandon the procession in view of the opposition. The threat of disorder was difficult to gauge and he concluded that the police would probably be able to deal with 'actual organized violence' but might not be able to prevent the procession from being broken up by a huge mob. 'I think the right course would be for you to write personally to Archbishop Bourne and ask him to abandon his procession on account of the risk of public disorder', he advised.[93] This sounds like his final considered view and was his most positive suggestion in favour of stopping the procession. Yet it was immediately modified by his report that Byrne (a Catholic and acquaintance of the archbishop) did 'not see reason to think that there will be serious opposition to the procession'.[94] Troup's main concern was that Gladstone protect himself against the possible subsequent accusation that he had not made it clear that the procession was illegal.

Meanwhile Asquith, already aware of the wider political danger of offending the nonconformists, was being pressed by the king to take action against the procession.[95] It was up to the home secretary to take into account these factors, together with Troup's analysis of the legal position and his estimate (albeit not altogether clear) of the danger to public order, and put fairly and squarely before the prime minister a firm recommendation. This he did not do. Thus, on 10 September, Asquith stepped in and asked the Marquess of Ripon – a Catholic member of cabinet – to approach the archbishop. The latter replied to Asquith that only a formal request from the prime minister would make him cancel the procession and if he received this he would vindicate himself publicly, whereupon Gladstone wrote to the archbishop saying that if the procession was to be 'identified with a ceremonial which is alleged to be inconsistent with the law . . . the difficulty of maintaining order is increased'.[96] The following day the archbishop very reluctantly agreed to abandon all aspects of ecclesiastical ceremonial in the procession. Troup was evidently not immediately informed of this decision, for late on Saturday afternoon (12 September) he was still trying to secure an interview with the archbishop to discover the outcome before proceeding to Scotland Yard to learn the arrangements for the following day.[97] On the Sunday he was again at his post informing Gladstone about the event. The size and activity of the crowd was somewhat worse than the Home Office had expected and the police had in some places had difficulty in containing it. Had there been a stronger hostile element they would not have been able to prevent it from overwhelming the procession. Thus, concluded Troup, 'the Archbishop by yielding *saved* the procession'.[98]

Home Office officials evidently thought all had passed off satisfactorily but this was not to be the case. First, Ripon resigned, allegedly through ill-health, but in fact because of the conflict he had experienced between his religious and political loyalties. Secondly, the king and several cabinet members blamed Gladstone for incompetence.[99] Asquith called for explanation and Troup, horrified and puzzled by the turn of events, set about producing an extensive justification for his chief. Troup's personal view was that if the cabinet had wanted the procession stopped on grounds of illegality, it was up to the attorney-general to do this. The function of the home secretary was to maintain public order; and since the Home Office (rightly or wrongly) had seen no indication that there would be a serious breakdown of order, the home secretary could not prohibit the procession on those grounds.[100] Troup hinted that if any official were to blame it was Henry – who was in a difficult position partly because he himself was a Catholic – since he had taken so long to inform the Home Office of the projected procession. Gladstone publicly defended Henry whose own personal account of events apparently went some way towards mollifying Gladstone's colleagues and possibly the king,[101] but not before Gladstone had suffered the further trauma of having his tendered resignation nearly accepted by Asquith.

The role of the pre-war Home Office official

The primary cause of change in the work and role of goverment officials during the period covered by this study was the phenomenon of legislative intervention to regulate large social and economic areas of men's lives. The Home Office still retained its non-legislative functions: it still acted as the liaison between the monarch and his subjects, advised the crown on royal appointments and on the award of honours, and drew up documents for the creation of titles. But these functions, which had loomed so large in the Home Office of 1848, were reduced to relative insignificance by the work introduced through legislation. By 1914 the formulation and administration of a myriad of parliamentary acts required a comparative army of civil servants: whereas in 1848 only two senior permanent officials with a staff of some twenty clerks advised the home secretary, now a first division of thirty-two, backed by a much larger executive staff and advised by inspectors numbering hundreds, were fulfilling that advisory function. The reforms of the 1870s, so effectively planned by Northcote and Trevelyan as necessary for the future of the civil service, had indeed proved essential in view of the work which followed that period. Their recommendation that the top level of university-trained officials assume a high degree of responsibility and leave routine matters to an executive class only began to assume reality within the Home Office after the turn of the century. By this time the increased volume of work, together with constant Treasury pressure towards the devolution of authority and its reluctance to admit staff increases, had created a situation where even junior first division officials found themselves 'acting' as more senior officials and in a position to make policy recommendations.

Greater complexity of legislation demanded increasing numbers of responsible officials on whom ministers increasingly relied. But it should also be noted that the new breed of post-open competition men generated work for their department simply by being energetic. They spotted administrative weaknesses and made recommendations which often required more time and more personnel. Their talent was there and put to use in the constitutional process; but at the same time they made sure that it was made use of.

Recently historians, politicians and political theorists have challenged the democratic orthodoxy which stated that government decided on policy priorities and put its programme before the legislature while the executive – the civil service – carried out measures approved by parliament. It is clear that civil servants in some departments played a crucial role in devising and promoting early welfare measures even before the first world war.[102] More recently, politicians have resentfully credited civil servants with being the real power behind the ministerial throne.[103] If this is true the foundations for such major official participation in the policy-making process were already laid by 1914.

Officials were able to influence policy in a variety of ways. First, they participated in committee work which often formed the basis for future legislation. By the early 1890s Troup and his contemporaries were finding an outlet for their talents by acting as secretaries to departmental and inter-departmental committees whose recommendations were increasingly the prelude to policy changes. Byrne was secretary to the inter-departmental committee on riots in 1894; Legge was secretary to the 1894–5 Home Office departmental committee on prisons; Aitken was secretary to the departmental committee on reformatory and industrial schools in 1896. After this there are increasing numbers of examples of official participation in committee work. In 1903, as a member of the Royal Commission on Alien Immigration, Digby opposed some radical proposals of the majority of commissioners in a separate, individual memorandum. The aliens bill of 1904 was a political bone of contention and failed because of the opposition's large number of amendments which echoed Digby's objections in many respects. In the area of factory administration, parliament was presented, between 1900 and 1914, with twenty-six separate reports of specialist departmental committees, usually concerned with technical aspects of factory work. These often led, if not to legislation, to new Home Office regulations.[104]

Secondly, officials played an important part in the actual formulation of legislation. They drafted memoranda on proposals which sometimes went to cabinet. During the passage of bills through parliament they drafted clauses; they received and minuted on suggestions from interested outside parties; they helped ministers receive deputations at the department; and they supported their minister, often by standing at his elbow in the House of Commons, as he piloted bills through parliament. Immediately following a new act they drafted explanatory circulars for the authorities concerned, and generally tried to get the new legislation effectively into operation.

Thirdly, they themselves effectively made laws, for they were increasingly delegated powers under major acts of parliament. Thus overworked legislators enacted the fundamental principles from which technical or administrative details were worked out and applied by the executive. Officials were delegated powers to make regulations, to add to the schedules of the acts, or to approve new rules made by a third party (such as managers of mines or prison authorities). An expert on delegated legislation commented in 1921 on what was happening: 'Everywhere in our statute book the same process is visible. The action of our Acts of Parliament grows more and more dependent upon subsidiary legislation. More than half our modern Acts are to this extent incomplete statements of law.'[105] In this system of lightening the burden on parliament, there were safeguards against the abuse of authority by the executive, such as the requirement that administrative amendments be subject to parliamentary scrutiny for a specified time. But MPs had less and less time to pursue this kind of paper and, in fact, the development of delegated authority gave officials considerable power to affect the lives of individuals.

Fourthly, civil service advice was a significant factor in a government's decision about whether to support non-governmental proposals for reform. In 1911 Mr Bryce and various other MPs put forward a private member's bill extending legal protection to women against procurement for prostitution. A minute on the Home Office file about this read: 'there are other and more important subjects to occupy the attention of the House of Commons and the Home Office . . . In these circumstances, I think . . . this bill . . . should be blocked.' Troup agreed.[106]

Lastly, officials were influential in the creation of policy simply through the way in which they interpreted and administered acts over a period of time. As their experience of a particular act grew, they built up a departmental view of how best to treat cases arising from it. Precedent was important. But cases varied enormously so that it was impossible rigidly to follow precedent. Some acts, particularly those which were roughly drafted, gave considerable leeway in interpretation. The 1905 aliens act, for example, gave the secretary of state wide discretionary powers to decide whether or not an immigrant might remain in Britain on the grounds that he was seeking political asylum. In fact immigration cases came up so often and had to be decided so quickly that officials frequently found it impossible to consult the secretary of state and had to make these decisions themselves according to what became a rough departmental rule for admission on grounds of political asylum.

Yet in the late nineteenth and early twentieth centuries major initiatives for legislative reform do not seem to have come from within the Home Office. Officials usually reacted to stimuli from their political masters rather than stimulate those masters with their own ideas for fundamental change. In the field of labour relations, for example, significant legislation on employers' liability and workmen's compensation was passed in 1881, 1897 and 1906. In each case senior officials struggled to try to work out acceptable and working compromises on individual clauses of the bills; but the government accepted the need for legislative action as the result of external pressures.[107] In the case of prison reform the 1898 prison act resulted from initial outside pressure on the department to relax rigid central control and consider new ideas about the treatment of prisoners. Even under the new regime Ruggles-Brise and the Home Office did not, in many people's eyes, go nearly far enough in their reforms.[108] Writing about Churchill's reform of prisons over a decade later, Butler commented: 'The old hands in the department were rather dismayed by the temerity with which he challenged the principles and practices which had remained sacrosanct for many years.'[109] A politician's account is naturally biased towards the idea that his role is the innovatory one. Nevertheless, a small comment by the parliamentary under-secretary, Herbert Samuel (later home secretary), on the preparation of the 1908 children's bill may not have been far from the truth: 'I decided that, instead of taking the more usual course of drafting a series of small departmental Bills, I would combine all the proposals into one comprehensive measure, and see what would happen... The Officials of the Home Office warmly welcomed the plan.'[110]

If they did lack an innovatory role they were not unique. Local Government Board officials have been accused of exhibiting a positively negative attitude towards the attempts of their political chiefs to introduce reforms.[111] In the Education Department, at least up to 1895, 'permanent officials were likely to respond only when politicians in turn prodded them'.[112] But this was not an inevitable feature of pre-war civil servants. In the Board of Trade 'labour officials played a highly innovative role in shaping the principles and structure of labour exchanges, unemployment insurances and the Development Commission'.[113] What, then, were the general features of civil servants which might have contributed to a lack of innovation; and what were the particular departmental features which tended to encourage this?

Part of the answer lies in the nature of the new type of open competition first division clerks who formed the decision-making élite. There was no doubt about their ability. Samuel later commented on 'the very able Home Office officials';[114] R. S. Redmayne, the chief inspector of mines, was 'impressed ... by their clarity of thought and their efficiency', and praised Troup's and Delevigne's minutes as 'models of exactitude, lucidity, and precision'.[115] But theirs was a particular kind of impartial ability, bred by an English classical education, which made them highly effective at analysing alternatives, at distinguishing points of value from irrelevancies, at ascertaining the best way of carrying out a policy, but which excluded zeal for a cause or idea. This quality could be suspect to those who were different. Even Redmayne could not help singling out Delevigne for possessing that rare quality among civil servants – imagination.[116] The inventive Cunynghame – one of the few departmental officials who delighted in leaving his desk and getting out into the real world of mines and factories – could not bear the calm objectivity of his colleagues. Significantly perhaps, he did not reach the top post.

In the equation of what makes up a departmental institution the factors include not only the nature and views of its officials but also traditional departmental views which are conditioned by its work. There was something inherent in the nature of Home Office work which made its officials particularly aware of reasons why changes should *not* be made. This derived partly from the legal aspect of their responsibilities and from departmental reverence for precedent which encouraged looking back rather than forward. It arose also from the fact that, as a government department, the Home Office often played a negative role. In the field of unemployment, for example, its function was not to devise ways of solving conflicts – that was left to the Local Government Board or Board of Trade – but merely to prevent their manifestations from disturbing the peace of the metropolis.[117] A certain conservatism was also the result of the crisis aspect of the department's work which put civil servants on their guard and made them cautious.

Looking back to pre-war days from the vantage point of 1950

Butler observed a different attitude in Edwardian civil servants which, if true, might account for a certain lack of aggression. He found the 'much less self-righteous officials of those days looked upon themselves as servants of the public not as their tutors or directors'.

> In those days it was a fundamental tenet of the Service that the public, like the customer, was usually right. After all it was their country, and within the limits of the law and common-sense they were entitled to have it the way they wanted it. That is hardly the present-day notion.[118]

He regretted, in retrospect, those days before, as he believed, 'the philosophy of *laisser-faire* had been ousted in favour of state interference'. Thus, in fact, might Troup or even Knyvett have argued about their early days in the office. Nevertheless, Butler correctly made the point that on the whole civil servants of his generation were less politically orientated than those of the post-second world war era. Indeed, at times they fought to be a-political. Pedder once refused to alter the licensing statistics 'to suit Winston Churchill's political views', and when Churchill altered them himself, Pedder would not sign them so that they were published unsigned.[119]

This small incident provides a clue to what was perhaps the best feature of the new generation of Home Office officials and of their successors. It is important to stress the positive aspect of their characteristic objectivity which sometimes annoyed their more zealous critics. Senior Home Office officials tried hard to be fair and to find solutions to problems which would be acceptable to all parties concerned. The underlying reason for this (unperceived by Butler) may have been fundamental self-interest: their social origins were not greatly different from those of their predecessors or from their political masters and they shared a common interest in the preservation of the social order which demanded the reconciliation of conflicting interests. This had been Lushington's objective; it was also Troup's. But because of intervening social changes between their periods of office as permanent under-secretary, Troup was more obviously and more frequently faced with situations where he had consciously to promote this kind of social control.

During the pre-war years of serious industrial unrest, while upholding local police and magistrates in their attempts to preserve public order, Troup was by no means always on the side of the big battalions. During the railway strike of August 1911, which drew sympathy from Liverpool dockers, a suggestion was sent to the Home Office that the trade unionist, Tom Mann, be arrested. To this

Troup replied: 'If Tom Mann is to be arrested there are one or two ship-owners who should go with him to prison.'[120] He also showed impatience with the constant pleas of manufacturers' associations for police protection from strikers.[121] During the coal strike of 1912, contrary to the wishes of the Monmouthshire and South Wales Coal Owners' Association, Troup was very cautious about the idea of sending in troops to quell local unrest in the Rhondda valley. Indeed, the Home Office at this time was consistently against the use of the military except as a last resort. During the London dock strike of that year, in a general guide-line entitled 'The General Principle of Protection', Troup firmly argued that individuals (that is, owners and managers) did not have an automatic personal right to police protection: '... when, where and how that protection is given must depend on circumstances on which police authorities must exercise discretion'.[122]

Troup's generation of officials, therefore, clearly played a role in the governing process which was unprecedented for career officials. The influx of large numbers of highly able higher officials in the late nineteenth century coincided with the vast extension of government activity in realms hitherto uncontrolled by central authority. This was partly the result of politicians harnessing the new talent at their disposal; it was partly the creation by civil servants of more work for themselves through their own activity, interest and energy. Even though pre-war Home Office first division officials may not have been highly innovative in terms of turning ministers in new directions and were influenced by a conservative departmental tradition, they were far from being negative. They were a positive force for furthering change when this was apparently desirable and was promoted by their political chiefs; and they were open-minded and flexible when it came to working out solutions to problems which involved reconciling a wide spectrum of interests.

5 The lower or second division: 1876–1914

Functions within the Home Office

The order in council of 12 February 1876 set out conditions for the recruitment and terms of service of the new lower division clerks who were gradually to replace the supplementary clerks, hitherto recruited through the Class II examination. Their function was to perform the bulk of civil service clerical work which the Northcote-Trevelyan report had described as 'mechanical'. At the Home Office they were directly supervised by various staff clerks – to whose posts they themselves aspired – who ranked immediately below the upper division. There was always a need for a more menial class of clerk than that of the lower division to perform the straightforward filing and copying. Thus by the same order in council government departments were allowed for this purpose to recruit fifteen to seventeen year old temporary boy clerks who could subsequently join the lower division. The Home Office also made use of temporary copyists, recruited through a central list kept by the Civil Service Commission until the late 1880s when the system ended. In 1891 the department began to recruit from a newly established class of assistant (or abstractor) clerks and found them so useful that by the end of the period they outnumbered the second division. The lower part of the office, therefore, consisted of four main classes of clerk: staff clerks, lower division clerks, assistant clerks and non-established boy clerks. Compared with the upper division this part of the office grew fast: between 1877 and 1914 it increased from twenty-one to 144 (see Table 7 overleaf). While the upper division increased from thirteen to thirty-two.

It is the lower division (or second division as it became in 1890) which is particularly interesting: it dominated the office numerically for most of the period; it supplied the staff posts (once the supplementary clerks had died out) with some remarkable men who were significant figures in the office; and it quickly provided the upper division with a vital back-up service in the form of three sub-divisions of the office whose methods became increasingly sophisticated.

Maconochie had predicted in 1873 that 'the second class will as a rule...be filled by clever boys of the lower middle class whose parents cannot afford to keep them long enough at school to fit them for the higher competition'.[1] In this he was probably correct. In 1886 when the Civil Service Commission investigated the occupations of the fathers of lower division clerks they found that the largest number came into the categories 'tradesmen' and 'artizans'. Subsequent categories were 'commercial clerks and travellers',

Table 7   Staff clerks, lower/second division clerks, assistant clerks and boy clerks at the Home Office in 1877, 1896 and 1914

	1877	1896	1914
staff clerks	clerk in charge of accounts (£400 × £20−£600)	clerk in charge of accounts (£400 × £20−£600)*	clerk in charge of accounts (£500 × £20−£650)
		assistant clerk in charge of accounts (£350 × £50−£400)	assistant clerk in charge of accounts (£315 × £50−£500)
	clerk for statistical returns (£350 × £15−£500)	clerk for statistical returns (£350 × £50−£500)	clerk for statistical returns (£350 × £15−£550)
	superintendent of registry (£350 × £15−£500)	superintendent of registry (£350 × £50−£500)†	superintendent of registry (£350 × £15−£500)
		assistant superintendent of registry (£350)	assistant superintendent of registry (£300 × £10−£400)
		senior clerk to chief inspector of factories (£250)‡	2nd assistant superintendent of registry (£200 × £10−£300)
		clerk for factory statistics (£230)‡	library and warrants clerk (£350 × £15−£450)
			clerk for factory statistics (£300 × £15−£450)
			senior clerk to chief inspector of factories (£250 × £10−£350)
Sub-total	3	7	9

	1877	1896	1914
minor staff clerks and 'higher grade' 2nd division clerks	–	3 (£250 – £350)[‖]	5 (£150 – £350)[‖]
special clerks[§]	3 (£100 – £550)[‖]	2 (£250 – £400)[‖]	6 (£80 – £350)[‖]
supplementary clerks	4 (£100 – £350)[‖]	–	–
lower/second division clerks (ordinary grade)	11 (£90 × 15 trienially – £250)	19 (£70 – £250)	33 (£70 – £300)
assistant clerks	–	9 (£55 – £150)	54 (£45 – £150)
boy clerks	–	4 (14/- × 1/- per wk)	37[¶]
TOTALS	21	44	144

Figures for numbers of lower division clerks, assistant clerks and boy clerks are taken from the annual estimates.

* Tripp (see below p. 102) had a personal salary ceiling of £700.

† Plus a personal allowance of £100.

‡ (So-called) temporary posts.

§ These were clerks with special titles (e.g. clerk for mineral statistics), including various inspectors' clerks, who were technically neither staff clerks nor straightforward lower/second division clerks.

‖ Figures denote the full range of the various salaries.

¶ No figures for wages given in annual estimates.

'lower grade civil servants', 'farmers' and 'schoolmasters', in that order.[2] The range of subjects for the Class II examination was that of 'an ordinary commercial education', and the age limits prescribed for candidates were seventeen to twenty. These factors virtually precluded their having been to a university. Of the 221 clerks appointed in 1885, 'as many as ninety-five received their education in National, British, Wesleyan, or Board schools; while of the residue, only about a dozen were educated at schools of so high a class as that to which Dulwich College, and the City of London School belong'.[3] Little is known about the education of Home Office lower division clerks, but W. Wheeler, who entered the office in 1877, had been at Surrey County School, Cranleigh, and had later attended evening classes at King's College, London.[4] Later analyses of successful Class II candidates show that their social and educational background had probably not changed much by 1911. That year the commonest categories in which their fathers were placed were 'merchant or shopkeeper' and 'artizan'.[5] Twelve out of sixty-six schools examined were grammar schools; four were listed as 'county' or 'high' schools and twelve merely as 'secondary' schools; and over twenty were schools with private (some religious) foundations, one or two of which were well-known day schools such as the City of London School. The 1911 analysis shows that a small majority of candidates had had 'special preparation' before taking the examination.[6] Both in 1886 and in 1911 a large proportion of the entrants (42 per cent and 57 per cent respectively) did not enter the competition straight from school or a crammer but from within the civil service – presumably from either the assistant or boy clerk classes.

1876 marked not only the inauguration of the lower division but also major internal reform at the Home Office whose work was redistributed among three departments.[7] Of these three it was the general department which absorbed most of the new lower division clerks: much of its own warrants and appointments work, requiring care, accuracy and experience, suited them; and it was the parent department for the registry, accounts branch and statistics branch.

The registry

The largest of the three general department sub-divisions was the registry, 'the mainspring of the Office', as Harcourt once described it.[8] A single, central registry had first been established in 1870 under Maconochie. It was divided into two sections. The 'in' section dealt with operations concerning all incoming correspondence: clerks opened, registered and docketed letters before delivering them to the relevant departments; they traced papers within the office and eventually filed them away with other relevant material. The 'out' section was responsible for despatching letters, for indexing and for entering copies in letter-books. Maconochie started a new system of numbered papers, marking all incoming letters on new subjects in a consecutive numerical series. Each subsequent paper was numbered similarly to earlier papers on that subject but with its own sub-number. Copies of Home Office replies to incoming letters were not attached to them but were bound together in separate letter-books.[9]

In 1876 G. Moran, an ex-supplementary clerk, became superintendent of the registry whose staff then consisted of one supplementary clerk, six lower division clerks and six copyists. Moran was to occupy this post for twenty-two years until 1898 during which period the registry began to develop techniques necessary for efficiently receiving, sorting, indexing, filing, despatching and storing an increasingly large number of papers. Butler's later description of this work as 'a highly skilled occupation' may have been an exaggeration,[10] but certainly it was essential for the smooth running of the office that it was effectively done.

Space was becoming a problem by 1880 when a Treasury Minute drew attention to the 1877 public records act which provided for the periodical destruction of certain papers.[11] This led Moran to change Maconochie's system of numbering incoming papers consecutively (although he retained the practice of sub-numbering). He had them divided into three categories according to their proposed eventual destruction: each paper was given one of three prefix letters indicating whether it merited preservation for five, ten or thirty years.[12] The system had the obvious defect that it was often difficult to foretell how important a subject might become, but it was at least an attempt to introduce a systematic method of destruction. Another reform changed the longstanding procedure whereby an incoming letter itself formed the file on its subject, being folded into four so that the blank front of the letter became the cover on which the paper was docketed and minutes were written. In 1885 new papers began to be put away flat and in white jackets, the front of which formed the first minute sheet. Extra minute sheets could be added inside if necessary. This practice gradually led, throughout the office, to a modern, organized system of writing minutes: the illegible scrawls, which had frequently been unsigned and undated, became neater, more expansive and were clearly initialled and dated.

Moran's new filing arrangements had not improved the defective cross-referencing system of papers. There were no effective subject indices and it was often impossible to look up previous Home Office decisions on a particular subject. It is alleged that on one occasion this confusion created some embarrassment when two local authorities submitted an identical form of bye-law within a few months of each other and one was confirmed while the other was disallowed.[13] By 1889 the enterprising Wheeler had become occupied with building up a much needed, alphabetically indexed 'notebook' of precedents of all important cases. This was a time-consuming occupation, which required the perusal of hundreds of papers, and Wheeler badgered Moran to be allowed to spend his whole working day at it. Moran's response was only lukewarm.[14] For he was secretly jealous of his powerful position whereby he was often the only person who could lay hands on a precedent. Wheeler's work did proceed gradually but Moran was reluctant to recognize the principle that an efficient registry could only be run on the lines that no one was indispensable. He had somehow contrived to keep to himself the work of dealing with all applications and licences under the vivisection act, guarding it 'with vigilance and ferocity', for he enjoyed the privilege of explaining the intricacies of these licences to the home secretary personally.[15] It was one of the last vestiges of the pre-reform days when precedents were few enough to be retained in the mind of a single experienced clerk and when clerks fiercely guarded their own specialist functions.

Never in the van of fashion, the Home Office was slow to adopt new office machinery. But after 1887 the use of copying presses (introduced at the Board of Trade in 1850) eased matters in the registry and reduced the need for copyists. By 1890 Moran had persuaded his superiors to order two typewriters. Unlike some departments, where 'lady typewriters' were employed at the machines, the Home Office set their boy clerks to using them. Senior officials alleged until the war that Home Office letters often contained subject-matter which was too distasteful for the eyes of women and, moreover, that there was nowhere women could suitably be kept away from the rest of the staff.[16] Typewriters and the increasing use of carbon copies in the 1890s contributed towards speed and clarity. By 1898 all letters were being typewritten (although a good deal of copying by hand was still being done). The first telephone appeared in the office in 1896 when it was connected with the Treasury exchange. Then, in 1902, both departments were connected to the General Post Office exchange system. The Home Office that year had only two instruments which were being 'largely used' and Byrne correctly forecast their increasing use.[17]

As the number of papers increased so did Moran's staff and prestige. Between 1889 and 1893 alone, incoming papers were estimated to have risen from 43,236 to 51,617.[18] Urgent storage problems led to the first floor corridor being crowded with new cupboards and to additional overtime work by registry clerks, set harder than ever to the task of weeding out old papers. By 1894 Moran – the doyen of the lower division – was so grand that he had his own separate room; and he managed to persuade his superiors that his 'personal allowance' should be increased from £50 to £100 and that he needed an 'assistant superintendent of the registry' (Wheeler) below him to supervise the registry staff.[19] Otherwise, Moran's staff in 1896 consisted of nine second division, four assistant and two boy clerks.

Despite the increasing flow of paper, registry clerks evidently led a cheerful existence under Moran:

Some of the staff used to leave the Office in mid-morning and go for a drink in the 'Red Lion'. The practice grew to such proportions that on occasion he had to send a messenger to the

'Red Lion' to request the gentlemen of the Home Office Registry to be kind enough to return and do some work. Eventually he succeeded in putting a stop to the practice by a compromise under which a messenger went across to the 'Red Lion' and brought the beer in cans hanging on a rod.[20]

Cricket in the registry corridors survived long after the turn of the century; and it was not unknown for registry clerks to keep bottles of spirits in their desks to fortify them for their work.

Moran's death in 1898 inaugurated a new regime for the registry under the superintendence of E. E. B. Boehmer, who had come to the Home Office as a lower division clerk in 1884 and succeeded to the post of assistant superintendent when Wheeler was promoted to the first division in 1896. Murdoch recommended him for the post on account of his 'great neatness', 'good capacity for order and management of men', and his concern ever 'to improve and reform the mode of conducting the work'.[21] The first event was a thorough investigation of registry work by Troup, Simpson and Byrne in November 1898. This committee found the general system of numbering, sub-numbering and filing 'excellent' and well suited to the special needs of the Home Office. But it suggested initially registering incoming letters under more effective subject headings so that an experienced person should have no difficulty in tracing a paper. A serious problem concerned overtime: too much of this had been allowed for years as a regular practice rather than in emergencies when the registry was pressed, and so payment for this work was considered by the clerks as a regular income. The committee wanted overtime to be done regularly only in the out-registry which had to be open late to send off letters at the end of the day. It suggested phasing out much overtime by increasing the flexibility of the clerks and by acquiring another typewriter to speed up production of items which were still being hand-copied. The committee found the staff of twenty-one quite adequate for its work – indeed, generous compared with comparable registries. It suggested various ways of rationalizing the working day of some of the staff (in particular that of the superintendent now that Moran had gone) and concluded that numbers might eventually be reduced or at least assistant clerks substituted for second division clerks.[22] Over the next few months the assiduous superintendent put these recommendations into effect.[23]

One of Boehmer's greatest assets was A. Locke who had been promoted in 1898 from a second division post to the recently created third registry staff post, second assistant superintendent. A large part of his duties included the noting work Wheeler had started.

'Full of fire and imagination and a zest for work which crackled in his flowing red moustache and bushy red hair', Locke had 'an uncanny nose for papers and a prodigious memory' which enabled him to set up an invaluable system of reference for the office.[24] By March 1901 he had not only absorbed 'the remainder of the miscellaneous collection of notes in the Registry into a more ordered system', but had cross-referenced all important precedents on about 4,000 cards.[25] These were listed under headings such as 'Home Office decisions on points of law', 'changes in Home Office practice', 'death sentences', etc. Thus a searcher could look up a general heading on the cards which would refer him to more detailed information in the notebooks. Boehmer was full of enthusiasm for Locke's system which provided 'a safe and ready means of tracing any decision however refined'; and Digby approved his request for funds for an 'up-to-date box as used in Libraries' to house the whole card index.[26] In 1902 he was allowed the help of an assistant clerk. The indefatigable Locke continued with the job of 'noter' until 1911 when he, like both his predecessor and successor, was promoted to become a junior first division clerk.[27]

His work was related to the destruction of documents. For it had become the office rule that virtually no paper recorded in the notebooks should be destroyed. As Boehmer speeded up the examination of old papers for destruction, he continually found noteworthy precedents in old papers which therefore had to be recorded and kept. In working out schedules for the destruction of documents Boehmer was concerned with questions such as whether or not they contained precedents, were of legal, historical, genea-logical or antiquarian interest, contained important information which could not be found elsewhere, or had been especially directed to be kept.[28] Now that more thought was given to the destruction of documents, Moran's system of classifying papers as they came into the office into three series, which immediately fixed their eventual destruction dates, had become antiquated. In September 1902 the registry reverted to the earlier 'omnibus' system whereby all incoming papers were simply numbered consecutively with no prefix.[29]

In 1908 Boehmer petitioned for a rise in salary and, as was customary with such memorials, listed his achievements. He then supervised a registry whose incoming papers had increased by 11,000 since he had taken over and which he had reformed according to the recommendations of the 1898 committee; he had dealt with fifteen years' arrears of documents due to be considered for destruction and, amazingly, had managed during one period of five years to destroy '12 tons of correspondence'.[30] He also requested a rise in status, suggesting that his position be dignified with the title 'Registrar and Superintendent of Records'. No one doubted his achievements. From Tripp to Troup it was generally agreed that 'the Registry under Mr. Boehmer is vastly more efficient than it ever was under the management of Mr. Moran'. Even Gladstone paid tribute to Boehmer's work. But his superiors felt unable to support either of his requests: his salary was as high as any other comparable officer in the civil service and remained static until the end of the period; and his title, wrote Troup, 'correctly describes the Office'.[31]

By 1909 the 'new offices' between Parliament Square and Charles Street were finally completed. The Home Office was at last able to expand into certain old offices of the Local Government Board next door and thus acquired a whole new set of extra rooms running along the north side of Charles Street. For the first time for many years, the registry found itself comfortably housed and its papers reasonably accommodated.[32] But further problems arose as the registry (like the divisions) began to experience serious problems in keeping pace with the expansion of work. Eventually, after an examination by the head of the Treasury registry in 1911, a second division clerk and three boy clerks were added to its existing staff of twenty-nine.[33] Two years later Troup was worried that the registry notebooks were not being kept up to date because of the increase of the day-to-day duties of the second assistant superintendent, A. H. May. Troup would have liked the noter to become a specialist appointment but for the time being the Treasury merely sanctioned an 'assistant noter' in the form of a second division clerk.[34] Despite such difficulties, however, the pre-war registry, built up by Boehmer and Locke since 1898, served the first division clerks well. It was later even used as a model registry, and was once alleged to have been 'the object of envy to every other department'.[35]

The accounts branch
The first specialist sub-division of the office was the accounts branch which started in a humble way in 1868 when Pennefather was recruited as 'a competent and skilled accountant'.[36] Pennefather was not officially accountable for the Home Office vote: that 'high and responsible position' was undertaken first by the chief clerk and later by the head of the general department. Pennefather's duties were described as 'of a technical character' and he was paid a mere £150 x £15 to £200.[37] His work soon proved more arduous and responsible than was anticipated. With no staff, he administered fairly large

accounts submitted by the inspectors; he endorsed, registered and filed all letters referring to accounts; he replied to all queries from the comptroller and auditor-general; and he prepared the Home Office annual expropriation account and annual estimates.[38] By 1876 his salary had taken three leaps so that the clerk in charge of accounts, as he was then called, had become the best paid of the three staff clerks, earning £400 × £20 to £600. Pennefather was evidently well thought of as an accountant outside his own department: the Treasury nominated him auditor of the patriotic fund accounts in 1882 and auditor for the Metropolitan Board of Works the following year.[39] In 1883 he left the Home Office to become receiver of the metropolitan police at a salary of £1,500 and eventually retired having earned a knighthood for his services.

Pennefather was succeeded by J. Simpson who had entered the Home Office as examiner of police claims in 1872 when it took over responsibility for the police vote. Simpson's work had been kept quite separate from Pennefather's but in 1884 the two aspects of accounts work were amalgamated. It was decided to create an assistant clerk in charge of accounts, to which post a lower division clerk, G. H. Tripp, was promoted.[40] This was the first Home Office promotion from the lower division to a staff post and the Civil Service Commission queried it; but it was allowed by the Treasury and Tripp's later career more that justified the appointment.[41] The arrangement lasted only until 1887 when Simpson died unexpectedly and Tripp suddenly found himself, aged twenty-seven, head of the branch, with a staff of five, earning over £400 a year within nine years of his having entered the department at a mere £95.

In 1887 Knyvett told the Ridley Commission that among the branches of the general department the accounts branch was the hardest worked.[42] But the following year the local government act reduced its work by abolishing direct grant-in-aid to police forces, thereby removing much of the work connected with the examination of county and borough police accounts. The duties which remained were divided into four categories: administering four parliamentary votes (for the Home Office and its sub-departments, the metropolitan police courts, 'special police',[43] and the reformatory and industrial schools); advising on financial questions connected with these votes and with the general business of the office; collecting exchequer fines inflicted by courts of summary jurisdiction in England and Wales; and receiving fees payable to the Home Office.[44] For this work Tripp's staff was reduced to his assistant and two lower division clerks.

Tripp's responsibilities, purely in terms of the Home Office vote, steadily increased: the annual estimates for 1887–8 amounted to £93,947; for 1897–8 to £123,566; and for 1908–9 to £224,667. Apart from this, where he proved an exceptionally useful and effective officer was in advising his seniors on any office business connected with finance. He understood what the Treasury would tolerate and was therefore influential in decisions about whether senior staff should support individual officers' requests for higher salaries or more staff. He often sat on departmental committees concerning staffing matters; and since finance and policy were closely linked he was frequently involved in policy discussion. In the field of social legislation he was drawn into debate about the controversial question of how large the factory inspectorate ought to be and in 1890 asked the home secretary whether, in view of the previous year's parliamentary discussion during the supply debates about the inadequacy of the inspectorate, he should include an additional item for extra inspectors in the new estimates.[45] He was involved in discussion about complex and politically difficult questions such as the extent to which reformatory and industrial schools should be centrally rather than locally or voluntarily aided.[46] Tripp was, in fact, so able that special arrangements were made for him to short-circuit the conventional minuting procedure. From 1896 he could, in certain cases, submit papers direct to an under-secretary rather than through the domestic department (which had taken over the accounts branch that year).[47] And in 1908 he personally was directed to submit all papers about metropolitan police finance direct to an under-secretary and not through division D.[48] His salary before he left the Home Office was on a personal scale of £700 × £25 to £800.

In 1909 when Tripp succeeded Pennefather as receiver to the metropolitan police, the Home Office felt the blow. Since 'a great deal of the work done by Mr. Tripp has been the work which properly belongs to Class I', and no one of Tripp's calibre was recruited from outside to replace him, completely new arrangements had to be made.[49] Troup proposed to transfer 'the higher administrative and advisory work' from the accounts branch to division D whose old loose supervision was now to be tightened up: the new clerk in charge of accounts was to work closely to the senior clerk of the division who was to submit all important matters through the principal clerk to the Home Office accounting officer – now Byrne, an assistant under-secretary. In addition, a junior clerk in the division was to specialize in accounts work.[50] The new arrangements meant that the separate divisions of the office dealt more with their own particular financial problems than they had done previously.

The new clerk in charge of accounts, S. M. Grunwald, was one of the last ex-supplementary clerks and had been Tripp's number two. His assistant was a second division clerk, W. C. Platt. Although much of the work involving policy recommendations had disappeared from the branch with Tripp, the Home Office was able successfully to put to the Treasury the case for a rise in salaries for Grunwald and Platt and for the creation of a minor staff post on the grounds that general duties had reflected the increasing complexity of legislation. The Home Office instanced 'the quarterly claims of the Medical Referees under the Workmen's Compensation Act and the examination of those claims' and also claims for reimbursement of deportation expenses under the aliens act as responsible and time-consuming.[51] Troup wanted more specialization within the branch and suggested a division of work among the staff clerks to facilitate this.

By 1912 Grunwald was requesting yet further salary increases. As the result of a Treasury investigation a formal letter was sent to that department arguing that since 1910 'the great increase of work in the Home Office has involved a proportionate growth of work in the Accounts Branch'.[52] Work singled out this time as especially time-consuming and difficult again included a variety of duties imposed by the workmen's compensation act 'which often involves very troublesome questions'; it also included processing the 330 inspectors' and 1,300 certifying surgeons' accounts, receiving exchequer contributions and fees due to the Home Office (which had doubled in five years), and preparing the annual estimates. The latter entailed

> ... repeated consultations with Heads of Departments with regard to the effect that new legislation ... will have on the expenditure of the coming year.
> Constant interviews are also necessary with Chief Inspectors as to enquiries and committees likely to be held and as to their scope as affecting their duration and the necessity of the experts and probability of carrying out experiments. It is also necessary to ascertain by interviews whether any charges are likely to occur which will influence the cost of travelling of their Staffs.[53]

The Treasury was unhappy that the accounts branch was dealing with anything other than work 'strictly relating to accounts', since this was out of line with other government departments, but it agreed to grant Grunwald and Platt incremental advances, raised Platt's salary ceiling again and created a second minor staff post in the branch.[54]

Thus the increased volume and complexity of legislation had a direct bearing on the growth of the accounts branch which between 1868 and 1914 grew from a single clerk at a very small salary into a sub-division of thirteen whose status was the highest among the three sub-divisions: its head and assistant head were the best paid of their peers; and it was the only branch to merit four staff posts even though it was not numerically the largest.

The statistics branch
It has already been observed that, unlike the other two branches of the general department, the statistics branch did not gain in prestige nor its staff clerk in importance during the 1880s because of the lack of Home Office interest in statistical developments.[55] After the overhaul of the judicial statistics their compilation was put into the hands of W. J. Farrant, a second division clerk, who remained head of the branch until long after the first world war. In 1896 the branch was transferred to the industrial and parliamentary department because its work was primarily concerned with parliamentary returns, and Farrant worked with a staff of two second division clerks.

The work of the statistics branch was kept quite separate from that of the factory and mining statistics clerks. The factory statistics, after their overhaul in 1894,[56] were entrusted to a second division clerk, who the following year was elevated to a temporary staff clerkship at a fixed £250 a year, and two assistant clerks all of whom worked in the office of the chief inspector of factories. After the 1896 rearrangements another temporary staff post, the 'clerk for factory statistics', was created at a fixed £230 a year.[57] There had existed a separate mineral statistics branch since 1883 when the old Mining Record Office, which had prepared statistics of the output and value of all minerals raised from mines, was transferred from the Department of Science and Art to the Home Office. From then a clerk for mineral statistics and a second division clerk worked on the annual parliamentary presentation, 'The Mineral Statistics of the United Kingdom'. In 1894 the departmental committee on mining and mineral statistics recommended, in the absence of a unified mines inspectors' report, the production of a general report on the mineral industry of the United Kingdom, based on the separate reports of the mines inspectors and on the 'Mineral Statistics'.[58] As a result a general report of this nature was produced from 1894 onwards (signed by a co-ordinating inspector)[59] and the mineral statistics branch was enlarged by two assistant clerks.

Troup thought that statistics work was ideal second division work. It was routine in the sense that a regular pattern of work was followed but it required intelligence and background knowledge.[60] In

1896 the major part of the work of the statistics branch was still the compilation for parliament of the now separate criminal and civil judicial statistics. The criminal statistics required 'an accurate and complete knowledge of criminal law and procedure, and of the functions, power, and territorial jurisdiction of the Courts and authorities administering the criminal law'.[61] Farrant alleged that he was ever mindful of the recommendations of the 1893 judicial statistics committee and that he constantly modified and extended the tables to suit legal changes, respond to external public criticism and follow useful foreign precedent. His branch worked out new forms from which to collect information and give guidance as to their compilation. With the classification of summary offences, for instance, the clerks had to induce the different police forces to produce comparable, useful returns. Once the statistics had come in, they were busy 'collecting, checking, and sifting the returns and enquiring concerning apparent errors and inconsistencies, compiling the tables from the returns, harmonizing the figures derived from diverse sources'.[62] It required experience to be able to adapt information from sources which were not designed specifically for their purposes.[63] They had to be wary of the peculiarities of English law and the differences of Scottish law which often made it difficult to produce general statistics for the whole of Britain.[64] One aspect of the presentation of these statistics which for some years was considered first division work was the writing of the introduction. This was composed by Troup from 1893 to 1896 and then by Simpson. After 1899 either a brief introductory résumé was compiled (and in later years signed) by Farrant or, occasionally, a detailed introduction was written by Sir John Macdonell, master of the supreme court. The latter also wrote the introduction to the civil statistics: their preparation involved a similar kind of work, but since Home Office responsibilities had little to do with civil law procedure, advice about improving or altering the tables tended to come from the lord chancellor's office.

Social legislation was the greatest generator of statistics. Workmen's compensation legislation is a good example. After the 1897 workmen's compensation act statistics of legal proceedings had to be maintained. Section 12 of the 1906 workmen's compensation act enabled the home secretary to direct employers in any industry to submit annual returns specifying the number of injuries in respect of which compensation had been paid by them under the act. Thus all employers in major industries began to submit such returns and in 1908 Byrne reckoned that this involved about 150,000 employers.[65] Licensing was another field where legislation led to more work. The

1904 licensing act led to the collection of statistics about the numbers of 'on' and 'off' licences granted and refused, and about payment of compensation for the non-renewal of licences; and its section 7 specifically provided for returns to be made to the secretary of state by quarter sessions about their own and about magistrates' actions in the granting of new licences.

Apart from such large new areas of statistical compilation, the branch was kept busy with ad hoc parliamentary demands for returns and with various miscellaneous statistics such as the compilation of the appendix to the annual reports of the inspectors of constabulary. Farrant consistently maintained that the work of his branch was more complicated and more responsible than that done by other government statistical departments because Home Office statistics involved 'an exceptionally wide range of subject matter' and required a great deal of background knowledge about each of the subjects concerned.[66] Two first division clerks in 1911 found some justification in Farrant's claim for a higher salary when they compared his duties with those of statistical officers in other government departments where comparable jobs were held by first division clerks.[67]

By 1909 the work was divided into three sections: the criminal section which included the criminal judicial statistics, the inspectors of constabulary tables and the probation officers' register; the miscellaneous section which included the licensing statistics, workmen's compensation statistics about county court proceedings and the civil judicial statistics; and a small section which dealt entirely with the annual compensation returns under the 1906 workmen's compensation act. Farrant's staff then consisted of two permanent second division clerks, four assistant clerks and a floating staff of temporary second division and boy clerks.[68] The acquisition of machinery had kept staff increases down: after the 1893 reforms the branch had first acquired a calculating machine and by 1912 it had four; from 1907 an addressograph helped to cope with the mass of correspondence with industrial employers; the following year an electrical adding machine was requisitioned; and the branch also had a duplicating machine. But by 1909 Farrant felt he needed more staff and salary increases, and this led to an investigation by Byrne and Tripp who found the branch 'well organized, the methods businesslike, and the output satisfactory'.[69] Their inquiry led to the addition of a second division clerk and two assistant clerks, the creation of a minor staff post for one of the second division clerks and a rise in the ceiling of Farrant's salary by £50.[70] By 1914 the salary of the other staff clerk had been raised and a further three second division clerks had been added to the staff of the branch.

It seems probable that statistical work continued to be under-valued at the Home Office. Despite the reforms of the 1890s the statistics branch always seems to have lacked status. By contrast the registry derived standing from being the largest sub-division; Troup considered it the most important sub-division.[71] The accounts branch had been given prominence by Tripp's authority, its senior staff clerk was the best paid and it had the most staff clerks. The statistics branch for some years lacked a satisfactory niche within the office: between 1876 and 1905 it moved from the general department to the criminal department to the industrial and parliamentary department; then Delevigne found this arrangement unsatisfactory because the branch dealt with many matters which were of no concern to his department and so, while its actual supervision was transferred to the domestic department, each department dealt directly with the statistics branch for purposes of its own statistics.[72] Troup always took an interest in statistics work but, while some other government departments regarded this as first division work, he felt that at the Home Office it was 'not at all on the same level with work done in the four divisions'.[73] Farrant clearly felt that his branch was under-appreciated. In 1917, he wrote:

> ... the work of the Statistical Branch has suffered lack of recognition because, owing to its technical and unusual character as compared with the ordinary business of the Home Office, its difficulty and importance is not realized, and further that the department has been prejudiced by the notoriously inefficient manner in which the work was carried on prior to the revision in 1892-3. I may, however, point out that this lack of efficiency existed in other departments of the Home Office, notwithstanding which no other department has been similarly penalized ... [74]

The first division clerks who supervised the statistics branch no doubt ensured that the statistics required by law or as the result of parliamentary query were efficiently produced. But did they set in train inquiry, for example about the implications of legislation, as the result of analyses made in the statistics branch? The attitude of senior officials towards the work of the branch and Farrant's feeling of neglect implies that they did not. This was perhaps another example of the Home Office reacting to external requirements rather than initiating political or social inquiry.

The large majority of second division clerks worked in the three sub-divisions of the office. Some worked in the offices of the inspectors where there were opportunities for staff clerkships. Only a few (three in 1909) worked in the actual division of the office because most of the non-first division work there involved letter-writing or typing which was done by assistant or boy clerks. But here there was one noteworthy second division clerk in charge of what almost amounted to a small branch. This was A. H. Eggett who, since the work of the library and the warrants section had been transferred from the old general department to the domestic department in 1896, supervised this work with a small subordinate clerical staff of assistant and boy clerks. Eggett was responsible for the 'highly technical duty of drafting and preparing for signature all Sign Manual and other Warrants and Appointments . . . their preparation not only requires great knowledge of precedents, but involves many interviews and much semi-official correspondence'.[75] Although in many respects the formal work had greatly diminished since the mid-nineteenth century, the growth of the honours system during the grand days of British Empire in the late-Victorian and Edwardian era created more work for the department. In 1910 Delevigne specifically mentioned honours as one part of division D's work which had grown.[76] By the same date Eggett's library work, which involved 'the care and arrangement of the General Library and Parliamentary Papers, the receiving and issuing books and papers to the Secretariat and the Staff, recording and cataloguing, and the answering of inquiries and searches for Reports, Returns etc.', had also 'grown into a very serious task'.[77] In one way Eggett appeared indispensable:

> When Eggett was sick, a warrant was sent to Buckingham Palace in another man's handwriting. 'What is this?' demanded Queen Victoria. 'This is not Mr. Eggett's writing. It won't do – and I won't sign it!' And, so the story went, she *didn't* sign it, until Eggett had written the warrant out again in his own crabbed hand.[78]

In 1910 a second division clerk was added to his staff of two assistant and four boy clerks, partly to learn the work connected with warrants (for Eggett could not last forever); and Eggett himself was made a staff clerk at a salary of £350 x £15 to £450.[79]

Soon after its creation in 1876 the lower division established itself as a vital part of the Home Office staff. Its clerks found they had an important role to play in supervising and staffing the branches of the general department which provided essential services for the upper division. Their techniques became more elaborate and their size rapidly increased as work was imposed largely through legislation. Developments in the first division were echoed in the second: increasing responsibilities without commensurate increases in staff led to the downgrading of work, particularly after the creation of the assistant clerk class; there was increasing specialization of duties among the clerks. Notable pressure of work around 1910, which reflected the extension of central government activity in spheres of social welfare administered by the Home Office, affected first and second division clerks alike. Legislation which seems to have imposed a particular burden on the second division included the 1905 aliens act, the 1906 workmen's compensation act, the 1904 and 1910 licensing acts; also, the expanding activity of some of the inspectorates – in particular the factory inspectorate – notably added to their duties.

The background of lower (or second) division discontent

The lower division was the first common class in the civil service and it is worth looking at the Home Office clerks in the context of their peers in other departments. As a class these clerks were generally discontented. In 1876 the *Civil Service Gazette*, journal principally of the lower grades, had forecast 'groaning and disturbance' about pay and conditions throughout the civil service, and this was indeed to be the case.[80] But the very fact that the lower division was now a single, service-wide class, subject to uniform conditions, gave these clerks power to improve their position collectively.

The order in council of 12 February 1876 had established their pay scale as £80 or £90 to £250 with triennial increments of £15.[81] These salaries could be boosted for some by the award of duty pay for specific tasks. The clerks argued that these salaries were too low, given their selection through a highly competitive examination and their performance of reasonably responsible duties. They found their triennial increments and their flat rate of progress to the upper limit of their class discouraging, particularly compared with the annual increments and varied salary scales of the upper division. A lower division man had to wait more than thirty years before he could reach his maximum of £250. They also considered the duty pay system awkward, unfair and grudgingly administered by the Treasury. It was intended to be awarded for specific duties which, if they were removed from an individual through no fault of his own (as they were in at least one Home Office case),[82] meant that he simply lost the extra pay. If a clerk were transferred or even promoted his duty pay could not go with him so that inter-departmental transfers were sometimes unpopular. At the Home Office the awkwardness of duty pay soon became apparent: constant increases in the work-load, without increases in staff, inevitably led to frequent demands for more duty pay and meant that the Home

Office was constantly badgering the Treasury for small amounts which were unsystematically awarded.[83]

The clerks were also discontented about their promotion prospects. At the Home Office the rigid rule of promotion by seniority meant that the staff posts – far from being rewards for good lower division men – were found to be convenient niches for redundant supplementary clerks whose salaries and standing had always been higher. Although Tripp had, against the odds, managed to become assistant clerk in charge of accounts in 1884, the future for other Home Office lower division clerks looked bleak: in 1886 they numbered sixteen and it was planned that they be increased to twenty-three, all of whom would be competing for four staff posts on much worse terms than the three remaining supplementary clerks. For this reason the department lost some of its best men who transferred to the metropolitan police courts where prospects were better, or even left the public service for City offices. Second division clerks generally resented their virtual exclusion from the upper division, promotion to which was permitted under the order in council but only 'exceptionally' and after ten years' service. The Home Office was not untypical in having made no such promotions. The *Civil Service Times,* the *Civil Service Gazette* and the *Civilian* saw the civil service as 'a new army, officered exclusively by learned young men, and with no promotion from the ranks'.[84]

The conflict between the militant clerks and the Treasury, on which they focused as the source of their troubles, is well documented.[85] The Home Office clerks first entered the fray in June 1880 when, with over six hundred others, they signed a memorial to the Treasury lords who were greatly alarmed by this new combination and eventually agreed to increase the starting pay by £5.[86] But the onslaught continued and groups of clerks in various departments, including the Home Office, – forbidden to approach the Treasury directly – presented petitions to their superiors. The Home Office petition listed a wide range of grievances but it gives an impression of discouragement with the system rather than hostility towards the head of department and senior officials. Indeed, the clerks recorded their special thanks to Harcourt for helping some of them transfer to metropolitan police court clerkships.[87] The Treasury lords could not ignore the cause which was now being aired publicly and had been taken up by various MPs. As a test case they had printed and presented to parliament the Colonial Office clerks' memorial together with their own reply. They took a tough line, based on the *laissez-faire* principle of a free market: that the public service offered a comparatively attractive career was proved by the fact that plenty of well-qualified candidates presented themselves for the lower division open competitive examination.[88] Opposition continued. Public meetings were held, many of which were attended by sympathetic MPs. There was correspondence and comment in the national press as well as in civil service newspapers which continued to encourage the 3,000 or so lower division clerks to press their common cause. By 1886 the clerks had organized a general committee which was busy preparing detailed statements of their grievances. In September of that year the government announced that another commission of inquiry was to investigate the working of the civil service.

Members of the Home Office were interviewed at length by the royal commission which was chaired by Sir Matthew Ridley. The staff clerks submitted a memorial to the commission requesting not only that their salaries be increased but also 'that they should rank between the senior and junior clerks of Class I'.[89] But the commissioners were more interested in the problems of the less fortunate lower division clerks who lamented that 'the conditions of their service are not only destitute of a single feature of liberality, but are such as must work positive injustice to most of those who are subject to them'.[90] They had, however, loyally pointed out to their department that none other had been 'more liberal to its Lower Division clerks, and that the Office has recommended more than the Treasury has been willing to grant'.[91] Their representative at the inquiry was Wheeler who particularly emphasized the lack of opportunity for promotion into the upper division, claiming that the duties of the lower division clerks overlapped with those of the juniors in the upper division. He even suggested that the only work which required 'special knowledge and exceptional training' in the Home Office could be done by three legally trained, highly paid officials who could be appointed by the home secretary from outside.[92]

This was not the view of Lushington, Knyvett, Murdoch and Moran. They were sympathetic to the plight of Wheeler and his colleagues whose work they complimented. They agreed that the system of triennial increments in a single salary scale, the award of duty pay and the limited opportunities for promotion to staff posts all contributed to a 'hopeless life' for these men. They made various suggestions for improving their lot. Moran felt that if the pay generally were improved, the starting pay might be reduced; Murdoch suggested dividing the lower division into two grades with the higher of the two having larger annual increments.[93] On one issue, however, Lushington, Knyvett and Murdoch – the three who spoke for the upper division – were unanimous: lower division clerks could not and should not take over the work of the upper division. Lushington even doubted 'if there was any junior clerk of the upper division the whole of whose work is not superior to that of the Lower Division clerks', although Knyvett and Murdoch confessed that there might occasionally be an overlap between the junior clerks' and the staff clerks' work.[94] Clearly the promotion of a lower division clerk into the upper division had never seriously been considered at the Home Office even though by 1886 some of these clerks had completed ten years' service.

The lower division was challenging the basis on which reformers, from Northcote and Trevelyan onwards, had wanted the civil service to be organized – that is, that the upper echelon, the decision-making body of clerks, should be staffed by a separate body of men having the breadth of experience imparted by a university training. Lower division clerks argued that it could equally well be staffed by men whose experience and training lay merely in years of practising civil service work. The views of Lushington, Knyvett and Murdoch about promotion were characteristic of many senior officials who believed with Sir Reginald Welby, permanent secretary to the Treasury, 'that passage from the second to the first division is not barred, nor ought it to be, but the exceptions ought to be reserved for *brilliant* men. Otherwise the upper division must go.'[95]

The outcome of the Ridley report was a new order in council of 21 March 1890 which regulated the conditions of service for the 'second division'. This was divided into two grades, the lower of which was sub-divided into three different salary scales (with annual increments) as follows:

higher grade: £250 × £10 – £350
ordinary grade: £190 × £10 – £250
                 £100 × £7.10.0d – £190
                 £70 × £5 – £100

There were efficiency bars at the £100 and £190 levels; only exceptionally able men were to be promoted into the higher grade and their names were to be submitted to the Treasury for approval. Duty pay was abolished. Promotions from the second to the first division could be made after eight rather than ten years although such promotions remained dependent on departmental recommendation. The Home Office reacted swiftly to the reform and immediately submitted the names of four second division clerks worthy of promotion into the new higher grade.[96] But the reaction of the Treasury boded ill for the future: in a reply which was sent sixteen months later they expressed the need to 'exercise sparingly the exceptional powers conferred on them' and would only consent to a single promotion.[97] The Treasury's reluctance to promote clerks into the higher grade was general; and the old pattern of public protest and discussion was resumed. In 1890 the Second Division Clerks' Association – one of the earliest staff associations – was formed to help better conditions; and discontent smouldered on. Meanwhile, some departments, including the Home Office, began to employ men from the new class of assistant clerks which were found increasingly useful. As their numbers gradually increased they too identified grievances about their conditions of service, formed combinations, drew support from sympathetic outsiders and eventually became an influential pressure group for reform.

Studies of lower middle-class occupational groups help to set these clerks in a wider social and economic context. In 1910 one contemporary observer, D'Aeth, suggested £150 as the lower and £300 as the upper end of the income band of the 'central lower middle class'. Below this level 'lay the poorer clerks for whom the struggle was often desperate, while above it were groups whose life-style and occupations became more and more akin to the substantial middle class'.[98] A more recent historian of Victorian clerks calls clerkships of £100 or less 'routine low-status': 'for the £80-£100 a year clerks the maintenance of a respectable image on a small income was a constant source of concern'.[99]

If one sets lower/second division clerks' salaries against these assessments it can be seen that those who did not manage to rise above the ordinary lower/second division class would virtually never be more than middle to low status in the clerkly world. Between 1877 and 1890 it would have taken a lower division clerk thirteen years to earn over £150 and he would not have reached his maximum of £250 until he had served thirty-four years when, if he had started at eighteen, he would have been fifty-two. After 1890 a second division clerk would have taken even longer – fourteen years – to reach £150, but he could expect to reach £250 after twenty-five years, or at forty-three for the man starting at eighteen. By contrast a sample of clerks in a 'typical medium-sized firm' in Liverpool, an insurance company where career opportunities and pay were 'equal to those in larger companies', did comparatively well. One who was earning £80 in 1890 at twenty-three had risen to £175 in ten years and £250 in fifteen. Another who was earning £100 in 1890 at twenty-seven had risen to £325 in ten years and £390 in fifteen.[100] When arguing their case in 1888 the lower division clerks argued that comparable clerks in the Sun Insurance Office and the London and Westminster Bank earned an average respectively of £48 and £65 a year more than they did in the civil service.[101] One must not forget the hidden benefits of job security and a pension within the civil service; but these were also normal benefits of old established firms.

The important thing, from the point of view of financial security, was to be promoted into the higher grade of the second division or to get a minor staff post which could secure a salary ceiling of up to £350 (over D'Aeth's 'central lower middle class' band) and could be the stepping-stone to a full staff post. What, then, were the prospects for such advancement in the Home Office? In 1877 the eleven clerks of the new lower division knew that they would be competing – and on worse terms – with four supplementary clerks for three staff posts. In fact, four of the initial eleven lower division clerks (or 36 per cent) eventually rose above the ordinary grade. In 1896 the situation had improved. Nineteen second division clerks had only two ageing supplementary clerks with whom to compete for vacancies among seven staff posts, while they also had the chance, if exceptionally good, of promotion into the higher grade – something that three of their erstwhile colleagues had achieved. In fact, of these nineteen, at least nine (or 47 per cent) had been promoted by 1914. By that time their chances still seemed good. Thirty-three second division clerks, with no competition from the now defunct supplementary clerks, had a chance of being promoted to nine staff posts; in addition, there were four minor staff posts. Thus, theoretically, they had a one in two and a half chance of some promotion. In fact, however, their chances were diminished by the simultaneous rise in the numbers of ancillary staff (assistant and boy clerks) which had grown from thirteen in 1896 to ninety-one in 1914. These more junior clerks were also to prove ambitious and capable of making it to staff clerkships, thereby lessening the overall chances of the second division clerks.[102] The relative change in size of the second division can be seen in Table 8.

Table 8   The changing clerical structure below the first division, 1877–1914, shown in rough percentage terms

	1877	1896	1914
staff clerks	14	16	6
other seniors*	33	11	7
lower/second division	52	43	23
ancillaries	–	30	63

*Supplementary, promoted lower/second division and special clerks.

Despite the absence of memoir sources we can attempt to construct the life-style of a diligent Home Office second division clerk. Let us assume that he entered the department at the age of eighteen in the mid-1890s. For his first six years he would have received £70 rising by £5 to £100. If he had had to support himself he would probably have found 'diggings' in some dingy metropolitan lodging-house.[103] Were he lucky enough to have a family in London, he would have managed well enough – even taking care to dress respectably for the office – and even contributed to the household purse. By the time his salary had climbed to between £150 and £200, during his thirties, he might have been able to install a wife in a rented semi-detached house in a clerks' suburb such as Kilburn or Peckham, commuting to Whitehall by train or underground.[104] Promotion on merit to a minor staff post would have helped him to reach this more secure – though hardly prosperous – position earlier. Promotion to a full-scale staff post would have made him comparatively well off and, socially speaking, set him substantially above his parents and the new second division clerks then entering the office. His salary, for instance, would have implied at least one living-in servant[105] and residence in a villa: Simpson, in the accounts branch, lived at 'The Close', West Norwood (although he left his wife in calamitous financial circumstances when he died in 1887, so perhaps he was living beyond his means).[106] Tripp's rise in salary from £95 to £400 within nine years was meteoric and most unusual but it showed what was possible with ability, diligence and luck. This upward social mobility, in which the lower middle class had particularly strong faith, was what second division clerks aspired to and this expectation explains why they continually fought for opportunities for promotion.

Second division grievances generally continued to centre around what they considered to be low pay and poor promotion prospects. In particular they wanted real, as opposed to illusory, promotion to first division posts and thereby access to salaries of over £600. 'So long as the Treasury refuse to adopt the principle which prevails in every other profession of allowing the best men to advance to the highest posts, without the imposition of artificial barriers that repress ambition and deaden zeal, Government Departments will contain a discontented body of men', wrote the *Civilian* in 1901.[107] Their discontent was undoubtedly aggravated by the fact that they were performing tasks hitherto carried out by more senior clerks, while they did not receive higher salaries. In the Home Office from the 1890s at least one staff clerk was performing first division duties[108] and second division clerks were doing what upper division clerks had done in the 1870s since the assistant clerks had removed most routine work from the second division. Improvements in pay and conditions were made: an order in council of 21 December 1907 increased the maximum of the second division salary to £300 while abolishing the 'higher grade', since clerks who merited this promotion were now being made minor staff clerks. But this did not stop discontent. After the passing of the 1909 labour exchanges act, when a large number of new civil servants were appointed without having taken an open competitive examination,[109] there was also strong opposition to what was called 'controlled patronage'. By this time it had emerged that what was required was 'that a formal negotiating procedure should be established together with facilities for conciliation and arbitration'.[110] Eventually in 1911 twenty-two different combinations, representing different interests in groups among lower paid civil servants, came together to form the Civil Service Federation, committed to advancing their common interests.[111] Agitation for another general inquiry into the civil service increased, and, eventually, in March 1912 the government appointed another royal commission on the civil service. The Macdonnell Commission implicitly recognized 'the new role which associations had started to play in the Civil Service as staff representatives'.[112] Its recommendations included a closer integration of the civil service examinations with the national educational system and a completely new system of grading all clerks below the first division. But the outbreak of war in 1914 prevented implementation.

Clerks from government offices such as the Post Office and the Board of Inland Revenue, which employed vast numbers of lower grade clerks, were particularly militant. By contrast there appears to have been no serious unrest at the Home Office. Certainly after the 1890 order in council second division clerks were frustrated at the Treasury's reluctance to promote them to the 'higher grade' and in 1893 they signed another service-wide petition demanding improved pay and prospects. But they characteristically modified the text to indicate that many of their requests for such promotion had at least received support from their Home Office superiors and they amended the general summary, assuring the Treasury that they had 'the good of the Service at heart'.[113] The Home Office clerks did take the opportunity presented by the Macdonnell Commission in 1912 to complain that 'their pay and their incentives to energy and efficiency . . . compare unfavourably with those of clerks in other departments and grades in the Home Office'.[114] Troup alleged to the commissioners that this referred to possibilities of promotion to staff posts and he argued that discontent was not a noticeable feature in his department.[115] There is no evidence to dispute this. Moreover he felt that the second division clerks 'certainly' had the 'opportunity of showing their ability and being picked out for promotion'.[116]

'The ultimate efficiency of any institution', wrote one Home Office official, 'depends more on the training and morale of the lower ranks than anything else';[117] and the morale among the Home Office lower ranks seems to have been good. Various reasons for this suggest themselves. First, there was growth, continuity and stability: able men such as Moran, Boehmer, Tripp and Farrant remained in office for years and provided a secure leadership at a time when work and responsibility in the branches was steadily increasing. Secondly, the creation in 1891 of a class below them to perform routine tasks, even though it provided an element of competition, may have raised their status. Thirdly, there was a strong corporate feeling within the office. Not only did staff clerks plead hard for better pay and status for their subordinates, but these pleas were often upheld in letters to the Treasury by senior first division men. The office was still small enough even in 1914 for the most senior permanent official to take a personal interest in the work and promotion of comparatively lowly personnel. This was a definite feature of Troup's regime. As permanent under-secretary he was involved in discussion and corrected draft letters about work arrangements and salary increases for staff within all three sub-divisions.

But this corporate feeling derived from a paternalistic outlook on the part of senior officials. However much they might promote the interests of their subordinates within their class, they discouraged the idea of promotion from the second to the first division. While admitting that 'the work of the staff clerks in the Second Division dovetails into the work of the lower officers of the higher division', Troup was quite clear that first and second division work demanded different qualities. Second division clerks required 'much carefulness and a good deal of intelligence' but 'not initiative or originality'.[118] He was not totally opposed to promotion: he thought that 'there ought to be occasional promotions of men of special capacity' but that 'speaking broadly' the first division should not be recruited from the second.[119] This attitude was characteristic of senior officials in the civil service, particularly in some of the older departments of state. Although the Home Office lagged behind the general average in these promotions, it was ahead of some departments. Between 1902 and 1911 altogether 248 new first division clerks were recruited to the civil service: 204 (or 82 per cent) came from outside; forty-four (or 18 per cent) were promotions from the second division.[120] At the Home Office between 1896 and 1914 thirty-one new first division clerks were recruited: twenty-eight (or 90 per cent) came from outside through the Class I examination; three (or 10 per cent) came from the second division. Between 1896 and 1911 neither the Foreign Office nor the Colonial Office had promoted any second division clerks into the first division, and the Treasury had promoted only one.[121]

The first such promotion within the Home Office was that of Wheeler in 1896. Troup considered it 'a complete failure'.[122] The second was in 1910 when Locke became a junior clerk. Then in 1913 A. Crapper, who had originally entered the department in 1890 as a mere boy clerk and who had followed Locke as noter in the registry, became the third and only other second division clerk to reach the first division before the first world war. Commenting later on the promotion of Locke, who eventually reached assistant secretary grade, Scott wrote: 'I had been to a university, and Locke had not: promotion from the ranks to the administrative class was rare indeed in those days, and it was a tragedy that because of the prejudices of the time he should have got his chance so late in life.'[123]

Part III Inspection: a Vital Tool of Central Government

Although the changing role of Home Office officials at the centre of the bureaucratic machine has been described, an important part of the story remains untold: that is, the nature and function of officials in the inspectorates. The circumstances surrounding the establishment and development of these well illustrate the forces which led to the great nineteenth-century extension of central government control in order to remedy social evils. The difficulty of presenting these sub-departments in a digestible form reflects the Home Office's difficulty in administering them. They all began at different times to cope with different problems and they developed in different ways. Thus each requires some individual attention before they are considered generally as significant phenomena in the changing political and administrative scene.

It has been decided to examine them chronologically within two periods. The first of these, 1848 to 1876, was the heyday of the inspectorates when their officials were pioneers of a new tool of central government. It is a period at present much under the searchlight of nineteenth-century historians trying to discern the rationale for the extension of central government control, the form which that extension took and the nature of those actively concerned in it. Several of these particular inspectorates have already been individually researched in detail. But it is important for the historian of the Home Office as an institution to try to look at them as a whole and see why they arrived at the home secretary's door and how his officials coped with the new work. The second period is 1876 to 1914 when many of the inspectorates were faced with new problems such as substantial bureaucratic growth, greater public interest and therefore political focus on their work, and frequent lack of funds with which effectively to carry out their legislative obligations which in themselves were not always clear.

6 The Home Office inspectorates: 1848–76

The increasing load of responsibilities which had worried Graham in the 1840s continued to press on his successors. For the home secretary found himself 'the key minister for co-ordinating the new departments of central control' which sprang up at this time to regulate those areas of people's lives where industrialization and population growth had created problems which could not be solved at local level.[1] This was simply because his sphere of control lacked definition and there was no other minister on whose shoulders to place many of the new responsibilities. The Home Office was the main central department concerned with internal domestic affairs other than those relating to revenue, trade, defence and the legal system. The Privy Council also concerned itself with social affairs but less actively than the Home Office. Recently-formed commissions also had extensive legislative powers. Notable among these was the Poor Law Commission, formed in 1834, whose general rules had to be sanctioned by the Home Office.[2] The important new method of regulation was government inspection by agents who were attached to the central department but outside it; and by 1876 the home secretary had become responsible for ten inspectorates many of which were not based in London at all. One reason for their growth outside the central department was the increasing attraction of the utilitarian ideal of in-the-field investigation and report by experts who understood the area of inspection. Another reason was the strength, within the Home Office, of traditional attitudes and patterns of work which would have made the assimilation of those newly-created experts inside the old framework very difficult.

The variety of new subjects which were attached to the Home Office between 1848 and 1876 was bewildering. Ten inspectorates were acquired in the following order: anatomy (1832); factory (1833); prison (1835); mines (1842); burial grounds (1854); constabulary (1856); reformatory and industrial schools (1857); salmon fisheries (1861); gunpowder (1871) which became explosives (1875); and cruelty to animals (1876). Diverse as they were in subject-matter, it is possible to classify them into groups. In the first group – the 'industrial' inspectorates – the factory, mines and explosives inspectors all had a policing role of enforcing acts regulating working conditions in industry. In addition, the factory and mines inspectors enforced certain minimum standards in the provision of education for children involved in the industrial process. Their ultimate sanction was to bring recalcitrant owners and occupiers to court for non-compliance with the acts. The role of the prison, constabulary, and reformatory and industrial schools inspectors, whose inspectorates form the second group – the 'law and order' inspectorates – was to oversee the efficiency of local authorities or private institutions which provided necessary services for the maintenance of law and order. Their authority was bolstered by power to withhold Treasury grants in cases of inefficiency. The third group – the 'medical' inspectorates – includes the anatomy, burial grounds and cruelty to animals inspectorates which regulated practices on the moral grounds that public decency demanded control (although the burial grounds inspectorate was primarily concerned with promoting public health). Inspectors from this group were part-time officials and medical men. The fisheries inspectorate, formed for economic reasons, stands on its own. This classification is artificial and not altogether satisfactory; nevertheless, it is useful to categorize these inspectorates in order to present a co-herent, and hopefully not too distorted, account.

The inspectorates will first be investigated within the groups described, in each case one being singled out for more detailed study, before the inspection phenomenon is discussed generally.

The 'industrial' inspectorates

The factory inspectorate
In 1848 it was fifteen years since parliament, acting on the recommendations of the Royal Commission on the Employment of Children in Factories, had empowered the secretary of state through the 1833 factory act to establish a factory inspectorate. There were four inspectors (three of whom had started in 1833), each covering his own geographical area of Britain with the help of fifteen locally based sub-inspectors.[3] Since 1844 there had been a central, statutorily appointed factory office at 10, Whitehall, staffed with clerk and messenger. The inspectorate was providing a new method of enforcing compliance with legislation regulating conditions of employment in factories. The idea of inspection had originally been put forward on the one hand by philanthropists, such as Lord Ashley, eager for more effective protection of the work-force, and on the other by employers, fearful of competition from rivals who evaded the law.

In the period under discussion the principal act under which the inspectors operated was the 1844 factory act. This had marked an important stage in the protection of women and children working in textile factories. Children over eight could only work six and a half hours a day; women and 'young persons' under eighteen were limited to twelve hours a day. There were important regulations about safety; others dealt with meal times, holidays and children's attendance at school. Occupiers had to report accidents causing bodily injury to the Home Office. Inspectors could bring charges against occupiers for offences under the act and could summon witnesses in prosecutions which were to be heard before magistrates. The latter section was a departure from the 1833 act which had given the inspectors far-reaching powers to act as magistrates and to make regulations. But the later act increased the powers of sub-inspectors who were enabled freely to enter and inspect factories. A significant feature of the 1844 act was the part played by the inspectors themselves in its promotion. It may be an exaggeration to claim that the act 'derived largely from the accumulated evidence... and teaching of experience contained in the annual reports of the factory inspectors'.[4] It has, for example, been convincingly argued that in the early forties 'Ashley, much more than the factory inspectors, was in the forefront of the accident question'.[5] But the very fact that they had been established as a monitoring force and enforcement agency to promote legislation protecting factory operatives made them an obvious consultative body when further legislative discussion about factory conditions arose.

Further than this, their motivation was the improvement of conditions. Horner 'used every means open to him to press his opinion on the public, on Parliament and in particular on the Home Office that this or that change or extension to the Act was necessary if the law was to be made enforceable'.[6] The inspectors, for example, soon discovered that the 1844 act could not prevent defiant manufacturers from evading parliament's intent by allowing different groups of protected persons their required breaks at different times of day so that production could continue for up to fourteen hours a day.[7] They fought hard for a change in this 'relay system' which was ameliorated by an act of 1853 that established a normal working day which could only extend from six in the morning until six in the evening for all workers.

The basic work was on-the-ground inspection which could be carried out by day or night, if necessary with a police constable and without warning to the occupiers. Inspectors could also enter schools for child operatives to ensure that the stipulated amount of education was being received. They appointed and worked closely with 'certifying surgeons' who provided essential certificates estimating the age of young children found working. They attended legal proceedings. They had to approve regulations made by occupiers about ventilation and sanitary arrangements. They prepared parliamentary returns and the annual report for which the sub-inspectors' statistics had to be collated. They occasionally sought the law officers' opinion about the interpretation of acts. They advised on the formulation and drafting of bills.

By 1850 the early principles of factory legislation were established,[8] and were gradually extended to related and to non-textile industries as committees of inquiry – taking into account inspectors' evidence – pointed out that employees needed equal protection in other areas.[9] An important extension came after the 1867 workshop regulation act. The outcome of the Royal Commission on Children's Employment of 1862–7, this act was an attempt to restrict the sweated labour of women and children in workshops. At first it was administered by local authorities which could appoint their own workshop inspectors. But local administration proved ineffective and full responsibility for inspection was transferred to the Home Office factory inspectorate in 1871.

The inspectorate faced immense difficulties which inhibited its effectiveness. Although some manufacturers had originally favoured inspection as a means of preventing unfair competition, when they found that inspectors tended to try to enforce laws which ran contrary to their own profit-making aims, they frequently thwarted legislative intentions. The social structure aided them: many manufacturers were the very magistrates before whom the inspectors brought those who would not comply with the law. Factory-owner magistrates could 'nullify the intentions of the Act and make fools of the Inspectors by returning not-guilty verdicts on a technicality, inflicting derisory fines or ignoring the blatant intimidation of witnesses dependent on the accused for employment and livelihood'.[10] Recent detailed research into the early inspectors' enforcement policy has shown that, partly because of this factor, the effect of inspection from the point of view of improving safety was strictly limited.[11] Difficulties encountered in getting prosecutions may well have caused the Home Office to stress the explanatory and advisory role of inspectors who could often, in the long run, be more effective reasoning with factory owners about methods of accident prevention or improvement of sanitation than constantly threatening prosecution.

Lack of uniformity of administration among inspectors was a

related problem. It was up to each inspector to find a balance between advice and prosecution and sometimes there was a definite inconsistency about this. In 1876 the Royal Commission on the Factory and Workshop Acts pointed out the different attitudes of Robert Baker and Alexander Redgrave who were inspectors simultaneously between 1858 and 1878. While Redgrave said 'he would not direct prosecution for unlawful employment on account of the mere presence of a woman or child in a workshop after legal hours . . . Baker stated that he had got convictions in such cases'.[12] Thus Baker annually undertook double Redgrave's number of prosecutions.

Another major difficulty was the sheer size of the task. The 1871 factory and workshop act added more than 90,000 establishments (workshops) to the inspectors' estimated total of over 30,000 (factories).[13] The size and structure of the inspectorate was altered in an attempt to meet new legislative demands. By 1876 the corps consisted of two inspectors, four assistant inspectors, thirty-eight sub-inspectors and eleven junior sub-inspectors. With 120,000 or so establishments equally apportioned, each inspector would have had 2,000 premises to inspect. The inspectorate could, therefore, hardly be an effective policing force.

In fact, each man did not supervise an equal number of premises. This comparatively elaborate inspectorate was beginning by the seventies to experience the problems of a growing bureaucracy. The two inspectors had been relieved of much of the daily round of inspection by the assistant inspectors and by 1876 were largely engaged 'in supervising and in arranging the work of a much larger staff'.[14] But the 1876 Royal Commission on the Factory and Workshop Acts regretted the assistant inspectors' lack of a supervisory role over the sub-inspectors which prevented uniformity: 'One sub-inspector would admit the manufacturer's objections to the required safeguards; another would overrule them; a third, perhaps, would see no danger to be guarded against. In such cases the larger experience of a controlling officer would be very valuable.'[15]

The inspectorate also experienced the problem of dual headship from 1862 when Redgrave and Baker were left as the only two inspectors. They strongly disliked each other and could agree neither about major policy recommendations nor about minor office arrangements. They came to such bitter blows in 1867, over a comparatively trivial matter, that the home secretary had to set up an embarrassing Home Office-Treasury committee of inquiry.[16] Even this did not prevent Redgrave from complaining about his colleague to a bewildered MP who commented to the home secretary on the 'great quarrelling and disorganization of the department'.[17] As a result the royal commission advocated a single head.

Improvement in working conditions even for employees in textile factories was not a steady process. A recent study of the fencing controversy between 1833 and 1857 shows that the inspectors felt that the 1856 factory act dealt 'a body blow to progress in fencing and compensation' because proposals had been emasculated through powerful lobbying from the National Association of Factory Occupiers.[18] Yet this fear did not ultimately materialize and over the period as a whole there is no doubt that working conditions for women and children (and men, following in their wake) greatly improved. Inspection made a vital contribution towards this. By 1859 Horner believed that 'legislative interference for the regulation of the labour of children, young persons, and women in factories is now viewed by a great majority of occupiers of those works as having done, and as continuing to do a great amount of good'.[19] By 1876 there was a new problem but this highlighted general improvement: if the factory owners were, by and large, attuned to the need for central regulation, this was not true of workshop occupiers who were disposed to infringe the law and 'derive safety from their number and obscurity; and while they are at least as slow as were the old factory occupiers to accept the interference of Government in their concerns, they are much slower to see the reason and benefits of regulation'.[20]

Horner, Baker and Redgrave stand out as inspectors during this period. Horner was born in 1785, the son of a prominent whig linen merchant. Educated at Edinburgh High School and university, he and his brothers moved in the 'highly educated and politically active coterie which formed the focus of the social life of their class'.[21] He became a partner in his father's firm, working and travelling between London, Edinburgh and the continent, continuing to move in whig circles and to pursue wide political, literary, educational and scientific interests which made him a fellow of the Royal Society and president of the Geological Society. Following a period as warden of London university, Horner sat on the 1833 royal commission. There is no indication that until then he had a particular interest in factory conditions but after his appointment as inspector he 'threw all his energies into his new work'.[22] The retirement in 1859 of this many-faceted man left the inspectorate in the charge of a different kind of official.

Redgrave and Baker were more bureaucratic and less wide-ranging in their interests and experience, having previously been sub-inspectors and thus made the inspectorate their career. Baker, probably more of an idealist than Redgrave, was drawn to factory work after he had qualified as a doctor in Leeds where he was affected by the plight of factory cripples. In 1830 he gave a piece of his mind to a mill owner, advised him to employ a medical consultant and thus began a practice of consultancy to mill occupiers.[23] Four years later, aged thirty, he was appointed a sub-inspector. Redgrave was the son of a manufacturer and spent nearly all his life from the age of sixteen in the Home Office where he started as a clerk. Having been private secretary to a home secretary and a parliamentary under-secretary, he transferred as a clerk to the factory inspectorate where in 1849, at the age of thirty-one, he was appointed a sub-inspector.[24]

'General intelligence, faculty of observation, discretion, tact, and firmness, united to a sufficient amount of bodily vigour and activity' were felt to be the appropriate qualifications for these inspectors.[25] From 1856 these were sought through the Civil Service Commission which examined all nominated candidates with papers designed for men of liberal education. Lowe replaced nomination with open competition in 1873 but this decision was hastily reversed by Cross who doubted that such a system could test the essential qualities of an inspector.[26] The backgrounds of the factory inspectors can be seen from a parliamentary return of 1880 which required details of the forty-one inspectors and sub-inspectors appointed since 1867. Among these men, whose average age was thirty-one, nine had entered the inspectorate from the army or navy; seven had been civil service clerks; six were either barristers or reading for the bar; four had recently graduated from Oxford or Cambridge; five had been secretaries, and three were tutors or teachers.[27] Only three had any apparent connection with manufacturing.

The factory, mines and explosives inspectorates compared

The mines inspectorate had two incarnations. The 1842 coal mines act, which excluded women and boys under ten from the pits and restricted machine-tending to those over fifteen, led the home secretary to appoint H. S. Tremenheere as commissioner or inspector. He saw his function as the general investigation of the social problems of the mining districts and operated virtually independently of the Home Office.[28] In addition, over the next eight years, various commissions of inquiry, usually consisting of two mining experts, reported on conditions in mines. Tremenheere, essentially an amateur inspector, pressed for the appointment of permanent qualified mines inspectors. He thus contributed towards the establishment of a new permanent inspectorate which was set up in 1850 after a series of pit disasters and an investigation by a House of Lords select committee.

As its responsibilities increased so the mines inspectorate was enlarged and its stucture made more complex. From a commissioner and four inspectors in 1850 it developed to twelve inspectors and twelve assistant inspectors plus two special metalliferous mines inspectors in 1872. But unlike both the factory and the explosives inspectors the mines inspectors had no central office in London. Instead, each inspector worked from his own home and submitted an independent annual report. This was later justified on the grounds that 'mines vary very much in different districts and the duties of the inspectors are chiefly the implementation of the Act with reference to these peculiar differences'.[29] But from the early 1850s they managed to meet occasionally to establish a modicum of uniformity; in 1859 they all contributed to a general report on proposed legislation; and by 1867 they held at least one general meeting a year.[30] There was no formal chief inspector of mines, although from 1872 one inspector, J. Dickinson, was granted a personal salary of £1,000 until he retired in 1891 and he was evidently known as the 'senior inspector'.[31]

Early coal mines regulation may have stressed the safety aspect of working conditions more than early factory regulation. But the mines inspectorate in many ways developed in parallel with the factory inspectorate. Initial extremely limited powers were gradually extended through additional mines acts which increased protection to employees (women and children first and then, inevitably, men) and thereby increasingly curtailed the freedom of mine owners to organize their mines as they pleased and obliged them to provide the government with information, such as details of accidents. In each case there grew up a comparatively large corps of inspectors, subject to the authority of the home secretary and submitting annual reports to parliament. Existing factory acts influenced the formulation of mines acts and vice versa. While the 1842 mines act had 'blazed the trail in the critical matter of protecting adult female labour', actual powers of enforcement through prosecution came later for the mines inspectors than for the factory inspectors.[32] The great consolidating mines act, which 'established a largely effective system of control' by allowing for flexibility of administration, came in 1872, six years before the equivalent consolidating factory act.[33]

As with factory administration, the central authority had to tread warily in its inspection. Indeed, the issue of private rights versus central interference may have been an even tougher one for the government in the case of mines inspection. One reason for this was the strength of the mine-owning lobby in the House of Lords where owners fought hard against restrictions on the industry.[34] This powerful lobby no doubt partly accounts for Home Office instructions to mines inspectors to tread warily:

> While you will afford to any parties who may solicit it, such advice or suggestion as your knowledge or experience may enable you to offer, you will abstain from dictation or any unauthorized interference . . .
> You will not fail to act with courtesy and forbearance in your official intercourse with all persons, and you will encourage a good feeling and understanding between the miners and their employers.[35]

The strength of the anti-interference lobby may explain the force of the argument – familiar to factory and explosives inspectors – that the existence of too many inspectors would relieve occupiers of the responsibility of ensuring safe working conditions. This hardly seems a danger when there existed, in the mid-1860s for example, only twelve inspectors to oversee 3,195 mines.[36] But it was the expression of a very real view that owners must exercise constant care in order to prevent the appalling pit disasters which aroused such intense concern. The importance of co-operation between owners, managers and employees was underlined by the 1872 coal mines regulation act which gave powers of inspection in each mine to representatives of the miners themselves.

The explosives inspectorate was formed out of the temporary gunpowder works inspectorate after the passing of the 1875 explosives act. This was inspired by a series of disastrous industrial explosions and was designed to protect employees involved in the manufacture, transport and storage of explosives.[37] By this date government inspection of factories and mines (with which the manufacture and use of explosives were closely connected) and of another large-scale scientific industrial process, the making of alkali, was well established.[38] There was no problem passing through parliament an act which equipped the inspectors with extensive and sophisticated powers. They could enter and search premises, give notice of dangerous practices, initiate legal proceedings for non-compliance, and confiscate potentially dangerous goods. Employers had to report accidents and they also had the right to make certain rules.

The functioning of explosives legislation differed from factory and mines legislation by controlling conditions through a system of licences which all large-scale factories and magazines had to obtain and review through the Home Office. The department could thereby keep a check on occupiers and change conditions if necessary. As far as the licensing and inspection of all small-scale works and the supervision of the transport of explosives were concerned, the act imposed responsibilities and powers upon local authorities which were encouraged to appoint their own inspectors. Thus the Home Office inspectorate started with only two inspectors and always remained small compared with the factory and mines inspectorates. Because of this system of local inspection, the early inspectors experienced great difficulty in ensuring that the act was effectively administered and at times almost despaired of local authority co-operation.

One feature which the three inspectorates shared was the observation of continental and American practices in attempts to improve methods at home. Horner wrote a comparative analysis of factory legislation in Europe in 1840;[39] Tremenheere made a professional visit to America;[40] Dickinson and J. J. Atkinson visited the mines of Mons and Liège to test mechanical ventilating machines;[41] and the early reports of the first inspector of explosives, Major V. D. Majendie, give examples of continental and American methods in the control of explosives.

Mines and explosives inspection, at least in the early days, was a far more technical business than factory inspection. It was essential for a mines inspector to understand the complications of mining machinery, underground ventilation and so on, just as an explosives inspector had to comprehend something of the chemistry and physics of explosives manufacture. Despite the increasing variety of industrial processes, a factory inspector needed far less technical know-how by comparison. This accounts for a fundamental difference in the type of men recruited to the inspectorates. While factory inspectors were gentlemen of liberal education who learned the job as they went along, mines inspectors after 1850 tended to have had previous experience of mining (often as engineers) and explosives inspectors were always royal artillery officers. For this reason they normally started their careers as inspectors later than factory inspectors. The mines inspectors of this period often originated from mining areas, rarely went to public schools or were university-educated. They often belonged, contributed papers and lectured to professional institutions such as the Geological Society, the Institute of Civil Engineers and the Institute of Mining Engineers. Some wrote technical works on their subject. Like the factory inspectors, the mines and explosives inspectors entered the public service through nomination by the secretary of state and examination by the Civil Service Commission. Once the very early factory and mines inspectors had been replaced, the normal career pattern of the inspectors was to remain in the inspectorate, often changing districts in order to gain experience. Explosives inspectors also tended to make their career in the inspectorate.

The 'law and order' inspectorates

The prison inspectorate

The 1835 prison act – the outcome of a House of Lords select committee – empowered the home secretary to appoint up to five inspectors to report on the state of all local British prisons.[42] The idea was to leave the building, expenditure, staff appointments and organization of prisons to local justices but 'subject them to the supervision and control of some central authority who should see that the duties were efficiently performed'.[43] This was an attempt to promote uniformity in prison administration. Although several eighteenth-century English prison acts laid down uniform regulations, local conditions varied to an extent which by this date appeared intolerable from the standpoint of criminal justice. Of the original five inspectors, four remained in 1848. Working from home, each covered a different area of the country and submitted an independent annual report.[44] One inspector, John Perry, later stated that their function was

> To examine all the books and all the salaries of officers of the prison, to hear complaints from prisoners, to visit every part of the prison, and to see as far as we can that the rules and regulations of the Secretary of State and the enactment of the law are carried out, and to report any deviation from them to the Secretary of State.[45]

In fact their powers were severely limited. Their only statutory authority was to approve or suggest alterations to prison rules. If their annual reports were critical the most that the Home Office could do was to reprimand local authorities; there was no effective financial sanction. As one of the inspectors later put it, 'we represent the eyes and ears of the Secretary of State but not his voice'.[46] Moreover, Grey, as home secretary, on the defensive about even this small extension of central control, assured parliament that the inspectors' right of reporting was minimal and that 'it was their duty to inquire into facts, rather than to report opinions or make recommendations'.[47]

Despite this, the inspectors did make some impact on the development of policy. An investigation into prison diet led in 1849 to the circulation of a suggested diet to the justices.[48] The inspectors' support for separate cellular confinement influenced various home secretaries and probably contributed to the requirement of the 1865 prison act that each prison should contain separate cells for this.[49] They influenced Grey in their opposition to fruitless forms of penal labour such as the use of the treadmill and crank, which were firmly supported by the 1863 House of Lords select committee on prison discipline.[50] When introducing the 1865 prisons bill, the home secretary proposed that nothing should be enforced statutorily about the use of these forms of penal labour and that discretion should be left to local visiting justices,[51] although the act itself was to stipulate that adequate means for enforcing hard labour should be found in prisons.

The inspectors were unsuccessful in carrying out their limited statutory functions. First, they were too thin on the ground. A request in 1846 for the aid of sub-inspectors in order that they might inspect all prisons at least once a year was rejected and by 1863 their numbers had been reduced to two which meant they were visiting their prisons only about once in eighteen months.[52] Secondly, local inertia, jealousy and therefore lack of co-operation with the central authority was a constant problem. Some gaols had not bothered to subscribe to the prison regulations which the Home Office had drafted in 1842 as a guide and 'in the remaining gaols the regulations vary indefinitely according to the views of the governing body'.[53] Perry claimed in 1863 that the Home Office had rarely exercised its power of altering the rules of local prisons because magistrates 'prefer making the rules themselves, and they often object to the alterations that are made, which leads to long correspondence'.[54] Local resentment was partly caused by bad liaison between inspectors and local authorities. After a visit the inspector was supposed to report directly to the Home Office without communicating with the justices to whom the home secretary subsequently wrote, if he felt it necessary, without showing them the reports. Inspector Herbert Voules tended to disobey regulations by conferring with the visiting justices.[55] But this lack of uniformity, together with not infrequent lack of agreement about policy among the inspectors, was undesirable. In 1850 Grey had pondered the idea of creating a chief inspector to co-ordinate policy.[56] But he did nothing about it and the inspectors continued in their isolated way, on the whole receiving little direction or encouragement from the Home Office. As a result Grey, in 1863, appeared to know surprisingly little about how they operated.[57]

The 1863 select committee found that 'for years past the inspection of prisons has . . . been reduced in most cases to a mere formality, both as regards the supervision itself and the subsequent use made of that supervision by the Secretary of State and the local authorities in counties and boroughs'.[58] It also found gross differences among local authorities in enforcing sentences of hard labour. The solution seemed to lie in giving greater control to the Home Office through its inspectors. It recommended that every gaol be governed by a definite code of rules, as had been the original intention of the legislature; and that, since the Home Office had failed to put this into effect, these rules should be embodied in a schedule to a new act reinforcing its power by giving it financial sanctions against authorities who refused to comply.

Accordingly the first schedule of the 1865 prison act set out a code of rules binding on all prison authorities. It was described by Grey as containing 'nearly all that was essential to the discipline and management of prisons'.[59] But the act delegated some power to the visiting justices who, with the consent of the Home Office, could make supplementary rules. The Home Office could, for the first time, enforce compliance by withholding the Treasury grant-in-aid (which no local authority wanted to manage without) towards the maintenance of prisoners. This important provision was modelled on the 1856 county and borough police act.

Firm instructions went out to local authorities giving detailed Home Office advice on how they should carry out provisions of the act relating to matters such as hard labour and diet; and Grey insisted on annual visits to prisons by inspectors or else an explanation of why these had not occurred.[60] The intention was above all to create greater uniformity in administration and, indeed, local authorities were brought more into line as the Home Office attitude towards recalcitrance and independence hardened. Yet still lack of uniformity remained a problem: the inspectors found, for example that they were unable to achieve standardization on diet, discipline and the carrying out of sentences of hard labour. Local authorities, on their part, found that one particular aspect of the act weighed heavily on them financially: the directive to build new gaols on the cellular plan.

It was to achieve greater standardization, to rationalize the number and size of prisons and to relieve ratepayers of expense that the Conservative government in 1877 passed the prison act which brought all English prisons under central control.[61] Thus the prison inspectorate was placed at one remove from the Home Office under the direct authority of a board of five prison commissioners who were responsible to the home secretary.

There were eight prison inspectors between 1848 and 1876.[62] Most is known about Frederic Hill. A member of an enlightened family which occupied itself with social questions of the day, he had been involved in the running of an experimental school in Birmingham. As an inspector Hill was energetic and active, first in Scotland where he was appalled by prison conditions. His reports contributed in 1839 to the creation of the semi-independent adminis-tration of Scottish prisons which he felt would lead to improvement. He wrote a book, *Crime, its Amount, Causes and Remedies,* published in 1853 after he had moved to the Post Office to aid his brother Rowland Hill.[63] The inspectors had a variety of backgrounds but there was a bias towards ex-army officers (with no connection with any particular corps since no specialist knowledge was needed). Two men with medical training were appointed specifically as 'medical inspectors'. The last inspector of the period, T. F. Powell, had been a prison governor, and this experience was to become the normal one for inspectors.

The prison, constabulary, and industrial and reformatory schools inspectorates compared

Population growth and urbanization had created a need for effective police forces. These were totally lacking in many areas until an act of 1835 obliged boroughs to form watch committees to ensure adequate policing, and another of 1839 allowed counties to do so. In 1856 the county and borough police act brought counties into line with boroughs in England and Wales by obliging magistrates to establish forces where these did not exist. It also provided for the amalga-mation of forces where this would lead to greater efficiency.[64] By January 1857, under this act, the home secretary had appointed three inspectors of constabulary for England and Wales. On the basis of their certification of forces as efficient, he could authorize the Treasury to allow grants-in-aid to local authorities towards a quarter of the cost of police pay and clothing. In his first annual report one inspector, Cartwright, described how he had communicated with magistrates and watch committees to offer his assistance and lay 'before them for their consideration a system more uniform than that existing as regard[s] strength of force, assimilation of pay and classification'. His intention was also 'to bring counties and boroughs into closer communication with each other, so that all forces should work together, and establish a complete system of co-operation throughout the district'.[65]

Although their powers were limited – for example, boroughs could still appoint, promote and dismiss members of their force and make regulations – the inspectors were on the whole successful. Unlike the prison inspectors they met with helpful local authorities. Cartwright had found 'an earnest desire on the part of the authorities to make their respective forces as efficient as possible'.[66] By and large they managed to persuade these authorities, particularly in the counties, to achieve and maintain efficiency. After two years only Rutland, of the county forces, remained inefficient. Moreover, 'the influence of the inspector was the main factor in raising the size of establishments'.[67]

One factor in their comparative success in the earlier period was their financial weapon, the threat to recommend the withholding of the Treasury grant, which they were not loath to use. Another may have been that they found it easier to produce an effective policy for improvement than did the prison inspectors who became involved in fundamental arguments over the value of different forms of penal discipline and the value of separate confinement. Although the efficiency of a police force might appear difficult of measurement, the inspectors worked out a straightforward formula for this: they looked at the size and discipline of a force. The former was related directly to the size of the population it policed, while 'the test of efficiency in discipline was that a force should have enough superior officers to supervise the constables on duty continuously and regularly'.[68]

Constabulary inspectors, like prison inspectors, were often retired army officers. Three of those appointed in this period had previous experience at the head of police forces. There were never more than three constabulary inspectors for the whole of England and Wales during this period but they were not overworked: the average number of forces for each inspector in 1857 was seventy-eight and in 1864 was seventy-three. Later on the Home Office felt that two inspectors could easily carry out the entire work of the inspectorate.[69] These inspectors also worked independently from their homes and so incurred the disadvantage of being isolated from their central department. At the same time they managed to obtain information from and influence police forces without undue Home Office interference.[70]

The inspectors of reformatory and industrial schools differed from their colleagues inspecting prisons and police forces in that, although they too were reporting to the government on what had come to be thought of as an essential service, it was one to which local authorities only contributed part of the finance and were not involved in running since these institutions were private and voluntary.

In 1857 the Home Office appointed an inspector of prisons with specific reference to reformatory schools. This inspector soon became involved in the administration of legislation concerning two types of voluntary school. Reformatory schools were institutions where a convicted child under sixteen could be committed by magistrates after the expiry of his sentence. The 1854 youthful offenders act stipulated that, if certified by the home secretary, these schools could receive a Treasury contribution towards the maintenance of a child. Industrial schools were designed to give an industrial education to vagrant, destitute or disorderly (but not convicted) children who could be committed up to the age of fourteen. By 1861 children at industrial schools – which until that date, when the Home Office took over, had been the responsibility of the Committee of the Privy Council – could also be partially supported by Treasury contributions. In 1866 the previous acts were replaced by two consolidating and amending acts which applied to reformatory and industrial schools in England, Wales and Scotland.

These schools received their funds from a variety of sources including voluntary subscriptions and donations, local authorities and parents who could be ordered by magistrates to help towards the cost of their children. But the largest source was the Treasury. Unlike the grant-in-aid for police forces, the Treasury contribution – which was reckoned per child – was fixed not by statute but by decision of the home secretary which meant that it had to be fought out between the Home Office and the Treasury. The inspectorate was responsible for two sources of finance: the Treasury grant and parental contributions. As time went on and the number of inmates increased, the voluntary contributions, which had hitherto been the second largest element of support, fell considerably. Thus the schools increasingly became government institutions, heavily subsidized by the Treasury and inspected by a central inspectorate. Like the prison inspectors, the reformatory and industrial schools inspectors worked at enforcing uniform standards in the interests of criminal justice. But the latter also emphasized local needs and characteristics in order to promote local voluntary interest and effort.[71]

Unlike the other two, this inspectorate was centred in London and it used provincial agents to collect parental contributions. It had developed from the prison inspectorate since reformatory schools were penal institutions. But the first full-time inspector, the Reverend Sydney Turner, a leading reformer in the field of juvenile crime, had himself run a reformatory school at Redhill, Surrey, and had never previously been a prison inspector. The scope of his inspection increasingly included methods and standards of education as well as of punishment. After the passing of the 1866 acts Turner officially became 'inspector of reformatory and industrial schools' and his association with the prisons inspectorate was nominal although inspectors of reformatory and industrial schools were still appointed under the 1835 prison act. Turner's sympathies lay fundamentally with those involved in the movement to found reformatory schools in order to reclaim young offenders for society. His aim in becoming inspector was to promote this: indeed, his annual reports have been described as propaganda for the work of this philanthropic movement.[72] From 1868 until 1875, when he became Dean of Ripon, Turner worked with one assistant, Henry Rogers, who was himself the son of a clergyman and had also worked at Redhill.

The part-time 'medical' inspectorates

The burial grounds inspectorate

By the mid-nineteenth century urbanization in Britain had produced a situation where the traditional English pattern of burial in local parish churchyards was becoming increasingly inadequate. Large new cemeteries, owned by joint-stock companies, had sprung up on the outskirts of towns. But in these and in the older, overcrowded parish graveyards a total lack of control had led to grossly insanitary conditions which were becoming a danger to health and to shocking graveside scenes 'arising from interments amidst the scenes of crowd and bustle of everyday life'.[73]

The situation was aggravated in 1849 by a severe cholera epidemic. The following year Edwin Chadwick at the General Board of Health and Dr John Sutherland, the Board's medical inspector, were among those who reported on the existing threat to public health and assault on the 'decency and solemnity' of traditional burial. Chadwick supported a radical scheme whereby all metropolitan burials would take place in public burial grounds, administered by a central commission.[74] This was not adopted but a burial act in 1850 gave the Board power to close burial grounds, to purchase land for the provision of new grounds, to make regulations for interment and to appoint local burial officers. The Board failed to bring about effective changes through this act. Chadwick's policies 'seemed to moderate people to be "too forward developments", and aroused an angry host of vested, threatened interests', while the government did not back the Board's schemes for buying up cemeteries.[75]

In 1852 a new burial act repealed the 1850 act and gave the home secretary power, through orders in council, to close metropolitan burial grounds which were dangerous to public health; to grant permission to local 'burial boards' (appointed by local vestries) to establish and manage new burial grounds for their parishioners; and to license the burial of persons in previously purchased graves and vaults. The local burial boards were given extensive rights to raise money and manage their grounds. Thus the government reverted 'to the more constitutional, simple, and less objectionable method, by which from time immemorial the parochial authorities had been intrusted with the burial of the dead'.[76] In 1853 a similar act extended the principle to other towns.

It was not until 1855 that the appointment of inspectors was mentioned in a burial act. But in late 1852 the home secretary, Spencer Walpole, appointed Sutherland to make preliminary inquiries about applications to close burial grounds. The following year two more inspectors, Richard Grainger and P.H. Holland, who were both from the General Board of Health, were appointed on a temporary basis, and provided with clerical assistance and an office in London. Although the 1852 act was a decentralizing measure, the Home Office took a fairly tough line over the closure of burial grounds. Parishes were frequently refused an extension of time or granted very limited time within which to close their grounds. Permission was frequently refused for people to be buried in family vaults.[77] By early 1854 two hundred and forty-two parishes had received notice and had been given a date for closure.[78] The inspectors were not required, even after 1855, to produce an annual report for parliament but they did submit some special reports on specific cemeteries whose practices continued to be obnoxious. Their recommendations contributed to a further burial act of 1857 which gave the home secretary greater powers to regulate practices in private and other cemeteries, to control the use of private vaults which were a potential health hazard, and to license the removal of bodies from one grave to another.

When asked about the success of the burial acts administration in 1869, Holland said that he thought it was a good illustration of effective, 'united action of the general and the local authorities – not by either alone'. He felt it right that the central authority should have the power to put an end to a nuisance (to close an unhealthy ground) while the local authority had the right to decide on improved measures (what new facilities should be made). During his fifteen years of inspection he had never had 'what may be called a collision with any local authorities'.[79]

The condition of burial grounds was obviously closely connected with the question of public health and local government. There were sections in the local government acts of 1858 and 1859 and the sanitary act of 1866 which related to burial grounds. Sir John Simon, in his eleventh report as medical officer of the Privy Council, complained of the fragmention of public health legislation, and it seems curious that burial inspection remained with the Home Office – particularly after the formation of the Local Government Board in 1871.

Being primarily concerned with public health, the inspectors were medical men whose knowledge of sanitation enabled them to frame useful regulations for burial boards, judge whether it was acceptable to disturb a grave, and so forth. Between 1852 and 1876 there were three inspectors, paid at a rate of three guineas a day on a part-time basis. Sutherland, one of the leading sanitarians of his day, was more of an adviser to the home secretary than a full-blown inspector and he did not remain long. A Scot who had been educated and qualified in Edinburgh, Sutherland had practised privately in Liverpool before entering the public service. He conducted various special inquiries, including one into the 1848-9 cholera epidemic, and later contributed to the reports of the royal commissions on the health of the army and its state in India. Grainger, the son of a surgeon, was educated at a grammar school in Birmingham and later at St Thomas's hospital where he eventually became professor of anatomy and physiology. For twenty years he was head of Webb's medical school, and was made a fellow of the Royal College of Surgeons and of the Royal Society. He remained a burial ground inspector until his death in 1865. After this, since the work had greatly diminished, there remained only his colleague, Holland, who worked effectively full-time as inspector until 1879.

The anatomy, burial grounds and cruelty to animals inspectorates compared

The anatomy inspectorate was the oldest Home Office inspectorate, having started in 1832 after the passing of the anatomy act. This was designed 'to remedy the great and grievous crimes, then recently come to light' – the secret digging up of corpses – 'to supply human bodies for the purpose of anatomical examination'.[80] The act recognized that human anatomical dissection, in which from the early nineteenth century there had been increasing medical interest, was essential for the advance of medicine. In order to control this practice it required anyone engaging in such dissection to do so in registered premises, to be medically qualified and to obtain a licence from the home secretary. Moreover, anatomy schools could only receive bodies with medical certificates showing the cause of death. The inspectors were to make quarterly returns to the secretary of state, detailing the numbers and types of bodies removed to anatomy schools. From 1843 there were separate inspectors for the metropolitan, provincial and Scottish areas, each of whom was locally based. An interesting feature was the method of their payment: each received an annual fee of £100 from the consolidated fund, rather than directly from parliament, because 'an annual discussion on this delicate subject is very much to be deprecated and would probably lead to increased difficulty (great enough already) in procuring bodies for dissection for the schools of anatomy'.[81]

The inspectorate functioned well and nearly forty years later, when methods of working out an effective policy for controlling the practice of vivisection were being discussed, it was referred to.[82] Like the 1832 anatomy act, the cruelty to animals act of 1876 was the outcome of a furor created by the development of new medical techniques. The science of physiology had, comparatively recently, begun to be taught in universities and medical schools where physiology and pathology laboratories were being established and professorial chairs in the field being set up. When it became publicly clear that medical schools were carrying out experiments on live animals for the purpose of instruction and research, formidable anti-vivisection pressure groups were formed, the issue was debated hotly and at length, and a royal commission reported on the subject.[83] The legislation which emerged, after stormy sessions and pressure from a powerful medical lobby, provided for a system of Home Office licensing and inspection not unlike that under the anatomy act. Applications for licences to practise vivisection, signed by leading medical authorities, were to be submitted to the Home Office which could inspect and register premises. By late 1876 the first part-time inspector, George Busk, had been appointed. Both the anatomy and cruelty to animals acts remained intact for many years and are partly in force today.

The legislative machinery regulating burial practice was obviously of a different type from that regulating anatomical dissection and vivisection. Yet the three subjects shared certain features. In each case legislation partly resulted from an outcry against activities which were felt to be offensive to public decency. It was hardly a matter of social deprivation whether or not vivisection was practised; yet it aroused one of the most vociferous Victorian public controversies. Even in the case of burial, where the threat to public health was the principal worry, the scandal of unceremonious treatment of the dead was never far behind as a reason for reform.

In each case there were the usual fears about central interference with local or private rights. The suspicions of the medical profession about control of anatomical dissection in the 1830s led the *Lancet* to deplore the use of central inspectors and argue that their powers could 'with much more propriety be thrown into the hands of the ordinary magistrate', even though the development of the inspectorate had the positive advantage for the profession of guaranteeing an adequate supply of corpses for the anatomy schools, which no magistrate would have been able to do.[84] In the case of burials legislation the government responded to pressure from vested interests by reversing its centralizing policy in 1852. And in 1876 the medical lobby proved strong enough to persuade the home secretary, Cross, to promote four significant amendments to the cruelty to animals bill, in their interests, during the second stage of its reading.[85]

In terms of their medical education and experience these inspectors had many links. Nearly all were fellows of the English or Scottish Royal Colleges of Surgeons or the Royal College of Physicians. They were attached to the same hospitals and university medical schools in London and Edinburgh. It was not only the inspectors of anatomy who were connected with its teaching: Grainger's medical school (Webb's) was a centre for anatomy instruction. One of the best known surgeons and anatomy specialists of his day, Sir Benjamin Brodie, recommended at least one of the anatomy inspectors to the home secretary in 1842 and was the friend and mentor of a later anatomy inspector, Charles Hawkins.[86] Brodie also gave evidence before the select committee on the health of towns about the effects of poor urban burial facilities.

All the medical inspectors were well qualified and highly respected in their fields. Among the anatomy inspectors, Charles Wood was president of the Edinburgh Royal College of Surgeons and Royal Medical Society; Hawkins was one of the most accomplished surgeons of his time. The credentials of the burial grounds inspectors have been observed. Busk, inspector under the cruelty to animals act, was twice vice-president of the Royal Society and president of the Royal College of Surgeons. These inspectors – with the possible exception of the later burial grounds inspector – were not in the category of professional bureaucrats, primarily attached to their government department. Rather, they advised the secretary of state on medical problems from within their own professions.

The salmon fisheries inspectorate
The salmon fisheries inspectorate for England and Wales was

established in 1861 for economic reasons in order to protect a popular source of food which, without central government intervention, was in serious danger of disappearing. By 1860 falling catches of salmon were causing prices, which earlier in the century had been low, to leap up dramatically. A royal commission of inquiry, which looked at earlier movements to protect salmon in Ireland and Scotland, revealed that protective laws were ancient but confused, and that the fish were endangered by irresponsible fishermen, careless of the need to protect spawning fish, by the dams and weirs of riparian mill-owners which prevented their migrating, and by the effluents of factories which poisoned them.[87] As a result the 1861 salmon act replaced all previous legislation on the subject. There was to be an annual close season and a weekly close time; mills and dams in future were to be built with fish passes to avoid obstructing the migrating salmon.

The two inspectors appointed under the act pointed out its severe limitations which derived from powerful vested interests and the lack of effective provision for local administration. The latter problem was remedied in a further act in 1865: 'fishery districts' were to be supervised by boards of locally elected conservators which could raise money by licensing fishing equipment and imposing a rate on fisheries. Fish yields improved and more effective apparatus to protect fish began to be constructed. An act of 1873, following a House of Commons select committee, completed the groundwork of fisheries legislation by giving the local boards the right to make their own bye-laws, subject to approval of the home secretary. A decentralizing measure, it was applauded by the inspectors because it provided for the adaptation of the acts to local needs while they themselves could ensure that overall standards were maintained.[88]

The inspectorate had an office in London. During this period there were four fisheries inspectors. With the exception of Spencer Walpole, the son of (and appointed by) the home secretary Walpole, they all had previous practical experience and knowledge of salmon fishing or natural history. The first two, William fFennell and Frederick Eden, had been closely connected also with the preservation of salmon in Ireland and both continued to be Scottish fisheries commissioners.

Although the Home Office was constantly acquiring work in diverse fields, salmon fisheries inspection was peculiarly unrelated to its other functions. The 1870 select committee recommended that, until there was a 'department of fisheries', the inspectorate be transferred to the Board of Trade; but its recommendation was ignored.[89]

The new instrument of central government

The early development of these inspectorates has been described in some detail in order to show how inspectors in the mid-nineteenth century were the new aid to central government in its attempt to solve problems caused by comparatively rapidly changing social, economic and scientific conditions. It was a critical period in administrative development and there are fundamental historical arguments about the reasons for change. No one doubts that the thought of Jeremy Bentham was a major influence on contemporary administrative developments. Although he viewed government in itself as 'one vast evil', he found in his *Constitutional Code* that 'wherever, by evil thus produced, greater evil is excluded, the balance takes the nature, shape and name of good; and government is justified in the production of it'.[90]

Elie Halévy, in his study of philosophic radicalism, showed that Bentham and his followers believed that a strong central administration under the control of elected representatives was justifiable in a democratic society as a counterbalance to the local power of a strong aristocracy. 'The organization of the state, according to Bentham and James Mill', wrote Halévy, 'is a representative and an administrative regime: for, in order that the functions of government may be exercised with the desired continuity and competence, they should be delegated to specialists.'[91] This interpretation of Bentham's thought was eventually taken up by more recent administrative historians who challenged the earlier, influential convictions of A.V. Dicey that the middle decades of the nineteenth century formed a period of individualism or *laissez-faire* and that this was due to Benthamism.[92] From the 1940s Dicey's view has been considerably modified by administrative historians who have shown how, in significant fields of social welfare such as the administration of aid to the poor, the protection of labour, the promotion of public health and sanitation, solutions were increasingly being sought in government control.[93] They stress that this tendency should not be regarded – as it had by Dicey – as a departure from the norm, but rather, as Professor Oliver MacDonagh argues, as a movement which amounted to a revolution in government.[94]

There have, however, emerged two schools of thought about the way in which changes occurred. The MacDonagh ' "organic" school of autonomous administrative history' places less stress on the influence of philosophical ideas than on the notion that reform came about almost piecemeal, with social problems engendering early tentative steps towards amelioration which subsequently led, through the experience of executive officers, to further legislation promoting increased government control. The school of Dr Jenifer Hart and Dr Henry Parris emphasizes the role of political philosophers – notably Bentham and J. S. Mill – who were a positive and direct influence on active reformers of the period and even on some of the executive officers who played a vital role.[95] Professor Harold Perkin, however, has recently argued that in a sense both sides are right and that reform is never a one-way process but the interaction of ideology and practice.[96]

The 'inner momentum' of bureaucratic development is consistently a feature in the progress of Home Office inspectorates. It is particularly well illustrated in the case of factories, mines and explosives inspection where the first few officials in the field, appointed after recognition of an 'intolerable situation', investigated, found the existing legislation inadequate for purposes of protecting employees and recommended further measures. Such measures were often more flexible and gave officials powers to adapt fundamental principles to special cases. More extensive protection to operatives or miners often meant expanding the bureaucracy. However, the time lag between the different stages of MacDonagh's well-known five-stage model varies considerably in different cases.[97] Also, this kind of development did not happen in the case of the anatomy or cruelty to animals inspectorates where one principal act regulated the field for decades: 'the peculiar nature of the moral reformers' problems ensured that they never evolved the progressively extending government machinery which the social reformers developed'.[98] Moreover, there was not an inevitable tendency towards centralization: the 1852 burial act reversed the Chadwick-Sutherland scheme for strict government control of burial grounds; and the 1873 fisheries act provided for greater local powers of administration.

Nor can the historian of these inspectorates fail to be aware of a direct link between the utilitarians and many of the inspectors. The classic example among nineteenth-century reformers is Chadwick, Bentham's friend and follower, and colleague of Sutherland. Horner, a product of the Scottish Enlightenment, was particularly close to his brother, Francis, whose circle of friends founded the *Edinburgh Review* and included James Mill.[99] One of Frederic Hill's brothers had been in touch with Bentham and he himself had been sponsored by the radical Benthamite MP, Joseph Hume, in his application for the post of inspector.[100]

Historical interpretation of Bentham may have shifted in recent years but one must not now over-emphasize the utilitarians' stress on the need in some areas for efficient central government admin-istration, and under-estimate their adherence to the classical economists' idea of a free market economy and desire for minimum possible interference. As J. S. Mill wrote in his *Principles of Political Economy*, 'laissez-faire, in short, should be the general practice: every departure from it, unless required by some great good, is a certain evil'.[101] The central and debatable point was, what 'great good' was sufficient to justify departure from the general practice? There was continual discussion about this among contemporaries in government and administration. Grey supported but was very cautious about inspection: he minimized even the limited powers of the prison inspectors in 1850 because of parliamentary opposition; he urged tact and caution to his mines inspectors in 1864; and he directed a temporary inspector of gunpowder, the same year, to bear in mind 'that legislative restrictions upon trade are only to be justified by the necessity of providing for the public safety'.[102]

Inspectors too were worried about intervention. In 1858 Turner, reporting on a new act of limited duration which allowed any person to bring a vagrant child before a magistrate, was aware that the act allowed for the 'interference with the common rights of parents for the purpose of preventing crime' and therefore felt it should be regarded as experimental.[103] Redgrave, soft on prosecution of factory occupiers, argued in 1867:

> it must not be overlooked that there is a very large number of persons, who . . . have strong objections to a greatly increased staff of government officers to exercise over such a vast number of establishments the right of making at their option constant visits, and who also object to any increased expenditure, the necessity for which is not clearly proved.[104]

Majendie claimed that the view that 'all state interference in industrial life is absolutely contrary to the first principles of economical science' had been ever-present in his mind when he worked on recommendations for new explosives legislation in 1872.[105]

Yet, if they did not start out as interventionists, inspectors often found from their experience as men on the ground that considerable departure from the ideal of *laissez-faire* was going to be necessary in order to right the social wrong with which they were dealing. This was partly because, as they became intimately concerned with their field, they became increasingly aware of the extent of the problems. It was also because, in some cases, they found a lack of local co-operation. Financial considerations, a tradition of local administration and the strength of the belief in non-interference had militated against the setting up of armies of powerful inspecting bureaucrats. Instead there were formed groups of mobile officials who advised ministers and frequently worked through justices, watch committees, vestries and so on. Yet it was often the very failure of co-operation from these authorities which led the central government to assume further powers. Thus the 1863 select committee on prison discipline recommended financial sanctions against recalcitrant prison authorities; and in 1871 the central government took over responsibility for workshops regulation.

It might seem remarkable that the inspectors made any headway. Their size makes their task seem daunting, to say the least. Those who worked from their homes were often geographically isolated. Perhaps most important, they all suffered from a lack of direction and co-ordination from the central Home Office.

All the papers which came into the department either to or from the inspectors passed through the domestic or the criminal departments and, in theory, were minuted as to action by the head of department before being forwarded to an under-secretary. Outgoing letters from the inspectorates were often written in the main department. Thus these new agencies of government, far from being autonomous, were responsible not merely to the home secretary himself, but to his office. Yet heads of internal Home Office departments before 1876 were not much of a filter: unless the cases were simple or there was a clear precedent to follow, they tended to pass the papers up to a higher level for action. An example will illustrate how the system worked in practice. In October 1875 the Board of Trade forwarded to the Home Office a letter from a gunpowder manufacturer who wanted his firm exempted from certain regulations under the new explosives act. The letter was registered and initially sent to Erskine, head of the domestic department. He obtained the authority of the parliamentary under-secretary to forward it straight to the inspector of explosives, Majendie, for action. Majendie found that the firm's reasons for making the request were based on a false premise, and that it could not therefore be allowed. His draft reply was then sent to the permanent under-secretary through the domestic department which simply suggested replying as Majendie had recommended. This course of action was approved by the parliamentary under-secretary and a letter was duly written out in the domestic department. Thus the departmental clerks had in no way deviated form the inspector's recommendation or contributed towards the Home Office's final reply.[106]

It is easy to understand why central officials below under-secretary level did not issue and rarely even proposed instructions to inspectors. The inspectors were experts in their own fields. Not only did they have practical experience within the area with which they were dealing, but they often knew more about the legislation they were administering than did the officials. Majendie, who had been largely responsible for drawing up the 1875 explosives act and was an artillery officer, knew far more about explosives administration than anyone else. Redgrave had worked in the factory inspectorate for most of his life and had published several guides to the numerous factory acts. Apart from anything else, the inspectors were often more highly educated than the career officials of this period. Indeed, in terms of education, experience and standing, the mid-nineteenth-century inspectors were more on a par with the under-secretaries than with the clerks.

Even the home secretary and his under-secretaries rarely attempted to co-ordinate the inspectors' activities or policies. All too often the hard-pressed secretary of state took little interest in their work. Palmerston once despaired of ever reading some prison reports.[107] The clerk for criminal business, Everest, once even said that it was not the duty of any particular Home Office department to consider reports from the prison inspectors, which raises the possibility that they might occasionally have remained unread.[108] Grey, in 1867, said that he had had 'little personal intercourse with the (mines) inspectors', and he showed no real interest in getting these comparatively isolated officials together for conference.[109] It was up to the inspectors themselves to organize this kind of activity and to pay visits to the Home Office when they needed consultation. For at this period the idea of dispassionate central officials comparing and co-ordinating the work of the field-workers was still embryonic. The advantage was that often – though not always – the inspectors' recommendations carried the day. The disadvantage was that they put forward conflicting recommendations in their isolation and often received little backing in their arguments with private manufacturers or owners, or with local authorities.

Even though they faced enormous problems, the important thing was that inspectors were established as a permanent feature of public administration. Furthermore, given the problems they faced, they were surprisingly effective. One reason for this was probably the nature of some of the pioneer inspectors. The first generation of 'amateur' inspectors, often described as zealots, tended to be men of wide experience, interests and often influence, extending far beyond the realm of their inspectorate. They did not scruple, moreover, to run counter to the developing idea of the anonymous public servant. The activities of men like Horner, Tremenheere, Sutherland, Hill and Majendie were frequently discussed and their views aired in the press and on other public platforms, sometimes to the embarrassment of their government department. Anonymity certainly did not apply to these men who have aptly been described as 'statesmen in disguise'.[110] The subsequent generation of inspectors, which tended to be more bureaucratic in experience and outlook, also injected important qualities and habits into public administration. Their professional technical experience made their connection with those they were inspecting close. Mines inspectors had often been mining engineers, constabulary inspectors were sometimes ex-chief constables, and so on. Their practical experience in the field created a direct relationship between central government and those it governed. And they recorded their experience and data carefully and often regularly in blue-books for public inspection and future reference. Their role was therefore quite different from that of central departmental officials. The question which now poses itself is, how complementary were the two types of official going to be in the formulation and carrying out of policy?

7 Extension of government control through inspection: 1876–1914

In 1914 the secretary of state was still responsible for ten inspectorates. Two had changed since 1876. In 1886 the Board of Trade took over the inspection of fisheries, and in 1900 the inspectorate of burial grounds moved to the Local Government Board, which had taken over all burials work relating to sanitation, leaving the Home Office with responsibility for the ecclesiastical aspect and for licensing exhumations. Meanwhile the Home Office had assumed responsibility for the inspection of licensed inebriate retreats under the 1879 habitual drunkards act.[1] In 1905 the aliens act imposed restrictions on the entry of immigrants into Britain and led to the creation of an aliens inspector, responsible to the home secretary, in order to supervise control. By the end of the period, therefore, the inspectorates might still be grouped into our previous three main categories: 'industrial' (factories, mines and explosives); 'law and order' (prisons, constabulary, reformatory and industrial schools, and aliens); and 'medical' (anatomy, cruelty to animals and inebriate retreats).

There would be little point in following the progress of each inspectorate for the later period of this study. But a detailed account of two of them will illustrate the process of bureaucratic growth, some of the external pressures on the Home Office, and the relations between central officials and the inspectors in the formulation of social policy during this period. The first study is of the factory inspectorate which remained the largest and one of the most important. Together with the mines inspectorate it exemplified the area of greatest growth and was much in the public gaze because it was concerned with problems which affected part of the population which was becoming increasingly significant politically. The second study is of the reformatory and industrial schools inspectorate which also greatly expanded but was not altogether successful. It shows the limitations of inspectors when their field of administration was not of great political moment and when there were major differences of opinion about policy. Finally, we shall consider more generally the points raised by these studies and try to see how the inspectors fitted into the administrative system when it came to policy-making.

The development of the factory inspectorate, 1876-1914
Governments continued to promote the interests of factory and
workshop employees in areas which by now were familiar: the
regulation of hours of work; the covering of machinery; the
provision of adequate ventilation, sanitation and lighting; the
education of children; the reporting of accidents. These were all
features of the consolidating 1878 factory and workshop act,[2] and
subsequent acts further refined these aspects. Sometimes new kinds
of obligations were imposed on manufacturers, such as the
requirement of 1891 that occupiers in the weaving industry should
have the 'particulars' about the cloth being woven and the machinery
involved publicly displayed for the benefit of the weavers who were
paid by the piece. Meanwhile, the provisions of the 1878 act were
gradually extended to industries hitherto untouched by factory legislation: laundries and docks in 1895, for example. Thus was built up a
body of law which was complicated to administer: it reached
different industries in different ways; the legal processes were
intricate; and, although the acts themselves were often detailed, they
allowed a good deal of delegated power to the Home Office which
continually had to work out new requirements for occupiers.

From 1878 the inspectorate was headed by a single chief inspector,
Redgrave. Under him were five superintending inspectors, thirty-
nine inspectors and ten junior inspectors. The total force numbered
fifty-five and that year cost the Treasury £28,144.[3] Redgrave's chief
inspectorship lasted until 1891 and it marked a period of conservatism.

By the last quarter of the nineteenth century this inspectorate was
in need of adaptation to new demands and requirements of the
social group it was originally intended to protect. During the 1880s
periodic depression and high unemployment led to working-class
discontent, contributed towards the growth of socialism and created
increasing concern about conditions of labour. Working men not
only saw factory inspectors as potential allies but also wanted to
have their own representatives within the inspectorate. This was a far
cry from the days of the paternalistic inspection of Leonard Horner
and his colleagues, 'drawn from the whig faction, the "Cousin-
hood" and its hangers-on'.[4]

Redgrave was hostile to the idea of 'working men' inspectors even
though trades unionists suggested merely that they work as 'sub-
inspectors' under the direction of a superior inspector.[5] Thus he came
into conflict with the home secretary, Harcourt, who, with characteristic impulse and enthusiasm, had taken up the working man's
cause on this, having convinced himself 'that the system has been

worked solely by men of the employer class and in their interests'.[6] In 1881 he appointed the first working man junior factory inspector[7] and by early 1886 there were nine more. Redgrave remained hostile, partly because he felt that they were unable to 'exercise discretion and display urbanity', but more tangibly because it proved difficult to utilize their individual experience by finding them vacancies in areas dominated by their own particular trades.[8] Also, the Treasury objected to their irregular appointment, made without examination. Although their recruitment position was regularized in 1886 they still did not fit happily into the inspectorate where their function had not yet been fully worked out.

The lack of rapport on this issue between the home secretary and his chief inspector is not difficult to comprehend. Redgrave, with his comparatively narrow experience in a single department, lacked the imagination to see that although there might be teething troubles in systematizing a new genre of inspectors, ultimately personal experience of working conditions might be a useful qualification at least for some inspectors and an acceptable substitute for urbanity. Harcourt, the impulsive liberal, was impatient with bureaucracy and – having made the bold gesture – was inclined to override any objection to the administrative problem of fitting a new type of inspector into a well-established framework. In Redgrave's defence it is worth quoting a later comment by Troup about the period when working men inspectors were recruited without examination: 'That is the time when we had the very worst specimens of factory inspectors we have ever had'.[9]

A problem which faced Harcourt's Conservative successor, Matthews, was the growing demand for more factory inspectors. There had been no increase in numbers since 1878 and there was clearly a feeling among workers that if only there were enough inspectors, problems such as safety at work would be substantially alleviated. There does not seem to have been a consensus about this at the Home Office. Redgrave infuriated Matthews in 1887 by responding to a demand for an increase from various trades councils by, on the one hand, deprecating 'an immediate and considerable addition to the staff', yet on the other, urging that 'an increase of the staff is really necessary'.[10] One of his staff was quite clear what he felt about this: J. B. Lakeman (an inspector in the east London area) told the House of Lords Select Committee on Sweating in 1888 that five, not two, inspectors were needed in his district.[11] But Lushington felt that too much was demanded of the inspectorate and argued that the government should take a firm line on its appropriate size, for a case could always be made out that more men were needed 'so long as there is not an army of inspectors'.[12]

The select committee urged that workshops required considerably greater inspection. It found that in hundreds of workshops, especially in the tailoring trade in London's east end, grossly insanitary conditions prevailed, unduly low wages were paid and excessive hours were worked. One problem was the inadequacy of the law. Section 69 of the 1878 act, which obliged inspectors to obtain a warrant from the secretary of state before entering a workshop which was also a home against the will of the occupier, made the detection of those evading the law difficult. Improvement of sanitary conditions was rendered difficult by an awkward system of dual control: sanitary requirements of the 1878 act were enforced through the inspectors while responsibility for ensuring compliance with public health acts lay with local authorities through whom the inspectors had to act where they discovered unsatisfactory sanitary arrangements. This caused considerable delay in the effecting of improvements.

It is difficult to judge how worried the inspectorate was about the very serious sweating problem. Following the report of the select committee, Matthews instructed Redgrave to put an additional inspector or two into the east end area to 'act vigorously, so far as the law allows, in prosecuting and enforcing cleanliness etc.' so as 'to show that we have done all that the present law enables us to do' before the government introduced a new factory and workshops bill.[13] The inspectorate's initial report showed that 20 per cent of inspected workshops were unsatisfactory in terms of ventilation, cleanliness, sanitation and so forth; nevertheless, the general impression conveyed was a certain complacency on the part of the chief inspector. Subsequently Redgrave was urged by the parliamentary under-secretary to pursue through local sanitary authorities those whose bad conditions were their responsibility. His jejune reply provoked the comment from Matthews that it was 'impossible from the above general observations to ascertain what number of these defective premises have been improved. I must request that the matter be dealt with in a more serious and businesslike fashion'.[14] Two weeks later the chief inspector reported that there remained only three unsatisfactory cases. A few months later, in the inspectorate's annual report for 1890, Lakeman optimistically applauded the recent growth in his area of combinations of unskilled workers (something the select committee had advocated) which had led to concessions from employers and 'great changes' in conditions.[15] In fact the sweating problem remained serious at least until the 1909 trade boards act attempted a new remedy.

Matthews' bill, which became the 1891 factory and workshop act, aimed at helping the factory inspectors keep a closer eye on workshops by empowering the secretary of state to require employers to maintain lists of contractors and outworkers. It eased the burden on the inspectorate by transferring to local sanitary authorities general responsibility for all aspects of sanitary supervision in workshops; but it gave the secretary of state special powers to enforce sanitary regulations through Home Office inspectors if he felt that sufficient measures were not being taken locally.

Matthews also successfully made out a case to the Treasury for an additional inspector and nine junior inspectors. But he was careful to emphasize that he

> had no intention of enlarging the scope of the duties of the inspectors or of introducing the notion that the state undertakes by means of its inspectors to supervise the manufacturers of this country. Any such attempt would be futile ... for it would relieve employers of the responsibility which now attaches to them and which they alone are capable of fulfilling.
>
> The most important function of inspectors is by their active influence to bring about a co-operation of employers and employed in the observation of the law. The utmost that inspection can accomplish ... is to render it dangerous for an employer to break the law.[16]

It was a conservative statement underlining the familiar nineteenth century dilemma of politicians and administrators: it admitted a clear need to protect the weak, yet implied that the government interference which this necessitated was a departure from the desired norm of freedom of contract. When Matthews left the Home Office, there were altogether sixty-nine inspectors responsible for administering acts affecting 'some 60,000 factories and an unknown number of workshops – probably between 100,000 and 200,000'.[17] Supposing there were 150,000 workshops, this would have given each inspector over 3,000 premises to inspect – a number which would hardly have permitted undue supervision of many manufacturers.

From the late 1870s there were growing demands for women factory inspectors from women's labour groups which felt that, since large numbers of women were employed in British factories (656,000 was the number suggested by the Women's Liberal Federation in 1893)[18] and even more in workshops, these employees should have access to female officials who might understand their problems. The Home Office was unresponsive. Redgrave was highly conservative about the social role of women and unable to conceive of a woman factory inspector 'conducting her case and having to submit herself in the witness-box to the cross-examination of an astute attorney'.[19] Lushington was 'decidedly against the employment of women inspectors'.[20] Neither Harcourt nor Matthews seems to have been in favour: in parliament the home secretary's standard reply to questions about this was that there were objections to women inspectors 'on grounds of administration, economy and practicability'.[21] The real reason for opposition may have been the conservative prejudice of a department where, as yet, there were no other female officers.

Another problem was the totally inadequate production of factory statistics. Unlike officials at the Board of Trade, where valuable statistics about strikes, the state of the labour market and related problems were being produced, Home Office officials were amazingly vague about statistics – for example, about actual numbers of workshops being inspected and facts connected with factory accidents. Information collected by the inspectorate was put before parliament in the chief inspector's formalized annual reports which had many deficiencies and took little account of statistical developments. A minute by the chief inspector in 1893 suggests that the inspectors had little taste for collating statistics, finding that 'preparing statistics for official purposes and parliamentary returns, seriously interferes with their duties'.[22] Yet there was no central branch of the department which specifically dealt with these statistics.

There was public criticism of Home Office factory administration. In June 1892 A. J. Mundella, president of the Board of Trade, complained to the prime minister about inefficient inspection of factories, workshops and mines.[23] J. H. Dalziel, another Liberal MP, put down a motion calling the government's attention 'to the necessity for the establishment of a department of labour, with a minister responsible to Parliament';[24] and a labour department bill was actually introduced (unsuccessfully) in the Commons. Sidney Webb suggested to the Royal Commission on Labour, then sitting, that a new department of labour might be formed by amalgamating the labour statistics branch of the Board of Trade and the 'Factory and Mines Department' of the Home Office.[25]

Such plans were abandoned after the arrival at the Home Office in August 1892 of Asquith and Gladstone. Three months later Asquith wrote:

> When I assumed office one of the first questions to engage my attention was the organization of the Factory Department, and from that time to this it has been the subject of my careful and almost continuous consideration. Mr. Herbert Gladstone also has devoted much time and thought to the matter.[26]

Asquith consulted his officials at some length, not least his new chief inspector of factories. Redgrave had retired, aged seventy-three, after fifty-seven years' service at the Home Office, in 1891. His post was filled initially by F. H. Whymper, a superintending inspector, but this was a temporary arrangement and caused some embarrassment for Asquith because there was pressure for him to replace Whymper with Henry Broadhurst, the trade union official who became a Liberal MP and served briefly as parliamentary under-secretary at the Home Office under Childers. Asquith found him 'wholly unfit for such a place'.[27] Gladstone considered the idea of having an assistant under-secretary in charge of the inspectorate based within the central secretariat. This would have been a major departure from having sub-departments separate from the main Home Office secretariat. But tradition was maintained and R. E. S. Oram, another superintending inspector, was appointed. Asquith gave credit both to him and to Lushington for their advice about reform. Oram stressed the need for a large increase in the inspecting staff to root out abuses in workshops. Lushington's role and views are something of a puzzle. In the autumn of 1892 he was much involved with another measure designed to help workmen - the formulation of an employers' liability bill – and was clearly anxious to work out a formula for reconciling labour's views with what he considered administratively workable.[28] He was not, however, in tune with demands for a large increase in the inspectorate and for women inspectors; and he was distinctly lukewarm about Oram's idea of creating a new 'inferior' grade of inspectors although this in fact was to be an important part of reform.[29]

In December 1892 Asquith drafted a statement of his recommendations. He suggested the creation of a new grade of low-paid inspectors, 'a set of energetic, quick-sighted, practical men, knowing the actual conditions of factory and workshop life, capable of giving clerical as well as other assistance to the inspectors, but not necessarily equal to the educational tests which are at present imposed'.[30] This grade of fifteen 'inspectors' assistants' was to provide a niche for working men inspectors whose prime function was to track down insanitary workshops where illegal sweating occurred. Secondly, he proposed the creation of regional inspectors' offices in Glasgow, Birmingham and Wakefield in the hope that these would become local centres of communication and statistical information 'not only for the inspectors of the district but for employers, trade union secretaries and other representatives of the workmen who wished to communicate with the inspectors'.[31] Thirdly, he proposed the appointment of two women inspectors, based in London and Glasgow but working on a peripatetic basis. The Treasury accepted these proposals which increased the inspectorate by seventeen and cost £2,679.

Finding the new scheme highly satisfactory, a year later Asquith proposed a second stage. Given that there were an estimated 3,270,000 factory workers (let alone hundreds of thousands of workshop employees) he found the previous year's expenditure of £36,300 on eighty-six inspectors justifiable. He now proposed further increases to various grades within the inspectorate, increasing it by eighteen, and the establishment of inspectors' offices in fifteen other industrial centres.[32] Again there was no apparent objection from the chancellor of the exchequer; 'perhaps because Harcourt had a lingering weakness for his old office', wrote Asquith, 'he accepted my proposals without even a momentary snarl'.[33]

Other aspects of Asquith's reforms were the improvement of the factory statistics in 1894[34] and a factory and workshop act of 1895. In a further attempt to improve sanitation in workshops the latter act stipulated the number of cubic feet to be allowed per employee, and for the first time required local sanitary authorities to inform an inspector of action taken following a complaint from him about sanitary neglect. It greatly increased the fine for workshop occupiers who defaulted on annual returns of employees and imposed on them the additional obligation of returning lists of all outworkers twice a year. It introduced important regulations about the provision of fire escapes (something which the inspectorate had pressed for). It also empowered a court of summary jurisdiction, on the recommendation of an inspector, temporarily to prohibit premises from being used as a factory until any specified danger had been removed.

The period following 1896 seems to have been one of high morale in the factory inspectorate. Industrial matters were given greater status within the office that year by the formation (with its own separate factory statistics branch) of the industrial and parliamentary department which had a strong staff.[35] Troup was principal, Byrne his senior and Delevigne his junior clerk. Delevigne, an Oxford first in greats who had entered the Home Office in 1892, was to become its authority on industrial matters and worked in harmony with the chief inspectors of factories and mines. Also in 1896 the home secretary appointed a new chief inspector of factories, Arthur Whitelegge. He had a medical background: educated at University College, London, and at Cambridge where he acquired a doctorate, he was an FRCP and had previously been a county medical officer of health in Yorkshire. Whitelegge was to provide the inspectorate with capable leadership and continuity for twenty-one years.

During his period of office a whole series of specialized departmental committees investigated different aspects of industrial work from the point of view of health and safety in places of work. Among the twenty-six subjects reported on to parliament between 1900 and 1914 were brass-casting factories, cotton-weaving sheds, electrical energy, file-cutting regulations, florists' workshops and the grinding of metals. Many aspects of safety were becoming technically more complicated partly because industry was stimulated by the discovery of new forms of power, such as electrity and new gases. In 1900 Whitelegge was concerned about ventilation fans which the Home Office required certain manufacturers to install under special rules governing dangerous processes. Since companies frequently installed fans – often at considerable cost – in such a way that they were useless, he drew up a circular for factory owners showing the more obvious causes of the failure of fans.[36] He also initiated an inquiry into the whole subject of ventilation, the results of which formed the basis of further guidance to both inspectors and factory owners on how to overcome the hazards.[37] In 1904 the chief inspector composed a memorandum for occupiers on the dangers (principally carbonic oxide poisoning) of new gases used in industrial processes.[38] Through this kind of investigation and report the inspectors followed scientific industrial developments and tried to promote the interests of employers and protection of employees.

Growth in the technical aspects of the work changed the nature of the inspectorate. First, an increasing number of specialists became attached to it: in 1892 the first inspector of 'particulars'; in 1898 the first medical inspector; in 1899 the first inspector for dangerous trades; and in 1902 the first electrical inspector. By 1913 two medical inspectors, two dangerous trades inspectors and the electrical inspector were formed into three 'special' branches of the headquarters staff. Women inspectors, who formed a separate branch which amounted to twenty-two in 1914, were specialists in problems affecting female employees. Secondly, even the ordinary inspectors themselves had to be far more technically minded than their predecessors, as they stressed once when pressing for higher pay:

> To efficiently carry out our modern duties ... an Inspector must possess an acquaintance which must often be more than super-ficial, with subjects entirely outside his province in 1872. Such for instance as with the symptoms and causes of industrial diseases; with chemistry, metallurgy, electricity; with building principles,

with dock construction, with the working of private railways, with scientific ventilation, with knowledge of the text, administration, and leading causes of many public Acts.[39]

Their qualifications therefore became more technical. They were still recruited through a system of limited competition after nomination by a small Home Office committee.[40] By 1903 they were obliged to take papers in English composition, arithmetic, sanitary science, law relating to factories and workshops, and elementary physics and mechanics.[41] In fact, the scientific knowledge needed to pass these was probably no more than any educated man could soon acquire which reflected the view of both Whitelegge and Troup that general intelligence and intellect, as much as scientific understanding, were the fundamental requirements.[42] Later the examination was evidently changed so that a candidate need have no technical knowledge.[43] Nevertheless, a parliamentary return of 1907 showed that the background experience of inspectors had changed and upheld a later contention that 'a large proportion . . . have had a previous training as engineers; some have been chemists or analysts; some have been managers of business firms; some have been sanitary inspectors; a few have had a purely academic training'.[44]

The inspectors' assistants were still recruited quite separately to a class of their own, on the basis of practical working experience. Their resentment about their pay and lack of promotion into the inspector class is reminiscent of that of the second division clerks. From time to time they petitioned the Home Office for improved conditions. Eager to alleviate discontent, Gladstone and Whitelegge in 1906 suggested reserving five inspectorships for promoted assistants. The Treasury agreed that in principle such promotions should be made possible but objected to places being specifically reserved for promotees. Delevigne's reply to this perhaps betrays senior officials' real views about such promotion: 'I think the Home Office idea in mentioning a number was rather to fix a limit which should not be exceeded than to establish any right of promotion to that number of posts.'[45] Two years later Whitelegge alleged that occasionally, 'in cases of exceptional merit', some were promoted.[46] Senior officials were anxious to improve the men's financial position and managed to raise the ceiling of their salaries from £150 to £200. These benefits were apparently gratefully acknowledged by the Association of Factory Inspectors' Assistants but discontent evidently continued as their petition in 1912 to the Macdonnell Commission shows.[47] In 1911 the departmental committee on factory accidents – which contained strong labour representation – in its majority report firmly supported abolishing the double system of entry and suggested that 'those who have been employed in one of the main factory or workshop trades for a period of seven years' would make ideal inspectors.[48] Sir William Cramp, deputy chief inspector of factories until 1909, associated himself, however, with the minority recommendation that, although promotion should be made more freely, two classes should be maintained because 'of the advisability of having upon the inspectorate men of a considerable variety of training and experience'.[49] The Home Office did not change the basis of recruitment.

The inspectorate was obviously an important influence on legislative developments. Inspectors continued to document abuses, report on further areas of desirable protection and point out where the law was not working satisfactorily. It made laws, in a minor way, through its powers of delegation, a good example of which was its (or the secretary of state's) authority from 1891 to make and modify 'special rules' for individual occupiers where machinery or processes were considered by inspectors to be dangerous.

Part of the history of the 1901 factory and workshop act illustrates the various factors which shaped an act.[50] This was a grand consolidating measure, designed to draw together various specific acts some of which had been found by the inspectorate to have ambiguous wording and contain various loopholes. It was intended specifically to alter the ruling on dangerous trades – modifying the procedure on 'special rules' – and further to tighten up sanitary regulations. Pressure for such a bill had been building up for some time: in 1899 a private member's bill, covering a wide field of protection, was introduced. It failed but some of its proposals were subsequently taken up by the Conservative government which introduced its first measure in 1900. Various aspects were opposed by labour. For example, the Industrial Law Committee and the Fabian Society disliked proposals to allow a two-shift system in some factories on the grounds that it would be impossible to control the employment of the same person in both shifts.[51] This proposal was omitted in the government's successful bill the following year. During the passage of the 1900 bill James Macdonald, secretary to the London Trades Council, complained of 'the autocratic power of the Secretary of State' and demanded the substitution of clearly defined provisions in all clauses for general statements of the law which left details to be worked out by officials. Interestingly, by this period, employees as much as employers were concerned about the growth of central authority which Digby, as permanent under-secretary, upheld in his public defence of delegated legislation.[52] The following year, in a cabinet memorandum about the new bill, C. T. Ritchie noted that earlier objections to 'wide powers' proposed for the secretary of state had led to a modification in the new bill.[53]

Within the Home Office the chief inspector of factories worked with the head of the industrial and parliamentary department and the permanent under-secretary on this as on the other factory and workshop bills. The normal form, when proposals were discussed, was for the inspectorate (usually the chief inspector) to make initial written comment, on the basis of which Troup, as head of the relevant Home Office department, put up his comment for under-secretaries and the secretary of state. This is not to say that the industrial and parliamentary department overrode advice from the factory inspectorate. On the contrary: Whitelegge and Troup worked together closely and usually in agreement. But central departmental officials had the final word and, indeed, might discuss the progress of clauses without reference to the inspectorate.[54]

Always controversial was the question of the desirable level of factory inspection. Not laid down by statute, this was left to be decided by the secretary of state and the Treasury. It was not merely that there was a steady increase in the number of works covered by legislation. Greater demands were being made on inspectors to whom factory occupiers, although they themselves were legally responsible for the safety of their employees, looked for warning about matters of safety – in particular, the guarding of machinery. The electrical inspector found that he had to spend what he considered too much time as a general counsellor, answering queries from occupiers and makers of appliances who would quite wrongly take his sanction as a mark of authorization.[55] In the House of Commons the home secretary was annually under pressure during supply debates from MPs sympathetic to labour who urged increases in the inspectorate. The subject was investigated in 1907 by a departmental committee which, while denying that inspection could ever be other than by sample, was nevertheless concerned about falling standards. The previous year 23 per cent of factories and 28 per cent of workshops had remained unvisited which showed a considerable departure from the golden once-a-year inspection rule.[56] The committee's report led to the addition of a second deputy chief inspector, two specialist inspectors, sixteen inspectors, eleven inspectors' assistants and five women inspectors. This brought the inspectorate up to 200.

It was difficult to measure the success of the inspectorate. One measurement might have been the changing accident rate. If preventing deaths and serious injuries was the prime object, statistics ought to show how these were being contained. Attention was focused on this after the revelation of a striking increase in the number of reported factory accidents which had risen from 79,020 in 1900 to 124,325 in 1907.[57] But the departmental committee on factory accidents not only exonerated the inspectors from blame but showed that accident figures were an unreliable guide to success, attributing the apparent rise to changes in the basis of reporting accidents. Anyway, figures about deaths and serious injuries by themselves gave rather a crude picture of conditions with which the inspectorate ought to have been concerned. From the 1890s increasing attention was given to longer term health questions. Inspectors began to investigate processes and conditions whose effects might only be recorded as accident statistics in the very long run. This was a refinement and showed that there was no absolute standard of safety: all the inspectors could aim at was constant improvement by following technological developments and setting new standards.

The inspectorate, in fact, came out well in the committee's report. There was some criticism about lack of uniformity in the inspectors' requirements. But the committee felt that 'the relationship between inspectors and occupiers reflects credit on both classes' and witnesses bore testimony to the 'competence and fairness of the inspecting staff'. It did, however, recommend increases in numbers.[58] This recommendation was taken up by Whitelegge and Delevigne during a further inquiry into the work of the inspectorate by a departmental committee in January 1913. The 1908 increases in staff had been outstripped by increases in work so that standards were slipping. At the beginning of its report the committee showed in tabular form (Table 9) increases in the inspectorate against the number of works and so forth under inspection.

Table 9   Staff and work-load of the factory inspectorate, 1901–11

Subject	1901	1906	1911	% growth 1901–11*
Staff (inspectors and assistants)	137	163	200	46
Expenditure	£65,557	£75,299	£100,315	53
Total registered factories and workshops	240,910	255,189	267,534	11
Works under regulations (except docks) and special rules	7,833	12,224	45,416	480
Docks etc.	2,367	3,242	4,079	72
Works under particulars section	10,203	24,661	32,150	215

*Author's addition.
(Accident details have been omitted.)

It is interesting that the recent expansion of work had come from an increase in the number of works under regulations and special rules, and from extended application of the 'particulars' section of the principal act, rather than from a straightforward increase in the number of factories and workshops.

The inspectorate was also experiencing organizational problems which arose from its size and dispersal, and also from the growth of paperwork. The latter phenomenon was causing serious problems for the staff at headquarters which was clearly in arrears. In the field the district inspectors were also finding paperwork a problem and there was a serious danger of their losing sight of important communications from London because of the mass of information they received. Moreover, the inspectorial districts were large and unwieldy: inspectors in charge, trying to cope with the office work, were often losing touch with occupiers as the actual work of inspection was being done by juniors and assistants. District inspectors were out of touch with each other which accounted partly for the lack of uniformity in their requirements. An interesting new idea suggested in the report was the 'thorough' visit: 'visits in which the works are inspected in an exhaustive manner in respect of all the matters arising under the Acts'. It was alleged that if such inspections of all important works were carried out every five, seven or even ten years 'an appreciable advance on the present standard would be made'.[59]

The committee suggested various remedies to ease the flow of paper, such as the consolidation and updating of instructions to inspectors in the field. But their major recommendation was an increase in the number – and therefore reduction in size – of the inspectorial districts from fifty-two to seventy so that district inspectors would be more in control of their staff and in touch with occupiers. The scheme would require an additional nineteen inspectors, most of whom were to be of a comparatively senior grade in order to create a more desirable balance of senior to junior inspectors and restore a reasonable flow of promotion. The Home Office requested the Treasury for an additional £10,000 to the annual factory inspectorate vote – an increase of approximately 10 per cent.[60]

The Treasury response was unhelpful and showed a lack of clear thinking about factory inspection. In a badly argued letter it suggested that annual inspections were not 'a vital necessity' and urged that trade unionists would point out to the Home Office any serious failures to observe regulations – a practice which, as Troup pointed out, his department had not invariably encountered. The

Treasury hoped that somehow the consolidation of instructions would 'simplify and lessen the work of factory inspection' and would only grant an additional £5,000.[61] This seemed to Home Office officials a cursory dismissal of ideas which were a matter of major policy concern:

> It is certain that any reduction of the standard to, say, one visit in every 15 or 18 months which would follow if the increase of staff is not given would expose the Home Office to severe criticism both inside and outside the House and would be stoutly resisted both by the Labour Party and by members on both sides of the House.[62]

But the Treasury remained intransigent and, although they refused to accept the decision as final, Home Office officials had to set about spending the money allowed as effectively as they could, compromising on the numbers of new districts and inspectors.[63]

The factory inspectorate was a major item of Home Office expenditure. The annual estimate for its salaries and other expenses in 1913–14 was £107,680. The comparative figure for the next most expensive inspectorate, the mines inspectorate, was £63,378. Factory inspectors' assistants and three grades of women inspectors. The inspectors. The factory inspectorate had become an elaborate bureaucracy with five grades of men inspectors (including the chief inspector but excluding the specialist inspectors), two grades of inspectors' assistants and three grades of women inspectors). The Home Office felt that the Treasury looked at such developments and comparisons in isolation without considering the statutory demands being made on the secretary of state or the increasing social importance attached to effective inspection. His statutory responsibilities for health and safety in places of work were far-reaching. Yet authority was useless without adequate means of enforcement. This had become a problem for the department in 1914.

The reformatory and industrial schools inspectorate, 1876–1914: financial problems of administration[64]

When Turner left the Home Office in 1875, Rogers became assistant to Cross's new inspector of reformatory and industrial schools, Colonel William Inglis.[65] In 1877 the inspectors were responsible for ensuring that 66 reformatory schools (having nearly 6,000 inmates) and 127 industrial schools (having about 13,500 inmates) merited the annual *per capita* Treasury grant for children committed to them through the courts.[66] The inspectorate was based near the Home Office in Delahay Street where, with a staff consisting of a chief clerk and four clerks, the inspectors supervised the work of nine local agents (often ex-policemen), who collected parental

Table 10   The proportions of the various sources of school funds in 1877

	Number in school	Treasury (£)	Parents (£)	Rates (£)	Subscrip-tions (£)	School boards (£)	Total schools expen-diture (£)
Reformatory schools	5,935	87,305	6,897	20,823	7,821	–	139,825
Industrial schools	13,494	144,369	16,133	24,318	44,412	40,213	292,280

contributions, and administered the central grant under the provisions of the 1866 acts.[67]

The withholding of the Treasury grant to the schools was a potentially powerful weapon in persuading school managers to maintain minimum standards in matters such as diet, discipline and industrial training. Table 10 gives an idea of the size of the central contribution in 1877.[68] Yet in fact the inspectors rarely even threatened such drastic action, which would threaten their very existence, and found that they were otherwise powerless to interfere in the organization of the schools. They had no powers to appoint managers or superintendents (heads). They could not force schools to receive children they chose not to. They had no power to initiate changes in rules although the fact that these had to be approved by the secretary of state gave some scope for control. This lack of central authority was due partly to the inspectorate's cardinal principle that schools must remain independent in order to stimulate local interest in their activities.[69]

Unfortunately local interest was dwindling. Few new schools were founded after 1876 and voluntary donations seriously declined. Yet the state was imposing greater burdens on the industrial schools. In 1876 the elementary education act indirectly compelled elementary school attendance and made school boards responsible for having truant children brought before magistrates who could send recalcitrants to industrial schools. Thus they were becoming overcrowded with a mixture of vagrants, potential criminals and truants. The central government found that magistrates were committing large numbers of truant children who immediately qualified their schools for an increased Treasury grant. School boards were empowered but not compelled to contribute to the schools and did not respond generously. Local authorities could found their own institutions but few did so.[70] The 1879 elementary education (industrial schools) act enabled school attendance committees to negotiate with managers of industrial schools to receive children for whose maintenance they could contribute a weekly allowance. In 1880 potential numbers of inmates were further increased by an act which authorized the commitment of the children of prostitutes. Lushington was repeatedly pressed by the inspectors and was himself concerned about this growing financial problem for the central government. He took up the matter in a confidential memorandum of October 1880, which was submitted to the cabinet, and concluded that 'on principle and expediency a portion of the charge now cast on the Treasury should be borne either by the parent, if not destitute, or, if he is destitute, by the local authorities'.[71]

The problem of how to treat juvenile offenders, increasingly regarded as a far-reaching social problem, raised the question of whether these schools were primarily penal or educational institutions. The original idea had been to separate convicted criminals (within reformatory schools) and potential criminals (within industrial schools) from dubious adult company.[72] Time spent by children in reformatory schools was also regarded as punishment. As Turner put it in 1870:

> Reformatories are not schools in the common meaning of the term. They are institutions for the custody, corrective training, and industrial instruction of their inmates, in fact a species of Juvenile Houses of Correction. The intellectual teaching which forms the staple of ordinary schools, is a very small element in their constitutions.[73]

However, now that industrial schools were associated with board schools and were taking in many children who clearly were not criminals, it was increasingly felt that the emphasis ought to be more on education and that the standard of teaching ought to be raised substantially. Philanthropists like Lords Norton and Leigh led a movement to transfer the whole administration to the Education Department. This was consistently opposed by inspectors and senior officials at the Home Office who argued that inmates of these schools had been deprived of their liberty and that the home secretary was the minister responsible for all that appertained to the liberty of the subject.[74]

Harcourt was particularly concerned about the problem of juvenile detention and conditions in penal schools where the occasional scandal revealed some shocking circumstances. In July 1880 he issued an instruction that prison governors should instantly report to the Home Office cases where children under fifteen had been committed for imprisonment. He closely supervised the returns of this order, and in some cases had extensive inquiries made, which had the effect both of discouraging unnecessary committals and of causing much public debate about the question.[75] In 1882 he proposed a royal commission, under the chairmanship of Lord Aberdare, to investigate the whole subject. Lushington set out the major issues.[76] First, was prior imprisonment appropriate for children who were to be sent to a reformatory school? The inspectorate was not entirely opposed to this but Harcourt was anxious greatly to restrict the number of commitments of children to prison.[77] Secondly, what was to be done about the effects of the education acts? The Home Office felt that truants were different from the ordinary inmates of industrial schools and that they ought to be the responsibility of local authorities. It also wanted the greater classification of inmates of schools. Thirdly, which department was to be responsible for inspection? On this the department took an unmovable stance. Fourthly, what was to be done about the financial burden on central government? The Home Office felt that local authorities should bear a greater burden and should take over the work of enforcing parental responsibility by collecting their contributions.[78]

Committee members were divided in their views. Their report of 1884, signed unanimously but with memoranda added, recommended that the Home Office should retain prime responsibility for the schools' administration and inspection while elementary education should in addition be inspected by the Education Department. Lord Norton, a member, reiterated his view that the schools should come entirely under the latter department. Preliminary imprisonment before confinement in a reformatory school was not opposed but it was suggested that magistrates be empowered to impose alternatives, such as corporal punishment. Two members (Broadhurst and Lord Dalhousie), however, opposed any form of preliminary imprisonment. The report wanted local authorities, in the form of poor law guardians, to contribute a fixed amount towards the upkeep of children in industrial schools in exchange for collecting and retaining parental contributions. It recommended that children not be confined to industrial schools for mere truancy.[79]

It was not until 1888 that a government found time for legislation on the subject. That year the Conservative government presented the House of Lords with two separate bills, based on the recommendations of the royal commission and intended to be comprehensive consolidating measures. They made little headway, only being read once. A major stumbling block was strong opposition from school managers and others to the system of dual inspection of industrial schools by two government departments.[80] Thus, to the regret of those like Lord Aberdare, who feared particularly for the standard of education, this provision was removed in new bills introduced the following year. These allowed magistrates various alternatives to sending children to both types of schools; they also raised the minimum and lowered the maximum age of detention in reformatory schools. Thus the government intended to reduce the numbers of inmates and therefore cut costs. There was to be a compulsory minimum contribution by local county councils (not poor law guardians) to industrial schools – partly to induce them to prevent the indiscriminate commitment of children to those institutions – in return for the collection of parental contributions. The latter, recommended in principle by the royal commission, was considered very important by the Home Office.[81]. However, so powerful was the local authority lobby against it that in standing committee compulsion was watered down to permission. The bills failed. In 1890 Lord Cross introduced two further bills which again proved too tough for local sensibilities. Not only did county and borough councils object to such obligations but industrial school managers resented the potential loss of custom and school boards disliked the curtailment of their powers to send truants to industrial schools. After this Lushington saw 'little compromise with these authorities' and thought his department 'should proceed in the assumption that legislation now will not take place'.[82]

A detailed study of the reformatory movement during this period argues that Lushington was the government's key adviser on industrial and reformatory schools and shows how he was not only responsible for the drafting of government bills but was also consulted on private members' bills. Although the former failed to be enacted, Lushington tried to put some of the intentions of the bills into effect by sending out circulars about treatment of convicted juveniles to local authorities.[83]

Successful legislation was left to private individuals. These bills were primarily aimed at improving the treatment of children rather than the schools' finances; but they did indirectly benefit the Treasury by allowing certain alternatives to committal. Howard Vincent's reformatory and industrial schools act of 1891 was intended to support school managers in their desire to counteract pernicious parental influence on children who had returned home. It enabled well-behaved inmates to be apprenticed or allowed to emigrate before their sentences expired. Lord Leigh's reformatory schools act of 1893, which allowed courts to send juvenile offenders to them without preliminary imprisonment, raised the admission age to these schools from ten to twelve for those who had not previously been convicted. It extended the minimum term of imprisonment in reformatory schools to three years but reduced the maximum age limit from twenty-one to nineteen. The industrial schools amendment act of 1894 (also introduced by Lord Leigh) kept inmates under supervision until the age of eighteen but enabled managers to let them out on revokable licence.

The long delay between the appointment of the royal commission and the department's acceptance that no large-scale legislative change was imminently likely caused problems for the inspectorate whose need for more staff and pay was for long held in abeyance. By 1890 numbers in reformatory schools, and therefore the Treasury grant, had somewhat diminished: 5,855 children were costing the central authority £78,862. However, the number of children in industrial schools had risen to 27,120 and were costing the Treasury £195,860.[84] From 1882 the inspectors' task had been eased through the addition to the inspectorate of an 'examining assistant' who accompanied them on their inspection, concerning himself largely with schoolroom work, and also a second division clerk and five copyists. Nevertheless, a Treasury-Home Office committee in 1891 supported their plea that their pay compared badly with that of officers in other departments, such as senior inspectors at the Local Government Board. It was also agreed that their accommodation was lamentable.[85] Salaries were raised (the inspector's to £800–£1,000) and a sub-inspector added to the staff. Less satisfactory was the move to new premises in Scotland Yard to which the staff strongly objected. Not only did the reformatory and industrial schools inspectorate remain the only Home Office inspectorate whose headquarters were outside the main department, but also the inspector's sensibilities remained offended by a lack of hygiene and by their situation between two pubs which he considered morally detrimental to visiting parents.[86]

The Treasury continued to be dissatisfied with the system of financing the schools; and the schools themselves, with voluntary donations still declining and costs rising, were beginning to experience serious financial difficulties. In 1895 Asquith set up an inter-departmental committee to look once again into the subject. Lushington, recently retired from the Home Office, was chairman. It was a disastrous committee. The main report was not signed unanimously and eight of the nine members signed separate critical memoranda, many of which, according to the chief inspector, J. G. Legge, were 'clearer and more crisp than the original propositions under review'.[87] The old arguments reappeared. Conservatives on the committee, who believed that the schools were doing excellent work, supported the inspector's view that they should remain under the aegis of the Home Office because the inmates were sent through the magistracy and because of the far-reaching responsibilities of the managers. They preferred boarding to daily attendance where this was an option.[88] The reformers, taking the earlier views of Lords Norton and Aberdare, questioned the very validity of the schools which they believed were based 'on a system which contains within itself grave drawbacks'.[89] One of these was Lushington whose views thus diverged from those of the inspectorate: with two others he argued that separating children from normal society, in institutions with prison traditions which were hampered by small funds and low grade teachers, stigmatized them for life. The reformers wanted the schools transferred to the Education Department.[90]

The majority report proposed inspection by the Home Office alone; it recommended the prohibition of preliminary imprisonment for children committed to reformatory schools and far greater restrictions on commitments to industrial schools. On finance it wanted a change in the law to facilitate the collection of parental contributions to discourage irresponsible commitments. It proposed that local authorities be compelled to contribute on a *per capita* basis for children in both types of school but that they should pay less than the Treasury for cases at reformatory schools and more for those at industrial schools. Thus it would be in the interests of these authorities to ensure that the schools were efficiently run. The report also proposed a new form of variable grant, designed to encourage efficiency, to be available from the Treasury for reformatory schools and from local authorities for industrial schools.

Once again the government was very slow to act. In 1899 the indefatigable Lord Leigh successfully sponsored a measure abolishing preliminary imprisonment for juvenile offenders committed to reformatories. Two years later the Conservatives' youthful offenders act, by altering the law on the sentencing of children and young persons, indirectly reduced numbers of committals to each type of school. Nevertheless, schools continued to be in desperate straits. There were constant pressures on managers, partly from the inspectors, to aim at higher standards for teachers, and to improve equipment and diets. But the inspectors lacked any financial inducement with which to tempt school authorities to comply. The average cost per inmate had risen steadily since 1870.[91] Many schools found that, far from being able to make improvements, they had few enough funds to pay superintendents and teachers. Some retained children longer than necessary in order to reap the financial benefit from their labours on uninstructive industrial employment. Ageing heads stayed on; good teachers were not attracted to the schools. The longer this situation continued the more evident became Lushington's criticism of them. Even Legge became so gloomy at one point that he wondered whether the Board of Education, after all, had better not take them over.[92]

But Legge was their official champion. His appointment by Asquith in 1895 was imaginative. Unlike his predecessors, he had been an open competition recruit to the Home Office. He was energetic and conscientious, and tried hard to persuade his department to adopt an enlightened financial scheme. He observed that the proportion of Treasury to local authority contributions towards schools expenditure was steadily changing. For, although not compelled to do so, local authorities were contributing increasingly generously while the Treasury grant was diminishing as a proportion of the total expenditure. By 1906, in the case of industrial schools, Treasury contributions had been overtaken by local authority contributions.[93] Thus, although he argued for increased local support through the exemption of reformatory and industrial schools from the rates, Legge also wanted a substantially increased central government grant, urging that this was quite as justifiable as increases made by the central government to managers of elementary schools.[94] In August 1904 he produced a scheme for an annual 'efficiency' grant – quite separate from the Treasury *per capita* grant – of thirty shillings a head to both types of school where standards of efficiency reached a high level in three areas: 'education'; 'industrial training and disposal'; and 'hygienic conditions and physical training'.[95] This was not unlike the variable grant proposed by the 1896 committee except that Legge wanted it to come entirely from the Treasury. The estimated cost was £24,459.

To achieve anything Legge required full backing from his department. This he did not always receive as inspector. In 1901 the then home secretary, Ritchie, had responded weakly and negatively to a visiting deputation from the National Association of Certified Reformatory and Industrial Schools which begged the Home Office for money and support.[96] Now his successor, Akers-Douglas, supported Chalmers's suggestion that a decision on Legge's plan be postponed until responsibility for the Scottish schools had been fully transferred to the Scottish Office (an outcome of the 1896 report).[97] Subsequently, in November 1904, on Chalmers's initiative, the whole matter of finance was submitted to yet another committee – this time containing representatives of the Treasury, Board of Education and Home Office – in order to strengthen Legge's case.

Once again, managers of the schools had to wait upon the deliberations of departmental officials.

Fully two years after Legge had proposed his scheme his committee reported. He had been a key witness and it adopted his idea of a variable efficiency grant, plus an increase to industrial schools in the fixed Treasury *per capita* grant, in a proposal now estimated at £41,000.[98] Action, once again, was held up and Legge was no longer there to add his insistent voice, for he had left in August 1906 to become director of education in Liverpool. The home secretary, Gladstone, was worried that the efficiency grant scheme would have the effect of giving most money to the schools best provided for. Therefore the new acting inspector, T. D. M. T. Robertson, Byrne and Tripp worked out yet another plan (this time estimated at £30,000) for an 'aid grant' which would be distributed carefully on an annual basis to schools where it was most needed.[99]

This was put to the Treasury in December 1906. Despite the fact that a Treasury official had sat on the earlier inter-departmental committee, whose recommended scheme was to have cost considerably more than the latest proposal, Treasury officials were uncooperative. They appeared unable to look at the schools' needs on their own merits, compare them with those of other types of school, or weigh up the social importance of effective management. They would not 'consent that the Parliamentary Votes should bear the whole cost of bringing up the schools to the proper standard of efficiency' and would only authorize something under £15,000.[100] This the Home Office decided to spend on grant aid to needy reformatories while increasing fixed grants to industrial schools where (to please the Treasury) local authority grants reached a certain minimum level. The outcome was disappointing not only to the inspectorate. The National Association of Certified Reformatory and Industrial Schools made their bitter disappointment about this first increase from central funds since 1866 quite clear to Gladstone at a meeting in the Home Office in late 1907.[101]

However, at that time Home Office officials were working on what was to become the 1908 children act, an important social measure which dealt with the whole field of protecting the young. A notable feature of this was the prohibition of imprisonment for all children under fourteen and (except in rare cases) young persons between fourteen and sixteen. In the area of reformatory and industrial schools it repealed and consolidated earlier legislation and imposed obligations at last on local authorities to support them. While the bill was being drafted Byrne observed that he did not think that there would be strong local opposition to this idea, at least in

England, where 'it is not a matter of first class importance'.[102] Thus had attitudes changed considerably since the late 1880s. Nevertheless, initially the bill retained the principle that Treasury funds to each type of school would be fixed and that local authorities might (but not must) contribute to the support of the inmates. In grand committee this was altered so as to make county or county borough councils (in the case of reformatory schools) and local education authorities (in the case of industrial schools) responsible for providing for reception and maintenance, although how much of the total maintenance they should pay was not fixed. Local authorities were given the right to inspect schools too.[103]

After the children act the duties of the reformatory and industrial schools inspectorate were indicated as follows:

> The Secretary of State certifies schools . . . appoints Inspectors . . . approves of the rules of schools . . . sanctions alterations in buildings . . . discharges or transfers inmates . . . sanctions the disposal of a child by emigration . . . decides, with the approval of the Treasury, the amount of the Government contributions towards the expenses of the children . . . remits payments ordered to be made by the parent . . . may send an offender, conditionally pardoned, to a Reformatory School . . . and makes various orders and regulations.[104]

The inspectorate was showing familiar administrative characteristics: bureaucratic growth and devolution of authority. In 1911 the permanent staff of inspectors (which had increased, proportionately to other Home Office inspectorates, very greatly) numbered seven, the clerical staff fourteen and the local agents fourteen. The annual cost of the inspectorate (including its provincial agents) was £11,561.[105] That year the Treasury spent a total of £202,000 on maintaining children in reformatory and industrial schools, while receiving £20,059 from parental contributions. Thus central administration of the system (in England and Wales) was costing about 6 per cent of the government outlay on these schools.

Expansion was not simply the result of increased numbers of inmates in schools; in fact, between 1890 and 1911 the total number declined from 32,287 to 28,632. Legislation had added to the inspectorate's functions. Also, what had seemed adequate inspection in 1876 did not twenty years later. In the mid-1880s the standard once-a-year visit, plus the occasional surprise visit, was the norm.[106] By 1913 each school was receiving between two and three visits a year and it was suggested that this be increased to at least four.[107] Inspectors still had no power to interfere directly with the running of the schools. Their one sanction remained the withdrawal of the central grant and they continued to be reluctant to use it. But through discussion, advice and encouragement they promoted higher standards in the educational and medical care provided and caused managers to consider aspects of children's welfare which had been little thought about in Turner's day. Like other inspectorates this one also began to recruit specialists: in 1903 the first woman was appointed; in 1910 a medical adviser was nominated and three years later this post was made full-time.

Nevertheless it felt chronically underestimated. Legge had felt its work was misunderstood. Once, when the Treasury proposed to re-classify the inspectors along the lines of Education Department inspectors, he minuted:

> It is difficult to realise that this proposal can be serious. It entirely ignores the difference between the range of inspection of an ordinary elementary school and that of a reformatory or industrial school. What sub-inspector under the Education Department ever had in his life to make the most delicate inquiries into the morals either of the children or the teachers of either sex, or to interview magistrates?[108]

In 1908 Robertson echoed earlier complaints when he grumbled that his department was 'regarded as insignificant'.[109] Aitken admitted in 1911 that his division did not have time to take as much interest in the schools as it would have liked.[110] In 1911 a further departmental committee on the reformatory and industrial schools was instigated by Churchill and chaired by successive parliamentary under-secretaries, C. F. G. Masterman and E. J. Griffith (Both Churchill and Masterman spoke for 'New Liberalism' which particularly sought, within the Liberal party, to provide new ways of tackling grave social problems.) The committee pointed out the serious consequence of underestimating this inspectorate: 'the magnitude and importance of the work have not been sufficiently recognized ... To the general failure to give to this branch of public work the share of attention and support it deserves, most of the deficiencies found in the schools are ultimately due'.[111]

The reason for this lack of attention had something to do with the whole status of these schools in terms of social reform. Despite increased recognition by governments (reflected in the 1908 children's act) that the welfare of under-privileged and criminal children was important, reformatory and industrial schools did not seem to receive the same attention as did either ordinary schools or the new borstal system of which the Home Office was so proud. For years the main incentive for government legislation had been desire for financial relief rather than for social improvement, and it had been left to private philanthropists to inspire changes benefiting the children concerned. As the 1911–13 committee forced Aitken to admit, prisons were presided over by men 'of considerably higher (social) rank' than those in charge of these schools. Prisoners' grievances could provoke public support far more easily than those of children in reformatory schools. As a reflection, prison inspectors – proportionate to the work involved – were more numerous and generally better paid than reformatory and industrial schools inspectors.[112]

The committee, which did extensive research into all the schools, found a wide variation in their efficiency. Progress had, on the whole, been made since the 1895 committee had reported but things had not moved fast enough because of the schools' severe lack of funds and because the inspectors lacked effective powers to enforce desirable changes. Altogether there was a need for vigorous insistence on minimum standards of efficiency in areas such as the classification of children and levels of teacher training and experience. The remedies proposed included the formation, within the Home Office, of a separate division to deal solely with problems connected with laws on children; the transfer of responsibility for the entire educational aspect of the schools to the Board of Education with co-operation and interchange among the two inspectorates involved; and a large-scale injection of public money into the schools through increases in the fixed Treasury *per capita* grant, the fixing of local authority *per capita* grants and the introduction of an additional, centrally funded variable grant, to be administered by the inspectors who would thereby have an inducement 'to stimulate managers to make desirable improvements'.[113]

The administrative recommendations were put into effect under McKenna. The formation of the new division D at the Home Office in July 1913 has already been observed.[114] The inspectorate was augmented by a medically qualified woman inspector and a full-time medical inspector, while the inspectors' salaries were slightly improved. The home secretary accepted the recommendation about the transfer of work to the Board of Education and arrangements were made for the co-operation of its inspectors. Over the financial recommendations the Home Office found the Treasury uncooperative: instead of the recommended £73,000 it sanctioned an increase of only £50,000. The Home Office therefore had considerably to trim the proposed scheme. It was decided that the most important aspect was the variable grant because the inspectors so badly needed the sort of sanctions it would give them.[115] This meant the abandonment of the increase to the fixed Treasury grant which, in turn, meant that the Home Office could not insist on specific and increased local authority contributions. (The chief inspector, in fact, later reported that on the whole these were made generously.)[116]

The committee, by and large, had been in favour of retaining voluntary management of the schools and this cardinal feature of Turner's, in fact, remained an ideal for years after 1914.[117] But, with the Treasury and local authorities contributing 85 and 82 per cent towards the total funds respectively of reformatory and industrial schools, they were hardly independent. Moreover, central control over their organization had advanced considerably since Turner's day: not only did the inspectorate take a much closer interest and demand higher standards, but Home Office approval of school superintendents had become a condition of the schools receiving their certificates and therefore their grants. This position of the schools – technically independent but vitally dependent on public funds from two often conflicting sources – had not made for an easy administrative situation for the Home Office inspectorate over this period. Its problems had been exacerbated by the Treasury's lack of co-operation over grants and by the inability of successive governments to achieve major reform.

The extended role of the state
Between 1876 and 1914 many political theorists were moving away from mid-nineteenth century liberalism, which had stressed the relative freedom of economic action and limited overall role of central government, and were arguing in favour of a more positive role for government in order to promote freedom for a wider section of society. T. H. Green, teaching at Oxford in the 1870s, viewed the state as a 'positive agency' whose function was to promote the general welfare of society.[118] During the 1880s and 1890s the Fabians reflected 'an important change in the climate of British political opinion, namely, a loss of confidence in the alleged social efficiency of private enterprise and an increased willingness to use the state's legislative and administrative power to correct its abuses and to humanize it'.[119] These ideas were formative to the growth of socialism – a concept deeply feared by some of the older, more conservative officials connected with the Home Office in the late nineteenth century.[120] Dicey too suspected 'socialism or collectivism'. His examples of legislation which wore 'all the marked characteristics of collectivism' included acts which affected the Home Office: the 1897 workmen's compensation act which compelled employers to insure their workmen against accidents at work; and the factory and workshop acts. He concluded,

The time is rapidly approaching when the State will, as regards the regulation of labour, aim at as much omnipotence and omniscience as is obtainable by any institution created by human beings. Wherever any man, woman, or child renders services for payment, there in the track of the worker will appear the inspector.[121]

The debate as to the value and desired extent of government interference therefore continued.

Home secretaries and government officials had to wrestle with the question: how positive a role should their department play? Matthews stated in 1892 that he had no intention of enlarging the scope of the factory inspectors' duties.[122] A mines inspector used the familiar argument to the royal commission on mines in 1906 that it would take an 'enormous number of inspectors' to ensure that the mines were always safe and thought that it would be 'very unwise to take the responsibility off the managers'.[123] Yet politicians were influenced by an increasingly vocal sector of the community which had once been the weak sector that philanthropists had laboured to have protected. It was now much better organized and in a position to press for greater state intervention where it felt that government could protect its interests – that is, especially in the field of labour. At the same time officials themselves, still impelled by the 'inner momentum' phenomenon,[124] could not resist the tendency towards increased intervention, again particularly in the industrial field.

The natural tendency of the Home Office inspectorates was to grow, although not all of them did so during this period. The constabulary inspectorate, which according to one central official offered some of the 'softest jobs in a hardworked department',[125] was actually reduced in size. The anatomy inspectors were slightly reduced. But the other inspectorates all expanded to some degree. In terms of pure percentage increase the greatest expansion was of the reformatory and industrial schools inspectors who increased from two to nine. But by far the greatest increase in terms of numbers was in the major 'industrial' inspectorates.

The Treasury was naturally suspicious of this tendency of certain inspectorates to expand, partly as the result of their insistence on higher standards of inspection, and this partly accounts for its reluctance to approve increased budgets. But expansion was also a matter of social policy. Parliament imposed new requirements on the factory inspectorate through the secretary of state, and his officials felt that these could only realistically be met by increasing staff and costs. Investment in penal institutions was also a policy matter. Numerous departmental committees, appointed by the home secretary, deliberated about the needs of the reformatory and industrial schools and, even if members disagreed on many points, they were at least agreed that the schools needed a large injection of public money to make them effective. In denying adequate funds for these social improvements the Treasury was thwarting demands made through the democratic process. Moreover, its replies to formal departmental requests – always set out in detail and carefully argued – were too often curt or hastily argued, showing little interest or attempt to understand the problems presented. Lord Salisbury's famous diatribe in 1900 against the extent of the Treasury's powers in governing every department of the government marked 'the collision of rival social, political and foreign policies. The issue at stake was essentially the survival of the Gladstonian tradition of rigid economy against the mounting demands of a nearly democratic state'.[126]

There were also tensions within the Home Office over the formation of policy. These, as we have observed in the case of the reformatory and industrial schools inspectorate, were sometimes the result of the different viewpoint of the officials in the field and those at the centre. The inspectorates had originally been tacked on to the central department, not incorporated within its existing framework. But over the years they had been transformed from isolated sub-departments into an integral part of the Home Office network. The move of the department into its new Whitehall home in 1875 brought under the same roof the inspectors of factories, explosives, burial grounds and – after 1877 – prisons. Thus, of the full-time, London-based inspectorates only the reformatory and industrial schools inspectorate remained physically outside the department. This change, together with the integration of most of the inspectors' clerks into the lower division in 1876, inevitably gave these sub-departments much closer links with their parent department. In 1878 Cross attempted to put communication with all the sub-departments on a more formal footing when he issued a standing order stipulating that for the first time he would interview the head of the inspectorates on a regular basis once a month and would also be accessible whenever necessary.[127]

From the 1880s the principal clerks were not only given new responsibilities by their superiors but also assumed a new authority over heads of sub-departments. Instead of being a mere post-box they became a filter between heads of sub-departments and under-secretaries. This has already been observed in detail in the context of the criminal department.[128] There are also examples in the domestic department. In 1881 Majendie suggested that the explosives inspectorate should not only by-pass the domestic department and the under-secretaries by reporting directly to the home secretary but should also refer only 'exceptional cases' to him. Lushington hastily scotched the idea, maintaining that Majendie's branch must remain on the same footing as the other inspectorates:

> My reason for this is simply the reason for the establishment of the Home Office at all – viz. that before the Secretary of State is personally committed to an opinion or course of action he should have the benefit not only of the Inspector's advice, but also whatever protections against mistakes are afforded by the Office system.[129]

This barrier at the level of departmental head between the central secretariat and the sub-departments was strengthened when the open competition men attained that level. Thus the attitude of the clerk heading an internal Home Office department became a matter of concern to an inspector. If Aitken was not enthusiastic about Legge's proposals for reform, or was less than appalled at Treasury meanness in responding to them, this was going to affect the final decision of his superiors, whose attention was occupied by a far wider range of subjects. When giving evidence in 1911 to the departmental committee on reformatory and industrial schools, Aitken made clear that the most important decisions were made within the central secretariat:

> The details of supervision of the schools are of course left to the Inspectorate, but all difficult cases or matters involving law or important principles are referred to the Secretary of State for decision, and he conducts the more important correspondence with justices, managers of the schools, police, and others.[130]

It is worth considering, with reference to the two inspectorates examined, the forces of these various factors on the development of policy. During the period 1876 to 1892 the Home Office tended to follow a conservative policy towards factory inspection, being unwilling, for example, to consider sympathetically many of the demands made by labour organizations. At this period the first 'heroic' wave of inspectors had given way to a cautious, less imaginative second generation, headed by a chief inspector whose experience had been limited to the Home Office. The permanent under-secretary, Lushington, held a traditional view of his department's responsibilities, instinctively giving priority to its law and order role. This was a view from which neither Harcourt nor Matthews dissented, although Harcourt's personal inclination to create working men inspectors – even though it conflicted with the views of his chief inspector – led to the appointment of the first of these, and Matthews put through the 1891 factories and workshops act. It was Asquith who changed the whole tenor of Home Office industrial policy and thus removed the faint threat of his department's losing this work. No doubt impelled by the ideas underlying the Liberals' Newcastle programme of October 1891,[131] he came into office determined to reform aspects of his new department which affected labour's interests. Thus he vastly expanded the inspectorate, created women inspectors, found a useful role for the working men inspectors and established a specialist industrial department within the Home Office. Then from 1896 the new and able chief inspector, Whitelegge, found a generation of sympathetic departmental officials, such as Troup and Delevigne, the formative years of whose careers had been influenced by this shift towards industrial affairs. They tended to support his proposals and fought the Treasury hard in 1913 for more money. Another feature which may have added weight to the views of this inspectorate was the technical nature of its work. However able they were, it was difficult for central officials to master the technicalities of ventilating machines or steam power and therefore on many matters they were bound to accept the views of the experts.

Children in reformatory and industrial schools were of considerably less political interest than factory workers (who were, after all, voters) despite a growing interest in children's welfare. They were not, therefore, of prime concern to most home secretaries, although exceptions to this are Harcourt and probably Churchill. There was always a handful of philanthropists who tried to exert pressure on the Home Office, but they were not always in agreement among themselves and sometimes found themselves out of tune with the inspectorate – for example, on the issue of the educational inspection of schools. In short, there was no strong combination of inspectors, central officials, local authorities, private pressure groups or politicians which might have brought about much-needed improvement in the schools. Members of investigating committees were greatly divided in their views, and their very differences were an excuse for a lack of positive government action for many years. This led to a feeling of helplessness and low morale in the inspectorate. Legge's appointment in 1895 injected spirit into it and he came up with constructive proposals for improving the schools' finances. But even Legge became discouraged and, although his ideas in a modified form won through in the end, he had by then already resigned his post, having met much procrastination from central officials. The head of the division which dealt with the inspectorate was Aitken, whom Legge failed to imbue with his fighting spirit. The Masterman/Griffith committee brought about some important administrative reforms but full financial proposals were blocked by the Treasury which does not seem to have been persuaded at ministerial level to relent. The inspectors, then, were influential in improving schools though their advice and guidance to managers and superintendents on matters such as discipline, education, accommodation and medical care. But as a force within the complex of the Home Office, Treasury and cabinet they were weak.

These two studies illustrate some of the factors which contributed to policy changes. Home secretaries, like all ministers, were subject to different, often conflicting pressures: from public bodies, such as trade unions, employers' federations and philanthropic movements, which were often represented on royal commissions and departmental committees; from party political decisions, such as the Liberal policy of 1891 to extend the appeal of the party to a more radical section of the voting population; from Treasury control of finance; and from internal departmental views. In addition their own personal predilections and convictions played a part: Harcourt's concern about juvenile offenders contributed to the formation of a royal commission and his impulsive desire to establish working men factory inspectors led to a change in recruitment policy; one small part of Churchill's conviction that his party must tackle important areas of social reform was his setting up of the 1913 reformatory and industrial schools committee under Masterman. Within the department the inspectors provided the expertise which formed part of the 'departmental view'. They offered advice based on their on-the-ground experience. But they were, in a sense, biased: on the one hand they could be complacent through the very fact that they were accustomed to conditions which outside observers, sitting on departmental committees, found objectionable; conversely, they sometimes pushed hard for reform in the interests of the sector of society which they had been appointed to protect. It was the role of the generalist officials in the secretariat to take a more objective view, taking into account those other ministerial pressures. Thus a home secretary turned instinctively for advice to his permanent under-secretary rather than to his chief inspector of factories.

But if the inspectors were not the only, or even the major, policy-makers, nevertheless there is no doubt that by the end of this period their expert advice had become an indispensable aspect of central administration and their work in the field the obvious way of enforcing certain kinds of laws. It is difficult to quantify the extent of their effectiveness. But enormous headway had clearly been made in ameliorating social conditions, and the inspectors had made a substantial contribution towards this. Central government inspection had been found a more or less effective way of galvanizing local authorities into action where new standards of protection were needed. Inspection was a means of aiming at national compliance and uniformity: an inspectorate established to enforce a series of laws could set – and raise – minimum standards which not only gave a guarantee of protection to citizens but also guided the institutions or firms involved. Furthermore, it was only the central government in Britain which had the resources to provide for experiments searching for new areas of control and for teams of statisticians to monitor incoming data. As an aid to government, inspection was well established and was to continue as a vital and expanding part of the administrative system.[132]

Part IV   Conclusion

8   The emergence of a professional civil service

The professional nature of the first and second divisions

By the beginning of our period there had taken root the liberal idea that it was educated, intelligent, trained men who ought to undertake those important services to the community which were coming to be known as professional duties and that these men were as socially valuable as those who had previously been the leaders of the community – men who had inherited titles, land and money.[1] The three ancient professions, 'divinity, law and physic', were being joined by newer professions, each with chartered, independent and (in most cases) controlling bodies whose aims were to promote the ideals of the profession and to maintain a high standard of service. Increasingly the latter was done by means of examinations which were also designed to protect members from unqualified competition. Taking the establishment of the professional body as the criterion for professionalization, civil engineers, architects and veterinary surgeons, for example, had become professional men by 1850; surveyors, teachers and accountants by 1900.

The Northcote-Trevelyan report had been part of the movement to promote education and training. Its authors had seen that in order to extend it to the functioning of government, competition and merit must be given priority. Decision-making within government was to be based on aristocracy of intellect. It is difficult to be precise about when civil servants joined the ranks of professional men because, although definitions of professionalism vary, civil servants did not share certain features usually included in definitions. A good recent one is: 'All "true" professions ... are characterized by expert, esoteric service demanding integrity in the purveyor and trust in the client and the community, and by non-competitive reward in the form of a fixed salary or standard and unquestioned fee.'[2] Civil servants had earned fixed salaries since the early nineteenth century when the Treasury had regulated salaries and then gradually abolished fees and gratuities. But they did not have a direct 'client' relationship with members of the community. Nor did they have a chartered body promoted from within the profession in order to regulate it. They did not possess a specialized expertise for which they had trained and qualified before starting their career. However, the civil service reformers had successfully aimed at establishing public trust and confidence in its public officials through the creation in 1855 of an independent body, the Civil Service Commission, to maintain high qualifying standards for entrants to the public service by examining and certifying them. The subsequent adoption by government departments of open competitive entry confirmed this aim and ensured for the community the recruitment of able men for responsible government posts. It soon became clear that the new breed of official had his own kind of expertise which was the ability to master social and political problems, and work out acceptable solutions to a wide variety of problems by absorbing information and applying administrative experience. Meanwhile the Treasury set out something comparable to a code of practice for civil servants, often in the form of official minutes. These developments, together with the increasing responsibility and constitutional significance of higher grade civil servants, not only made them professional men but gave their profession high status.

What, then, were the special characteristics of civil servants and their profession? One way of illustrating these is to examine an important aspect of the professional idea of 'service demanding integrity in the purveyor and trust in the client and the community'. In 1867 Dicey commented:

> The chief difference between a profession and a trade or business is, that in the case of a profession its members sacrifice a certain amount of individual liberty in order to ensure certain professional objects. In a trade or business the conduct of each individual is avowedly regulated simply by the general rules of honesty and regard to his own interest.[3]

An adherence to an ethical code of conduct or an accepted manner of working and behaving, which imposed obligations in the interests of those for whom they were working, was developing for civil servants from the mid-nineteenth century. The corollary of this was the simultaneous development of certain benefits for members of this new profession.

Civil servants did not have the direct and personal client relationship of a doctor and his patient. But the 'clients' of civil servants were, in a sense, members of the community as a whole, or – more directly – members of the existing government (in particular their own departmental minister) whom the enfranchised had put into power. In theory permanent, a-political officials were servants of the 'state', which in constitutional practice meant that they acted as the executive arm of the elected government for its duration. Thus early civil service reforms were aimed at the transformation of irregularly recruited and paid officials into full-time, salaried employees of the government. At the Home Office the remnants of an allowance system existed as part of the pattern of individual clerks having their own specialist functions until Grey's reforms.[4] In 1849 he stipulated that individual salaries were to die out when the clerks concerned retired.[5] For years clerks continued to request gratuities for specific work which they considered beyond their routine, although the Treasury showed increasing reluctance to entertain such claims. In 1868 it refused a request for gratuities for extra work done during the Fenian outrages.[6] It did grant Maconochie £30 for preparing a new edition of *The Statement of the Powers and Duties of the Secretary of State* in 1872, but after this it insisted that the work should become a regular part of office routine.[7] (Up until the end of the period, however, it did allow clerks gratuities for serving as secretaries to departmental committees.)

The Home Office parliamentary under-secretary had agreed with the 1848 select committee on miscellaneous expenditure that the receipt of regular salaries 'should be considered as imposing an obligation on the persons who receive them to devote the whole of their time to the public service'.[8] Subsequent select committees and royal commissions also pressed the point that in return for reliable and good salaries, officials must give their work total attention during the official working day. They needed to do so for hours were highly elastic. Despite the nominal six hour day of the 1860s, Maconochie, a comparatively assiduous clerk, frequently caught an afternoon train from his suburban villa in Wimbledon to town where he put in a brief appearance at the Home Office.[9] Twenty-two years later Knyvett assured the Ridley commission that an official 'at the Home Office or anywhere else, is expected to give all his time to the service of the state'.[10] He knew of only one upper division clerk from his department who had an additional job (as a university examiner) although work outside official hours was not discouraged. The order in council of 1890, which regulated conditions of service for the new first division, underlined the requirement that civil servants should have a total commitment to their jobs. It forbade officials to participate in the management of any trading, commercial or financial company which required their attendance between the hours of ten and six. It also stipulated that daily attendance books were to be kept – a practice which Home Office clerks found contrary to the ethic of trusting the timely execution of work to official discretion, and to which they had hitherto refused to conform.[11]

The relationship between a professional man and his client has always demanded a commitment on the part of the former beyond the strict call of duty: thus a doctor goes out to a sick patient, or a clergyman to a dying parishioner, in the middle of the night. For civil servants service to their political masters began to require that while certain fixed office hours existed, a responsibility for finishing the work of the day must be recognized even if this meant working beyond official hours. The leisurely habits of the Home Office were beginning to change as work mounted and the separation of 'intellectual' and 'mechanical' duties became real. During the various crises of the early 1880s Erskine and probably Campbell were taking office work home. In 1885 Troup complained that he had to do three or four hours overtime every day.[12] Lushington reckoned in 1887 that each day some of the staff stayed late in the office: 'We tell them what work to do, and it is done as a matter of course', he told the Ridley commissioners.[13] From then on, as we have observed, this was a regular feature of office life although officials, particularly at the lower level, did not hesitate to use it as a bargaining counter in pleas for higher salaries.

Another rule in the developing code of conduct involved professional secrecy. Doctors, lawyers and clergymen had their own code of secrecy which again related to their client relationship. Within the civil service, rules preventing the disclosure of official information were being formulated to protect governments. In 1873 there occurred various 'highly irregular' cases in which civil servants leaked official information to the press. The Treasury thereupon threatened to dismiss the perpetrators of any future leaks, and in February 1875 reiterated in a Minute that no official information might be communicated to public journals without sanction from 'responsible heads of Departments'.[14] In 1889 parliament passed the first official secrets act. Intended primarily to prevent the disclosure of military secrets to foreign countries, it included the unsanctioned publication of official information by those holding offices of the crown. Offenders were liable to imprisonment. This was reiterated in the 1911 official secrets act. Over and above this, senior officials had a special relationship with ministers and were expected to be discreet about policy-making – a characteristic which originated from the concept of collective ministerial responsibility.

One obligation which was peculiar to a civil servant's profession was his duty to serve with equal loyalty whatever political master the electorate chose to put into the seat of government. Even by 1848 the period was long past when officials who owed their position to a patron had to abandon office when their patron relinquished power.

Nevertheless, as long as senior officials were appointed from outside the public service they were open to the accusation of having some special loyalty to the party which appointed them. Although an admirable civil servant, Lushington, who had been appointed by a Liberal home secretary, appears to have been more sympathetic towards Liberal than towards Conservative policies. Indeed, Salisbury was so suspicious of his reputation that, despite the fact that in 1885 Lushington was the obvious candidate to succeed Liddell as permanent under-secretary, the prime minister was reluctant to agree to his appointment.[15] With the later generation of senior civil servants, appointed from within the service, this vestige of political patronage disappeared.

The ideal of the political detachment of officials had been held since the eighteenth century: in 1741 it was enacted that they could vote for but not become MPs. But the niceties of the connection between political and executive activities were still being refined during the nineteenth century. In 1884 the Treasury had embodied in an order in council the general 'usage' that a civil servant seeking a seat in the Commons resigned 'as soon as he issues his address to the electors, or in any other manner announces himself as a candidate'.[16] The situation in reverse touched the Home Office in 1885 when Cross offered Pemberton, then a Conservative MP, the post of legal assistant under-secretary. The actual moment when he must vacate his seat had to be clarified by the law officers who gave this as the moment when he was officially appointed.[17] Other political restrictions were also being set out. In 1889 the first lord of the Treasury would not allow a permanent member of the civil service to act as secretary or registration agent to any political party. But, he added, 'much must be left to the discretion of Civil Servants themselves'.[18]

'Discretion' also related to financial probity and personal integrity. In 1886, for instance, the Treasury tried to stop the practice (graphically depicted by Anthony Trollope in *The Three Clerks*) of young clerks signing 'accommodation bills' and thereby subsequently getting themselves involved in the financial difficulties of others. It argued in a formal minute that governments and parliament had recently tried 'to raise the Civil Servants of the Crown in efficiency and general estimation' and that this could only be done if they were above financial reproach.[19] Officials were also admonished against using their official positions and knowledge to benefit themselves financially. In their private lives they were expected to observe conventional patterns of respectable behaviour. In 1869 a temporary supplementary clerk was dismissed from the Home Office without notice because he had become involved in divorce proceedings.[20] Guillemard received a shock one morning in the mid-1880s while he was at the Home Office when, as he sat dishevelled on a bench in Hyde Park after a night on the town, Lushington rode by. Luckily the young clerk was later able to report to his chief that he had been 'quite sober'.[21]

Table 11   Salary prospects for first division clerks, 1848–1914

	1848	1876	1896	1914
Top post open to career official	chief clerk £1,000–£1,250	principal clerk £900–£1,000	assistant under-secretary £1,000–£1,200	permanent under-secretary £2,000
Post which competant man could expect to reach	1st class clerk £600–£800	principal clerk £900–£1,000	principal clerk £900–£1,000	assistant secretary £1,000–£1,200
Usual initial post	3rd class clerk £150–£300	junior clerk £200–£600	junior clerk £200–£500	junior clerk £200–£500

In return for such curtailment of their liberty as these obligations involved, civil servants derived substantial benefits. For 'professional status is . . . an implied contract; to serve society over and beyond all specific duty to client or employer in consideration of the privileges and protection society extends to the profession'.[22] One of the main benefits was a good salary. Table 11 shows the changing financial expectations of upper or first division Home Office clerks over the whole period. The salaries of officials at each end of the three levels considerably improved over the period as a whole. In addition, average real incomes were rising between 1850 and 1900, and rising particularly steeply after 1880.[23] Therefore Troup's generation of higher officials was, for a while, doing financially even better in comparison with the preceding one than the table implies. In the general rise of incomes it seems likely that the middle classes, and probably professional men as a whole, were doing particularly well.[24] Until the latter part of our period it is hard to make meaningful salary comparisons between civil servants and other professional men because contemporary sources give both vague and differing information about incomes. More precise figures about average professional earnings in the twentieth century show that those of Home Office first division officials – who were among the best paid in government departments until the standardization of their salaries after the first world war – compared well with their peers among barristers, solicitors and doctors at the lower and medium levels of their careers although not as well at the top for there were no opportunities to make the enormous incomes which could, for example, be made at the bar. Any first division man who did not blot his copybook could by then expect, in due course, to reach over £1,000 – an annual salary which 'at any time before 1914 . . . represented considerable worldly success, though not great wealth, and placed a man, economically speaking, well towards the top of the middle classes'.[25]

In addition to their salaries, from the passing of the superannuation act of 1859, all permanent civil servants could count on a retirement pension. These were awarded on a fixed and fairly generous scale: a man who retired after forty years in the public service received two-thirds of his annual salary. In 1909 pension terms were improved so as to allow payments to the representatives of those who had died in the service. Pensions were not only an aid to discipline in that those who were dismissed for misconduct lost their pension rights, but their award justified the introduction in 1890 of compulsory retirement (then set at sixty-five) which finally put an end to situations where ageing clerks hung on to posts which could more usefully be filled by younger men.[26]

Civil servants also had the advantage of continued employment – in default of gross misconduct – and steady promotion to a certain level. Basic security of tenure was necessary as an antidote to a political spoils system but it had the obvious disadvantage that the inefficient were difficult to dislodge. The civil service reformers had done their best to erode this feature in the interests of public efficiency but met with resistance from longstanding tradition. At the Home Office Lushington's orthodox view was that 'advantage arises from the feeling in the service that stability is one of its characteristics. You get a better class of men in consequence of the knowledge of the fact that they are not liable to be sent away by the caprice of their superiors, or in bad times.'[27] Although security of tenure remained a feature of the civil service, increasing emphasis was placed on merit. In 1894 the Home Office for the first time promoted an able young junior, Simpson, over the head of a more senior clerk, E. S. W. Johnson. The following year Johnson had to retire, through 'inability', after only fourteen years' service. (Even so, he was awarded a pension.) With Troup's generation merit did count, as his own and Delevigne's careers demonstrate.

Terms of service, then, were good in the civil service. There was, in addition, the reward increasingly granted to its senior officials as their influence grew and as they rose in public esteem: public honours. In the mid-nineteenth century it was not customary to reward civil servants with honours; but by 1914 able, hard-working officials could almost count on this form of acknowledgement. At the Home Office the tradition of awarding the permanent under-secretary a knighthood began with Liddell in 1867 (at about the time that top retired civil servants were first awarded peerages[28]). However, this honour was a gift from the prime minister and Lushington found that it was by no means an automatic one. We have already noted Salisbury's antipathy towards him.[29] Despite the strong recommendations of the home secretary (Matthews) and his argument from 1887 onwards that Lushington was at a disadvantage in not having a knighthood compared with other departmental heads, it was not until 1892 that the prime minister at last relented and Lushington was awarded his KCB.[30] An honour could be a useful compensation: Knyvett gained his KCB when Murdoch was promoted to become assistant under-secretary in 1896; Cunynghame gained his after Troup's appointment to the permanent under-secretaryship – although evidently this consolation was granted with some reluctance.[31] Troup's generation was the first to be awarded honours on a wide scale: of the first division officials recruited to the Home Office between 1880 and 1896 all those who devoted their working lives to the public service gained some honour. Six earned knighthoods, four of which – Troup's, Delevigne's, Byrne's and Pedder's – were awarded for service in the Home Office.

Working commitment to the state, maintenance of professional secrecy, impartial loyalty towards the policies of the government in power, abrogation of direct political activity, and general integrity: these were the obligations, some of which the Treasury had codified, which had developed for civil servants. Their rewards were a good and regular salary, security of tenure, the knowledge of certain promotion to a reasonably high level, and the recognition of the importance of their role through the award of public honours. They had become first class professional men, sharing with their professional peers that freemasonry which derived from a common education, often at the same schools and nearly always at the same universities. Their upper middle-class incomes enabled them to have a similar life-style in terms of servants, holidays, and where they lived.[32] They often continued to share the same social activities: as Scott observed, the pre-war Home Office was still 'influenced by the rhythm of the London season'; and its first division officials nearly all belonged to clubs, one of the most popular of which was the

Athenaeum – haunt of eminent lawyers, ecclesiastics, academics and public servants. They also shared *mores* about personal habits, such as dress:

> No young secretary of a committee would ever dare to arrive in the office in tweeds . . . Whatever the weather, he wore a morning coat and top hat; and he was expected to present himself in the same attire when asked to luncheon with his superiors at the week-end.[33]

This pattern of life, which gave the first division officials strong links not only with other professional men but also with their political chiefs, was what identified them as 'gentlemen' and, incidentally, set them apart from those below them in the office.

Second division men were not professional men of the first rank; indeed, many contemporaries would have denied that they were professional men at all. Yet they had to qualify, in the sense of passing an examination, before entering a career in the civil service and they earned a salary; and 'qualify', 'career' and 'salary' were all words used to describe the life of a professional man. They performed a valuable role in the civil service and, to a limited extent, they followed the same code of conduct, were subject to the same kind of obligations and received some of the same benefits as their superiors.

The more senior men in the second division were expected to work beyond the call of official duty without extra pay: in 1887 Moran claimed that he regularly worked an extra two hours a day in the registry for six months of the year.[34] In 1909 Farrant alleged that he had put in two to three hundred hours of his own time over the course of a year.[35] But at a lower level second division clerks showed a growing tendency to ask for overtime payment for work done out of office hours. This the first division clerks on the 1898 committee investigating the registry found 'contrary to the principles which govern employment in the Civil Service'.[36] Certainly the Treasury disliked it. But the salary structure of parts of the second division was such that there was room for manoeuvre over pay. Staff clerks had individual salaries and, although these were roughly equated with those of comparable clerks in other departments, they were subject to re-negotiation with the Treasury as these men acquired more responsibilities. Ordinary second division clerks had opportunities to negotiate for improvements through additional duty pay (until 1890), overtime payment or having their posts turned into minor staff posts.

Second division clerks were just as much bound by civil service rules about non-participation in politics and the maintenance of professional secrecy as were their superiors. They were obliged to respect rules prohibiting commercial, industrial or financial activity during office hours – a rule which may have been a restricting factor to those involved, for example, in the running of civil service co-operative societies. Since these were often the focal point for activity in the promotion of second division combinations, it is just possible that this regulation, embodied in the 1890 order in council setting out conditions for the second division, was deliberately designed to discourage such activity at least during the official working day.

In return for such restrictions they too had the benefit of a regular income with guaranteed increments and a retirement pension, regular holidays, a half-holiday each Saturday after 1890 and stipulated terms about sick leave. All this was set out by the Treasury through orders in council so that they were in no way at the mercy of capricious employers. They even occasionally merited public honours: Tripp was given a CB, one or two staff clerks were awarded the ISO (Imperial Service Order) after its creation in 1902, and others were awarded coronation medals in 1902 and 1911. Overall they consciously benefited from what Wheeler called that 'certain dignity attaching to the Civil Service' which gave them social standing.[37] Even though to many of their first division contemporaries they might not have been bona fide professional men, those second division clerks who made it to staff clerkships probably regarded themselves as such. And if one can distinguish between higher and lower professions, theirs certainly comes into the latter category.

The second division clerks' fight for better job opportunities is interesting in two ways in the context of discussion about professionalism. First, it was because of the lack of a pre-career specialist training for civil servants that the militants were able to put forward the argument that apprenticeship at the lower end of the service was as good a preparation for higher responsibility as was a university training. Secondly, second division clerks wanted better pay and career opportunities partly in order to acquire the elusive attributes of gentlemen and yet, paradoxically, set about obtaining these things in a way which their superiors found distinctly ungentlemanly: that is, by using their new-found, service-wide strength to combine in trade union-type activity.

That second division men wanted to be professional men and gentlemen, and that they feared that they might not be, is indicated by their sensitivity on this point. In 1888 the *Civil Service Gazette* portrayed outraged indignation against the secretary of the Post Office for expressing his feeling of social superiority:

According to Sir Stevenson Arthur Blackwood, KCB, the members of the Lower Division are not gentlemen, and, what is even worse, that Division is not recruited from the social class which the Secretary of the Post Office thinks men in the service of the Government occupying responsible positions ought to come from, and been brought up in [sic].[38]

This 'craving for recognition' had various manifestations which have been found characteristic of the lower middle class as a whole at that time.[39] In the first place, second division clerks tended to be very rank conscious. In 1887 the Home Office staff clerks presented their own petition to the Ridley commissioners asking that they might formally be ranked between the upper division junior and senior clerks. On one occasion Farrant, lower in order of seniority than the recently appointed assistant superintendent of the registry, Wheeler, was promoted to become clerk for statistical returns which was head of a branch of the general department. Wheeler immediately requested that his technical precedence be made quite clear in the published Home Office lists so that the outside public might not feel that he had been passed over.[40] Secondly, having arrived at positions of relative security, the more senior clerks tended to emulate their superiors rather than fight to better the condition of those from whose ranks they had risen. The Home Office staff clerks regarded themselves as quite separate from the lower grades of which they were in charge and more like first division officials. Moran, when interviewed by the Ridley commissioners about how to deal with lower division grievances, expressed no views which singled him out from Lushington, Knyvett and Murdoch. Tripp, after his appointment to the headship of the accounts branch, clearly became more or less an emancipated colleague of the principal clerks. And there is no indication that Wheeler, the angry young lower division clerk of 1888, took a lead in trying to better the lot of his erstwhile colleagues after his promotion to the first division in 1896.

Yet the staff clerks at the top of the second division did not really shade into the junior clerks at the bottom of the first division. The fact was that the social and educational cleavage between first and second division clerks by 1914 was much wider than that between established and supplementary clerks in the pre-reform Home Office. In the 1850s divisions in the civil service had been vertical as much as horizontal: departmental barriers had been more important than class levels and whether a clerk worked in the Home Office or the Admiralty was more important to him than whether he was a supplementary or an established clerk. In the days of patronage a supplementary clerk might well have had the same social background as an established clerk, and the jump from the lower to the higher class was not only much easier than it later became but it did not necessarily imply a stunted career in the higher class. Compare the success of Maconochie (who started as a supplementary clerk) with the failure of Wheeler, following their respective promotions into the upper or first division. From the 1880s Home Office upper or first division officials felt quite different from those below them. This accounts for why, although there were good opportunities for clerks to rise as far as the level of staff clerk, beyond this there was – if not an 'inexorable barrier'[41] – at least a clear bar to advancement.

It is interesting to set the characteristics of the civil service second division, as viewed through the Home Office, in the context of Geoffrey Crossick's essay on wider aspects of the British lower middle class in the late-Victorian and Edwardian period.[42] The civil service second division, which greatly expanded over the period, seems to have exhibited the frustration of unfulfilled ambition and those characteristics of social insecurity which Crossick finds in other low middle-class groups. A particular parallel seems to have been the school-teachers: they too had a strong sense of professional identity; and they also formed combinations which at first emphasized professional and even social interests but were driven by their frustrations to more trade union-type of activity.

The 'consolidation of a caste' within the civil service may have been part of a more general phenomenon identified by historians of this period.[43] We have already observed that developments in education were making it even more difficult for clever children of poor parents to receive the same kind of privileged education as those of rich parents; that Oxford and Cambridge colleges and the older public schools were ceasing to maintain the tradition of reserving certain scholarship places for poor and local children.[44] Even by 1864, evidence to the Taunton Commission on secondary education showed that trustees of local grammar schools, themselves educated at such schools, were sending their sons away to public boarding schools thereby separating them from local contemporaries and ensuring that their future friends and associates would be the sons of those who could afford this kind of exclusive education.[45] By the turn of the century a whole new generation of public schools had become established and were turning out alumni destined for the higher professions, including the public service. Improvements in transport, together with crowded urban conditions, led to the development of specifically lower middle-class suburbs. Socially mixed areas were giving ground to more socially stratified housing zones: first division clerks walked to work from Pimlico, or came in by omnibus from Kensington, while poorer clerks commuted by underground from Holloway. At a lower level there was a self-conscious and political identification of interests among labour as a whole. Among voters, the drift of lower middle-class Liberals away from their erstwhile working-class political allies and towards 'villa Toryism' is seen as an example of the end of cohesive high Victorian Liberalism, once constructed as community politics but by the end of the nineteenth century beginning to fragment and contributing towards the emergence of class politics.[46]

The professional nature of the inspectors

The word 'professional' also had a more specific meaning than that referred to above: it also meant 'trained' or 'expert'. Government inspectors were professional men, not only in the wider sense of being roughly equated with higher civil servants in terms of the service they gave to the community, their standing in society and their salary levels, but also in the narrower sense of having a specific expertise which allied them, not with generalist first division officials, but with other experts in similar fields. Their expertise had been acquired either through previous training (as with the inspectors of explosives), or through previous relevant working experience (as with the inspectors of constabulary who had been chief constables), or simply through their apprenticeship within the inspectorate (as with the factory inspectors). The civil service recognized the need for this rather different type of official in two important rulings: section four of the 1859 superannuation act allowed specialist civil servants to add to their years of service for the purpose of computing pensions; and clause seven of the 1870 order in council exempted them from examination where the Civil Service Commission deemed that this was fit. None of the Home Office inspectors in 1914 had been recruited through open competitive examinations. The factory, mines, and reformatory and industrial schools inspectors were nominated before undergoing a competitive examination conducted by the Civil Service Commission. All the others were nominated by the secretary of state and appointed without examination.[47]

Certain basic activities were common to all inspectors: on-the-ground examination of the premises and people covered by the legislation under which they were appointed; compilation of regular reports, based on their statistical data; and correspondence, on behalf of the Home Office, not only with those whose work and premises they were inspecting but also other interested parties. These activities gave them a much more direct relationship with the public than that of officials who worked in the central secretariat. Their faces were known; their official reports were signed and published; their opinions canvassed and given. However much their expressed views represented the official departmental view, the very fact that theirs was more personally given and not merely presented in an anonymous letter, tied the inspector himself to that view. This exposure to the public meant that the inspectors sometimes found it more difficult than their comparatively secluded generalist counterparts to adhere to the code of conduct which was developing for all civil servants.

Inspectors too were officially bound by conventions regarding professional secrecy although these did not necessarily refer to the interests of national security. Factory inspectors might gain industrial information which could be of use to industrial competitors: they were instructed to 'appreciate the confidential character of the work' and 'not to prejudice any private interests by disclosing in any unofficial communication...matters which become known...in the course of...inspection, such as the extent of the works, the number of people employed from time to time, the nature of the work carried on, the sort of machinery used, etc'.[48]

Secrecy, in the broader sense of loyalty to the department, was expected by senior officials and ministers from a fairly early date although this obligation was not always met. During the period of open warfare between the two factory inspectors, Redgrave and Baker, in the 1860s, Redgrave at one point informed an MP, Edward Baines, of a state of disorganization and chaos in the factory department. This embarrassing incident led the secretary of state, Bruce, to deliver Redgrave a severe reprimand, emphasizing that such behaviour was 'detrimental to the public service'.[49] A striking example of the head of a Home Office sub-department being considered openly disloyal to his department concerns not an inspector but the commissioner of metropolitan police, Warren. The actual occasion for Warren's resignation arose from his publication in *Murray's Magazine* of November 1888 of an article entitled 'The Police of the Metropolis', in which he openly criticized successive governments for not having the courage to take a stand against a small but vociferous minority of the population and for having given way before 'tumultuous proceedings'. During the course of embarrassing scenes in the House of Commons, Matthews mentioned a Home Office rule, embodied in a minute of May 1879, which echoed the Treasury Minute of 1875:[50]

The Secretary of State having had his attention called to the question of allowing private publication, by officers attached to the Department, of books on matters relating to the Department, is of opinion that the practice may lead to embarrassment, and should in future be discontinued. He desires, therefore, that it should be considered a Rule of the Home Department, that no officer should publish any work relating to the Department, unless the sanction of the Secretary of State has been previously obtained for the purpose.[51]

It was Warren's refusal to agree that his department was a sub-department of the Home Office (and therefore that he was bound by this ruling) that led to his resignation.[52] Later in our period – possibly because a more bureaucratic generation of officials had emerged – there appear to have been fewer examples of such indiscretions. But rules continued to be elaborated: in 1900, for example, the chief inspector of factories proposed that the preparation and reading of a paper by an inspector before a public body was to be considered tantamount to its publication in the press and therefore to require Home Office sanction.[53]

The ideal that officials should have no personal involvement – either financial or any other – in the management of enterprises or institutions which they were inspecting led to restrictions on non-official activities. Mines inspectors could not simultaneously be practising land agents, mining engineers, managers or viewers; in 1893 the new factory inspectors' assistants were prohibited from accepting any duties, such as rent collecting, which might give them an indirect interest in the places they inspected. Inspectors were discouraged from promoting, however inadvertently, the interests of other private firms: factory inspectors were circularized that they were to collect information as to the best means of fencing machinery, but were to avoid 'writing letters recommending inventions or contrivances which could be used for advertisement'.[54] Non-involvement was particularly important in the case of inspectors of factories and mines where conflicting interests of employers and employees might be involved. A new mines inspector was told: 'he will be specially careful to conduct himself with strict impartiality in all matters, and where an opportunity offers for him to assist in promoting good feeling and understanding between employers and employed, he will take advantage of it'.[55]

Nevertheless, this ideal of impartiality may, at times, have been difficult to attain. The majority of mines inspectors had had previous experience as managers, assistant colliery managers or viewers and may unwittingly have sympathized with management rather than with the miners – about the desirable extent of government inspection, for example.[56] There were two inspectorates in particular where the inspectors were closer to those they were inspecting than to their official colleagues: the anatomy and cruelty to animals inspectorates. One inspector under the cruelty to animals act, Dr Thane, was professor of anatomy at University College, London, and was almost certainly a close colleague of the doctors who worked in the physiological laboratory (in the same building as his own room) which was licensed by the Home Office, through him, to practise vivisection.[57] There is nothing to show that Dr Thane was not utterly scrupulous; but one wonders whether an inspector in such a position might possibly – again, even unwittingly – have overlooked some small infringement of the act in the interests of his own profession.

In 1914 an interesting case, involving the ideal of official detachment, arose in connection with a prison inspector. Dr Mary Gordon, the first woman inspector in this field, was a suffragette sympathizer. That year the assistant commissioner of the criminal investigation department forwarded to the Home Office a collection of letters which the police had found during a raid. These not only revealed that Dr Gordon's connection with one of the leaders of the movement, Mrs Pethwick-Lawrence, was very close and that she was contributing funds to the cause, but also that she was sailing very close to the wind in trying to help suffragette prisoners through her official position. 'Don't be afraid to ask me anything whatever for the prisoners. *All* prisoners are entitled to be kept well and warm and well nourished and in good spirits (!) as far as possible and that is my job', she had written.[58] Troup's reaction to this 'astonishing series of letters', which 'might well justify her dismissal', was that she should be asked formally to dissociate herself from the objects of the movement and be debarred from visiting suffragette prisoners. This Dr Gordon craftily refrained from doing; yet the Home Office was persuaded by Ruggles-Brise to accept her rather 'disingenuous and unsatisfactory' explanation of events and to keep her on as inspector, partly because by that time all suffragette prisoners had been released.[59]

In 1914 pay and status of the most senior inspectors was roughly comparable to that of senior departmental officials.[60] The chief inspectors of mines and of factories earned salaries equivalent to an assistant under-secretary though not to the permanent under-secretary. Below this level, considering the stage which they had reached in their careers, the inspectors did comparatively less well. The deputy chief inspector of mines earned less than the assistant under-secretaries, and the deputy chief inspector of factories earned barely more than the senior clerks. The range of salaries of the ordinary factory inspectors and the junior mines inspectors (roughly their equivalent), who would remain in those classes for many years, was similar to that of a junior clerk. In the other inspectorates salaries of the inspectors were comparable to those of senior clerks. (The chief inspector of reformatory and industrial schools earned slightly more but not as much as an assistant secretary.) The inspectors' services too were recognized, towards the end of the period, through the award of honours. The later chief inspectors of mines and of factories tended to receive knighthoods: C. Le Neve Foster (mines) in 1903, Redmayne in 1914 and Whitelegge in 1911. Other inspectorates did less well although there was generally a sprinkling of CBs and ISOs among worthy inspectors.

The first professional women in the Home Office were inspectors. This was a direct result of the fact that the inspectors were in greater contact with the outside world than the higher officials, imprisoned behind their Whitehall desks. The original women factory inspectors were an immediate success and more were soon recruited. By 1914 there were twenty-one women factory inspectors, one woman prison inspector (who also acted as an assistant inspector under both the inebriate acts and the reformatory and industrial schools acts) and a woman reformatory and industrial schools inspector. The factory inspectors included former secretaries to the royal commission on labour, private secretaries and sanitary inspectors. The prison inspector, Dr Gordon, had trained and qualified as a doctor in Edinburgh and Glasgow. There was a certain amount of friction from time to time between the chief inspector of factories and some of the women inspectors, such as Adelaide Anderson, Mary Paterson, Rose Squire and Hilda Martindale, about the functioning of their branch of the inspectorate.[61] Dr Gordon presented the Home Office with various problems.[62] But such altercations demonstrated the tenacity of these pioneers whose zeal is reminiscent of the early, mid-nineteenth-century inspectors. Spurred on, not cowed, by the attitude of many of their male colleagues – whose suspicion was partly reflected in the inferior salaries awarded to the women[63] – they broke new ground for women in government service. Their breakthrough into the ranks of the first division did not occur until 1921, when Rose Squire became a principal. But Troup and his peers were already adjusting to the idea of professional women working within departments under the Home Office.

The dominance of a generalist élite
Troup, Byrne and Delevigne were among the first of successive generations, throughout the civil service, to exhibit those characteristics

which the liberal reformers of the mid-nineteenth century had sought to promote among higher officials. Selected from a group of highly intelligent young men, educated in liberal arts subjects at the best universities, they were well equipped, once they had acquired administrative training within the service, to perform their most important task of advising on the formulation and execution of policy. Their Oxford tutorials, where 'the effort is submitted to a ferreting, worrying, persistent examination, accompanied by suggestions to the student, recommendations of further or alternative reading, the indication of alternative solutions or points of view', enabled them to present their political chiefs with 'the sharply focused white light' of concise recommendations. For an official's effectiveness 'depends not on what he knows but on how he can handle his knowledge to solve a problem'.[64] They were incorruptible: they had been recruited without patronage, on their intellectual merit; salaries and pensions were good so that they were financially secure. Imbued with the civil service ethic of loyally serving any politician in charge of their department, they viewed issues with impartiality. They had a strong sense of public duty – inculcated in many cases from public school days – and were admirably conscientious and willing to subordinate personal interests to those of the service. This sense of moral purpose derived from their seeking rewards less from great financial gain and obvious power than from the stimulus of constant intellectual exertion, the involvement in matters of state, and the security of a financially comfortable life together with a comparatively high social standing. Above all, their education and the developing traditions of the service gave them liberal, tolerant minds which did credit to the reformers and educationalists – followers of Bentham and J. S. Mill – who had devised the new system of public administration which selected these officials. They led a civil service which was admired from abroad,[65] which – at least in its upper ranks – had self-confidence and therefore high morale, and which was highly effective.

In many ways the second division too had proved a success. This completely new large class of officials, headed by men with managerial talent, formed the bulk and backbone of the civil service. By running and staffing the back-up departments, such as registry and finance branches, it allowed the first division to spend time on more intellectually exacting tasks. As the third tier, the abstractor class of the service, grew, the second division itself was relieved of purely mechanical work and found a role performing duties which required knowledge, experience, intelligence, care and sometimes organizing ability.

Yet the reformed civil service contained inherent problems which Trevelyan, for all his insight into administrative requirements, could not have foreseen. His ideal was to be challenged by criticism which derived from the rapidly changing nature of society in the decades following the second reform act of 1867. The democratic idea that opportunities for advancement should be spread more evenly in society began to gain ground; and the dominance of the liberal arts in education was challenged, as science was given standing at institutions such as Imperial College, London, and at the new provincial universities. Admirable leaders of a parliamentary bureaucracy though they were, higher civil servants from Troup's generation onwards have been criticized for being cautious, negative, conservative, narrow-minded and lacking drive. Some of these charges arose almost inevitably from the nature of the work. Often the detached official must produce the lowest common denominator, the policy which is most acceptable to the largest number of people. But a more serious basis for such criticism was that these men were a narrowly based élite, a small unrepresentative group which was playing an important role in a society where the principle of democratic representation had been recognized as essential.

Our sample of Home Office officials from Troup onwards, with their predominantly public school, Oxford and Cambridge, middle-class backgrounds, was more or less typical of the first division as a whole at least until the second world war.[66] Between the wars critics began to wonder whether the recruitment of higher civil servants from such a narrow stratum of society made them unaware of a wide spectrum of social requirements.[67] Was official detachment such a desirable ideal after all?

If their [civil servants'] composition included the memory of misery, hunger, squalor, bureaucratic oppression, and economic insecurity, perhaps a quality would be added to their work in the highest situations which could not fail to impress the minister at a loss for a policy or argument.[68]

This criticism of the higher civil service is, of course, an indictment of the educational system – and, *au fond*, of the English class system – which gave an automatic advantage in the civil service examinations to candidates from Oxford and Cambridge and therefore from good schools. It is possible that had more higher civil servants originated from less secure backgrounds they would have been more of a force for urging faster application of social benefits such as workmen's compensation or unemployment pay. But the system certainly was capable of throwing up officials imbued with a sense of urgency about social reform as various memoirs and recent studies of the period show.[69] Also, the argument against the élite system presupposes that, having risen to the security and comfort of the higher civil service, men of relatively humble origin would have had a particular sympathy towards the problems of the social strata from which they came; and study of second division attitudes does not necessarily imply that this would have been the case.

Criticism of the narrow social background of first division officials was highlighted by the discontent of the second division. An American observer of the British civil service in 1914 found the second division's frustration the most disconcerting feature of an otherwise admirable institution. He quoted a professor of the London School of Economics who had told the Macdonnell Commission that he had seen so many capable second division men that he doubted 'whether the present chasm between the two divisions is expedient'.[70] Discontent among the second division, or executive class (as it became), was a continuing problem and change was slow. To the Tomlin Commission of 1929-31 a senior official portrayed a situation which remarkably resembled the pre-war decade: 'The different classes are treated as "castes", determined by a man's entrance examination, and special promotion into the upper caste is very rare.'[71] At that time the Home Office permanent under-secretary, Sir John Anderson, took an enlightened view about this, evidently encouraging the principle that wherever possible promotion to assistant principal level from within the department was desirable.[72] But, in fact, the percentage of promoted executive-class men in the Home Office administrative class (as the first division became) was then only 2 per cent higher than it had been in 1914.

In assessing the problem of the second division one must weigh the disadvantage of having a large group of discontented employees in a service headed by a narrow élite against the danger of that able élite being unduly diluted by men who might not be capable of filling senior posts. Clearly serious discontent in a class which formed the bulk of the service was undesirable; and governments recognized this by appointing the Ridley and Macdonnell Commissions partly to investigate the problem. But maintaining excellence in the higher reaches of the civil service was important, and recent researches have indicated that promoted men have not been as capable as graduate entrants at performing the higher tasks of administration.[73] Anderson was probably correct in 1929 in his statement that 'a typical administrative class examination man and a typical promoted man . . . are not absolutely equivalent', and that the important thing was for each department to assess the correct balance of the two types for its own particular work.[74]

Some of the earlier quoted criticisms of the narrowness of higher officials and of their lack of drive arose from the fact that the large majority were recruited in their early twenties, immediately following graduation. This gave rise to the danger that years of similar work in the same department and the lack of stimulus from another type of work or discipline, combined with long periods of intense overwork, would lead to even erstwhile brilliant officials becoming 'played out' in their forties and fifties and failing to realize their early promise. Sir George Murray, ex-permanent secretary of the Treasury, hinted at this to the Macdonnell Commission; and later critics were to make the same point.[75] Another worry was that the entry of these men at such an early age into a rather closed world meant that there was too little opportunity for senior officials to bring to bear on their work the fresh eye of someone who had had personal experience of other aspects of professional life. In this sense Lushington's pre-office experience may have given him a wider vision than Troup's. The Northcote-Trevelyan plan had tried to guard against these dangers by encouraging inter-departmental movement. Although this did increase, especially after the first world war, it has never been the rule of the British civil service.

The new breed of open competition officials, with their lack of specialist training prior to entry to the civil service, had to rely for expertise on the specialists attached to it. This brings us to the peculiarly British phenomenon of the separation of the central corps of higher administrative officials from the specialist branches of advisers. It was a situation which may have led to friction even in the period of this study. On the whole relations between inspectors and first division officials at the Home Office were good. But the inspectors did not always acquiesce happily in the superior status of the arts-trained graduate over the scientifically-trained expert. Redmayne complained that

in the majority – the great majority – of instances, the technician in the Civil Service is subject to clerical control, and he has not, for instance, direct access to his Minister except upon rare occasions . . . all his plans, ideas, and activities in connection with matters coming within his purview are subject to filtration and interpretation of an officer or officers who must, in the nature of things, be less competent to appreciate their significance.[76]

He went on to lament the invariable practice of excluding 'officers of the expert class' from senior administrative posts. There was increasing frustration on the part of specialists at their not being able to provide another kind of experience to that of the generalist official in the highest ministerial counsels.

In 1929 the specialist staffs of the civil service pressed the Tomlin Commission for reform through their own trade union, the Institution for Professional Civil Servants. The commissioners offered them little of substance in their recommendations. They uttered pious exhortations towards 'effective and harmonious co-operation' between generalists and specialists. They agreed that the latter had the right to be consulted on matters regarding their fields. But specialists could not necessarily expect their advice to be taken: at the top of 'normal' administrative departments there should be one officer responsible for ministerial advice and the conduct of the department, and that was the permanent secretary. As far as promotion to such senior posts was concerned, while pointing out that two existing heads of department had, in fact, started their careers as specialists, they regarded it as 'inevitable that most high administrative posts should continue to be filled by officers with administrative rather than specialist experience'.[77]

Much more recently, in 1968, the Fulton Committee on the Civil Service considered these problems. It recommended denying the 'cult of the generalist' which meant that an official was often required to make decisions about subjects he did not fully understand. The non-specialist official should be taught the 'basic concepts and knowledge' which related to his particular sphere of administration. Reform should include giving specialists in the civil service more opportunity to contribute to policy-making and management. It should also include abolishing rigid 'classes' in the service since they caused 'frustration and resentment' and impeded 'the entry into wider management of those well fitted for it'. In addition, the committee recommended various features designed to counteract the lack of contact between civil servants and the rest of the community.[78]

To justify the dominance of generalists one can only return to the definition of their role. The statement that, while France 'made a science of the service of the State', England 'considered it a task for intelligent amateurs' was not altogether accurate.[79] 'Intelligent', yes; 'amateurs', no. For the higher civil servants of 1914 and their successors did possess a definite and highly developed skill which required an academically-trained mind and a certain pragmatic ability, and was sharpened through years of experience at their work. They alone could provide the link between politicians and executors in the carrying out of policy. They alone were able to apply a wider view to conflicting interests in the complex problems presented to them; to assess the weight of specialist advice against administrative feasibility, Treasury demands and political acceptability; and to present their considered advice – the 'departmental view' – to their minister in a form in which he could justify it to parliament. That was their profession which had grown out of the British political tradition.

The outcome of the Fulton recommendations is beyond the scope of this study. But it is relevant to note that this committee received no brief to alter the underlying relationship between ministers and civil servants which derives from the historical development of Britain's parliamentary democracy. As long as political theory dictates that sovereignty rests with an elected parliament to whom the prime minister and his cabinet colleagues are accountable, and that the legislative and executive arms of the constitution are basically separate, ministers must be guided by official advisers whose profession is to reconcile political, administrative and expert interests. Although the Fulton report spotlighted serious flaws in the modern civil service, recent developments have not yet denied the need for the generalist higher civil servant of which Troup and his generation were the prototype.

Appendix A

Home secretaries between 1848 and 1914	Date of assumption of office
Sir George Grey, Bart	6 July 1846
Spencer Horatio Walpole	27 February 1852
Henry John, Viscount Palmerston	28 December 1852
Sydney Herbert (Lord Herbert of Lea)	8 February 1855
Grey (again)	28 February 1855
Walpole (again)	26 February 1858
T.H.S. Sotheron-Estcourt	28 February 1859
Sir George Cornewall Lewis, Bart	18 June 1859
Grey (again)	23 July 1861
Walpole (again)	6 July 1866
Sir G. Gathorne-Hardy (Earl of Cranbrook)	17 May 1867
Henry Austin Bruce (Lord Aberdare)	9 December 1868
Robert Lowe (Viscount Sherbrooke)	9 August 1873
Sir Richard Assheton Cross (Viscount Cross)	21 February 1874
Sir William Vernon Harcourt	23 April 1880
Cross (again)	24 June 1885
H.C.E. Childers	6 February 1886
Henry Matthews (Viscount Llandaff)	3 August 1886
Herbert H. Asquith (Earl of Oxford and Asquith)	18 August 1892
Sir Matthew White Ridley, Bart (Viscount Ridley)	29 June 1895
Charles Thomson Ritchie (Lord Ritchie)	12 November 1900
Aretas Akers-Douglas (Viscount Chilston)	11 August 1902
Herbert John Gladstone (Viscount Gladstone)	11 December 1905
Winston Leonard Spencer Churchill (Sir Winston Churchill)	19 February 1910
Reginald McKenna	24 October 1911 (to 27 May 1915)

Source: F. Newsam, *The Home Office*, pp. 211–12.

Appendix B

Biographical information about Home Office permanent officials, 1848–1914

Key

f.	=	father
*	=	name appears in *Burke's Peerage and Baronetage*
educ.	=	educated
c.	=	circa
ret.	=	retired
d.	=	died
C of E	=	Church of England
matric.	=	matriculated
lit. hum.	=	literae humaniores
cl. mods	=	classical moderations
PUS	=	permanent under-secretary
ch. clk	=	chief clerk
pr.	=	principal
sr	=	senior
jr	=	junior
cl.	=	class
clk	=	clerk
asst	=	assistant
u.-sec.	=	under-secretary
suppl.	=	supplementary
Adm.	=	Admiralty
CO	=	Colonial Office
CS	=	civil service
HC	=	House of Commons
ICS	=	Indian Civil Service
Inl. Rev.	=	Inland Revenue
LGB	=	Local Government Board
PO	=	Post Office
T	=	Treasury
WO	=	War Office

N.B. Officials are listed within each category in order of precedence. Only the highest honour is noted. Records of major public schools and all universities have been extensively searched; therefore where these are not mentioned the likelihood is that they were not attended.

A major source about the careers of officials up to 1870 has been Sainty, *Home Office Officials 1782–1870*. Otherwise, for sources, refer to the bibliography below.

Permanent under-secretaries

Phillipps, Samuel March (1780–1862)
 f. landowner; educ. Charterhouse, Cambridge (maths, 8th wrangler); barrister; PUS 1827–48

Waddington, Horatio (1799–1867)
 f. C of E clergyman; educ. Charterhouse, Cambridge (maths, 18th wrangler); barrister; PUS 1848–67.

Liddell, Adolphus F. O., KCB (1818–85)
 *f. MP, cr. 1st Baron Ravensworth; educ. Eton, Oxford (cl. mods 3rd); barrister, QC; PUC 1867–85.

Lushington, Godfrey, GCMG (1832–1907)
 *f. MP, admiralty judge; educ. Rugby, Oxford (cl. mods 1st; maths 4th); barrister; HO 1869 legal adviser; asst. u.-sec. 1875; PUS 1885–95.

Digby, Kenelm E., GCB (1836–1916)
 *f. C of E clergyman; educ. Harrow, Oxford (lit. hum. 1st); barrister, academic; PUS 1895–1903.

Chalmers, Mackenzie Dalzell, KCB (1847–1927)
 f. C of E clergyman; educ. King's College, London, Oxford (cl. mods 2nd); ICS, barrister, parl. counsel to T; PUS 1903–8.

Troup, Charles Edward, KCVO (1857–1941)
 f. congregationalist minister; educ. Scottish parish school, Aberdeen (mental philosophy 1st), Oxford (BA); HO jr clk 1880; asst. u.-sec. 1903; PUS 1908–22.

Other senior officials

Pemberton, Edward Leigh, KCB (1823–1910)
 f. C of E clergyman; educ. Eton, Oxford (BA); barrister, MP; HO legal asst u.-sec. 1885; ret. same 1894.

Cunynghame, Henry H., KCB (1848–1935)
 *f. army officer (general); educ. Wellington, Cambridge (moral sciences 1st), Royal Military Academy; barrister; HO legal asst u.-sec. 1894; ret. same 1913.

Murdoch, Charles S., CB (1838–1900)
 f. chairman Colonial Land and Emigration Commission; HO 3rd cl. clk 1856; asst u.-sec. 1896; ret. same 1903

Blackwell, Ernley R. H., KCB (1868–1941)
 educ. Glenalmond; barrister; HO legal asst u.-sec. 1906; ret. same 1933.

Byrne, William P., KCVO (1859–1935)
 f. 'gentleman'; educ. St Cuthbert's College, Ushaw, London (3rd); CS (PO) 1881; HO jr clk 1884; asst u.-sec. 1908; chairman Board of Control 1913.

Delevigne, Malcolm, KCVO (1868–1950)
 f. wine merchant; educ. City of London School, Oxford (lit. hum. 1st); CS (LGB) 1892; HO jr clk 1892; asst u.-sec. 1913; ret. deputy u.-sec. 1932.

Clerks (establishment, upper division, first division)

Plasket, T. H.
 f. wine merchant; HO clk 1794; ret. ch. clk 1849.

Noble, R. H.
  HO clk 1797; ret. 1st cl. clk 1849.
Mills, F. R.
  f. C of E clergyman; HO clk 1798; ret. librarian 1849.
Walpole, F.
  HO clk 1811; ret. 1st cl. clk 1849.
Currie, F. J. G.
  f. MP (from banking family); HO clk 1817; ret. 1st cl. clk 1852.
Dawson, R. S.
  HO clk 1819; ret. 1st cl. clk 1850.
Knyvett, H. J.
  f. chief paymaster, Isle of Wight; HO clk 1820; ret. ch. clk 1865.
Fitzgerald, C. R.
  f. naval officer (vice-admiral); HO 3rd cl. clk 1823; ret. ch. clk 1868.
Leslie, F. S. (1805–c.1881)
  f. landed gentleman; educ. Trinity Coll., Dublin (BA); HO 3rd cl. clk
  1827; ret. ch. clk 1876.
Redgrave, S.
  f. manufacturer; educ. 'night school'; HO suppl. clk 1818; asst keeper of
  criminal register 1828; ret. keeper of criminal register 1860.
Streatfield, F. (1811–83)
  f. landed gentleman; HO 3rd cl. clk 1828; ret. 1st cl. clk 1876.
Erskine, C. (1813–c.1886)
  HO 3rd cl. clk 1834; ret. ch. clk 1885.
Kitching, J. F.
  HO clk for aliens business 1836; ret. librarian and registrar 1865.
Dillon, A. E. D. (1812–92)
  *f 13th Viscount Dillon; educ. Oxford (BA); HO 3rd cl. clk 1840; ret. 1st
  cl. clk 1869.
Maling, H.
  HO 3rd cl. clk 1841; ret. 2nd cl. clk 1854.
Joseph, A. G. (became Uttermare 1874) (b. 1821)
  HO suppl. clk 1839; asst keeper of criminal register 1845; ret. 2nd cl. clk
  1876.
Everest, G., CB (1805–85)
  Public service (convict hulk establishment) 1828; HO asst clk for criminal
  business 1845; ret. clk for criminal business 1876.
Gilly, F. D. (1831–c. 1881)
  f. canon Durham cathedral; educ. Eton; HO 3rd cl. clk 1847; ret. 2nd cl.
  clk 1871.
Arbuthnot, R. C. (1830–91)
  f. sr T official; public service (T) 1847; HO 3rd cl. clk 1849; ret. 2nd cl. clk
  1871.
Maconochie, A. (c. 1826–84)
  f. governor Birmingham gaol; HO suppl. clk 1848; 3rd cl. clk 1849; d. in
  office 1884 pr. clk.
Noyes, T. H. (b. 1827)
  f. barrister; educ. Rugby, Oxford (lit. hum. 3rd); HO 3rd cl. clk 1850; ret.
  2nd cl. clk 1861.

Sanders, H. W. (1806–77)
   Public service (office of keeper of signet and privy seal) 1825; HO clk for signet business 1851; ret. same 1876.
O'Grady, P. S. (1835–77)
   *f. 2nd Viscount Guillamore; HO (?) 3rd cl. clk 1852; ret. (?) 1856.
Perceval, J. S. (1832–63)
   *f. MP (ex-HO parliamentary u.-sec); educ. Harrow; HO (?) 3rd cl. clk 1852; ret. (?) 2nd cl. clk 1856.
Knyvett, C. J., KCB (1833–1908)
   f. ex-army officer, banker; educ. Cambridge (matric. only); HO 3rd cl. clk 1852; ret. pr. clk 1898.
Hobhouse, E. A. S. (1833–1908)
   *f. private sec. to brother (later Lord Broughton); public service (Ordnance Office) c. 1850; HO 3rd cl. clk 1854; ret. sr clk 1885.
Murdoch, C. S.
   See above, 'Other senior officials'.
Campbell, C. G. (1832–88)
   f. naval officer (admiral); educ. Cheltenham; HO 3rd cl. clk 1856; ret. pr. clk 1886.
Wharton, R. (1835–1908)
   f. barrister; educ. Eton, Cambridge (BA); HO 3rd cl. clk 1860; ret. 2nd cl. clk 1876.
Stapleton, E. J. (1839–96)
   f. commissioner of customs; educ. Oxford (matric. only); HO 3rd cl. clk 1861; d. in office pr. clk 1896.
M'Clintock, F. R. (b. 1842)
   f. country gentleman; educ. Trinity Coll., Dublin (BA); HO 3rd cl. clk 1865; ret. sr. clk 1894.
Deffell, C., ISO (1843–1908)
   f. merchant and company director; educ. Harrow; HO 3rd cl. clk 1865; ret. registrar of imperial service order (pr. clk) 1904.
Mitford, R. S., CB (1849–1931)
   f. auditor; educ. Merchant Taylors'; HO 3rd cl. clk 1868; prison commissioner 1882.
Orr, J. S. (1847–1922)
   f. C of E clergyman; educ. Radley, Oxford (BA); HO 3rd cl. clk 1868; ret. same 1870.
Fitzgerald, G. B. (b. 1849)
   f. C of E clergyman; educ. Oxford (matric. only); HO 3rd cl. clk 1868; ret. jr clk 1881.
Dunbar, W. C., CB (1844–1931)
   *f. 7th Baronet of Mochrum; HO 3rd cl. clk 1869; asst u.-sec. Scottish Office 1885; registrar-general England and Wales 1902.
Graves, A. P. (1846–1931)
   f. bishop of Limerick; educ. Windemere Coll. and Trinity Coll., Dublin (BA); HO 3rd cl. clk 1870; inspector of schools 1875.
Gernon, W. J. (c. 1847–90)
   f. high sheriff of Drogheda; CS (Chief Secretary's – Ireland – Office) 1865; HO 3rd cl. clk 1875; ret. same 1881.

Troup, C. E.
See above, 'Permanent under-secretaries'.

Ruggles-Brise, E., KCB (1857–1935)
f. country gentleman; educ. Eton, Oxford (lit. hum. 1st); HO jr clk 1881; prison commissioner 1891; chairman same 1895.

Johnson, E. (b. 1858)
f. dean of Wells; educ. Oxford (lit. hum. 3rd); CS (PO) 1881; HO jr clk 1882; ret. same 1895.

Byrne, W. P.
See above, 'Other senior officials'.

Simpson, H. B., CB (1861–1940)
f. 'gentleman'; educ. Winchester, Oxford (lit. hum. 1st); HO jr clk 1884; ret. asst sec. 1925.

Reynard, R. F., ISO (1862–1926)
f. country gentleman; educ. Uppingham, abroad; CS (Inl. Rev.) 1878; HO jr clk 1885; ret. asst pr. 1921.

Guillemard, L. N., GCMG (1862–1951)
f. C of E clergyman; educ. Charterhouse, Cambridge (classics 1st); HO jr clk 1886; transferred T 1888; Governor of Straits Settlements 1919.

Harman, E. G., CB (1862–1921)
f. C of E clergyman; educ. Uppingham, Cambridge (classics, aegrotat); CS (Adm.) 1886; HO jr clk 1886; transferred T 1889.

Legge, J. G. (1861–1940)
f. Oxford professor; educ. Oxford (lit. hum. 2nd); CS (Adm.) 1885; HO jr clk 1888; inspector of industrial and reformatory schools 1895.

Dryhurst, F. J., CB (1855–1931)
f. master builder; private sec. to MP; CS (PO) 1882; HO jr clk 1889; prison commissioner 1903.

Delevigne, M.
See above, 'Other senior officials'.

Aitken, G. A., MVO (1860–1917)
f. farm bailiff; educ. King's College School, London (no degree); CS (PO) 1883; HO jr clk 1893; d. in office, asst sec., 1917.

Eagleston, A. J., CVO (1870–1944)
f. ironmonger; educ. Oxford High School, Oxford (lit. hum. 1st); HO jr clk 1894; ret. registrar of the baronetage (asst sec.) 1932.

Pedder, J., KBE (1869–1956)
f. C of E clergyman; educ. Bath College, Oxford (lit. hum. 2nd); schoolmaster; CS (PRO, LGB) 1892; HO jr clk 1895; ret. pr. asst sec. 1932.

Lubbock, C. (1872–1956)
*f. banker; educ. Eton, Oxford (lit. hum. 1st); CS (WO) 1894; HO jr clk 1896; ret. same 1901.

Wheeler, W. (b. 1859)
Educ. Surrey County School; HO lower div. clk 1876; jr clk 1896; ret. acting sr clk 1908.

Waller, M. L., Kt Bach. (1875–1932)
Educ. Rugby, Oxford (lit. hum. 1st); HO jr clk 1897; prison commissioner 1910; chairman same 1921.

Elliott, F. L. D., CB (1874–1939)
 f. lieu.-gov. Bengal; educ. Harrow, Cambridge (classics 1st); HO jr clk 1898; asst commissioner metropolitan police 1914.

Bannatyne, R. R., Kt bach. (1875–1956)
 Educ. Rugby, Oxford (lit. hum. 1st); CS (Adm.) 1898; HO jr clk c. 1901; ret. asst u.-sec. 1939; re-joined HO 1940; transferred Ministry of National Insurance 1945.

Harris, S. W., KCB (1876–1962)
 f. merchant; educ. St Paul's, Oxford (lit. hum. 3rd); CS (PO) 1900; HO jr clk 1903; ret. asst u.-sec. c. 1946; Br. rep. to social cttee United Nations 1946.

Bettany, T. E. (b. 1874)
 Educ. Leeds Grammar School, Oxford (lit. hum. 3rd); CS (LGB) 1899; HO jr clk 1903; ret. sr clk 1914.

Dixon, A. L., Kt bach. (1881–1969)
 f. Wesleyan minister; educ. Kingswood School, Bath, Cambridge (maths, 9th wrangler); HO jr clk 1903; ret. asst u.-sec. 1946.

Maxwell, A., GCB (1880–1963)
 f. clergyman; educ. Plymouth College, Oxford (lit. hum. 1st); CS (Estate Duty Office) 1903; (Inl. Rev.) 1904; HO jr clk 1904; chairman Prison Commission 1928–32; HO PUS 1938–48.

Henderson, J. F. (b. 1881)
 Educ. Liverpool College, Oxford (lit. hum. 1st); HO jr clk 1904; ret. asst sec. c. 1940.

Moylan, J. F., KCB (1882–1967)
 f. barrister, educ. Bedford School, Cambridge (classics 1st); HO jr clk 1905; receiver metropolitan police 1919.

Chrystal, G. W., KCB (1880–1944)
 f. professor; educ. George Watson's College, Edinburgh, Oxford (lit. hum. 2nd); CS (Adm.) 1904; HO jr clk 1906; perm. sec. Ministry of Research and Information 1919.

Kennedy, W. T. (b 1882)
 Educ. Cambridge (history 1st); CS (WO) 1907; jr clk 1908; ret. same by 1914.

Butler, H. B., KCMG (1883–1951)
 f. fellow of Oxford college; educ. Eton, Oxford (lit. hum. 1st); CS (LGB) 1907; HO jr clk 1908; 1919 transferred Ministry of Labour; director International Labour Office 1932.

Balfour, H. R. C. (1882–1964)
 *f. lord justice-general, Scotland, 1st Baron Kinross; educ. Cheltenham, Oxford (lit. hum. 2nd); CS (HC clk 1907; HO jr clk 1908; invalided and ret. 1917.

Markbreiter, C. G., CBE (b. 1885)
 Educ. Dulwich College, Oxford (lit. hum. 1st); HO jr clk 1908; ret. asst sec. 1945.

Hestletine, M., CB (1886–1952)
 f. C of E clergyman; educ. Winchester, Oxford (lit. hum. 2nd); CS (Office of Works) 1909; HO jr clk 1910; pr. sec. National Health Insurance Commission 1912.

Locke, A., CBE
 HO 2nd div. clk 1890; jr clk 1911; ret. by 1935.
Scott, H. R., GCVO (1887–1969)
 f. craftsman; educ. Sexey's School, Bruton, Cambridge (history 2nd); HO
 jr clk 1911; chairman Prison Commission 1932; commissioner metro-
 politan police 1945.
Whiskard, G. G., KCB (1886–1957)
 f. bank manager, educ. St Paul's, Oxford (lit. hum. 1st); HO jr clk 1911;
 transferred CO 1924; perm. sec. Ministry of Town and Country Planning
 1943.
Robinson, C. D. C., CB (1887–1958)
 f. barrister; educ. Winchester, Oxford (lit. hum. 3rd); CS (HC clk) 1911;
 HO jr clk 1912; ret. asst u.-sec. 1947.
Finlay, E. N. A. (1889–1916)
 Educ. Eton, Oxford (lit. hum. 2nd); HO jr clk 1913; d. on active service.
Whitelegge, M. H. (b. 1889)
 Educ. Cambridge (classics 1st); CS (PO) 1912; HO jr clk 1913; ret. asst
 sec. 1949.
Parsons, A. L. R. (b. 1888)
 Educ. Oxford (English 2nd); CS (HC clk) 1912; HO jr clk 1913; T private
 sec. 1916.
Crapper, A. (b. 1873)
 HO boy clk 1891; 2nd div. clk 1892; jr clk 1913; ret. asst sec. c. 1937.
Holderness, E. W. E., Bart. CBE (1890–1968)
 *f. ICS, 2nd Bart; educ. Radley, Oxford (cl. mods 2nd); CS (LGB) 1912;
 HO jr clk 1913; ret. asst sec. c. 1952.
Johnson, F. C., CB (b. 1890)
 Educ. Cambridge (natural sciences 1st); HO jr clk 1913; receiver metro-
 politan police 1945.
Sheepshanks, W. (1890–1917)
 Educ. Oxford (lit. hum. 2nd); HO jr clk 1913; d. on active service.
Sandon, F. (b. 1891)
 Educ. Cambridge (maths, wrangler); HO jr clk 1913; left HO by 1920.
Buckland, G. R. A. (1889–1968)
 f. doctor; educ. Winchester, Oxford (maths 1st); CS (LGB) 1914; HO jr
 clk 1914; u.-sec. Ministry of Labour and National Insurance 1942.
Eady, C. W. G., GCMG (1890–1962)
 f. engineer; educ. Clifton, Cambridge (classics 2nd); CS (India Office)
 1913; HO jr clk 1914; Ministry of Labour pr. clk 1919; HO dep. u.-sec.
 1938; jt 2nd sec. T 1942.

Appendix C

The division of work in the Home Office from November 1913
Abbreviations: as = assistant secretary; sc = senior clerk; jc = junior clerk.

Division A
Staff: 1 assistant secretary; 2 senior clerks (one junior 'acting' as senior); 2 junior clerks

Responsibilities: factories, workshops, etc.; mines and quarries; workmen's compensation; truck; shops; other industrial questions.

Division B
Staff: 1 assistant secretary; 1 senior clerk; 3 junior clerks.

Responsibilities: licensing; naturalization and nationality; aliens; public bills not specifically relating to work of other divisions; private bills; provisional orders; bye-laws.

Division C
Staff: 1 assistant secretary; 1 senior clerk; 2 junior clerks.

Responsibilities: prerogative of mercy except *re* sentences of penal servitude and preventive detention; extradition; prisons; probation except *re* children under 16; criminal lunatics; police, county and borough; disturbances and riots; coroners; production of prisoners; commissions rogatoires; colonial prisoners' removal; salaries and fees of justices' clerks and clerks of the peace; other matters relating to administration of criminal justice.

Division D
Staff: 1 assistant secretary; 1 senior clerk; 1 junior clerk;*

Responsibilities: reformatory and industrial schools; children – protection, cruelty, probation, etc.; children's courts; employment of children; probation officers; white slave traffic; obscene publications; HO staff.

Division E
Staff: 1 assistant secretary; 1 senior clerk; 2 junior clerks.*

Responsibilities: prerogative of mercy *re* sentences of penal servitude and preventive detention, including petitions, licences, revocations and forfeiture of licence and administration of convicts' property; explosives and petroleum; burials and cremation; vivisection; anatomy; merchant shipping; fairs; honours and creations; medals; addresses; appointments (outside HO); title royal; civil petitions; commissions; exequaturs.

*A new junior clerk, about to be added to the staff, was to divide his time between divisions D and E.

Division F
Staff: 1 assistant secretary; 1 senior clerk (junior 'acting' as senior); 1 junior clerk

Responsibilities: metropolitan police; street traffic; metropolitan police courts; minor police questions not assigned elsewhere; asylums and lunatics; defectives; inebriates; entertainments; aeroplanes; wild birds; Channel Islands and Isle of Man; HO estimates and accounts; HO library.

Source: Table on HO45 11095/B27590/2.

Appendix D

Biographical information about Home Office inspectors and assistant inspectors, 1848–76 (to show qualifications for appointment)

Key (see also key, Appendix B)

ARSM   = Associate of the Royal School of Mines
Ed.   = Edinburgh
FGS   = Fellow of the Geological Society
FRAS   = Fellow of the Royal Astronomical Society
FRCP   = Fellow of the Royal College of Physicians
FRCS   = Fellow of the Royal College of Surgeons
FRS   = Fellow of the Royal Society
FZS   = Fellow of the Zoological Society
GBH   = General Board of Health
LRCS   = Licentiate of the Royal College of Surgeons
RA   = Royal Artillery
RMA   = Royal Military Academy

Note: The inspectorates are listed in the order relevant to the categories described in Chapter 6. Scottish inspectors are included where they reported to the Secretary of State.

In the case of the coal mines inspectors Tremenheere was a different type of inspector from the others (see Chapter 6, p. 128). Because of the large number of mines inspectors during this period and the dearth of biographical material about them, it has not been considered useful to list them all separately, even though in listing only three a slightly misleading impression may be given. These include the initial inspector and the two who at some time in their careers acted in the capacity of 'senior' inspector. Foster and T. F. Evans were metalliferous mines inspectors.

Name	Date and age on appointment	Father's occupation	Education	Previous and relevant professional experience, and qualifications	Rank or honour gained apropos of work as inspector
FACTORY					
HORNER, Leonard	1833 (48)	linen merchant	Ed. university	member 1833 Factory Commission; FRS, FGS	
HOWELL, Thomas	1833 (40)	judge	Westminster School Cambridge Lincoln's Inn	judge; commissioner W. India islands relief	
SAUNDERS, Robert	1833				
STUART, James	1836 (58)	minister, doctor	Ed. university legal training	assistant commissioner for Scotland, Factory Commission	
REDGRAVE, Alexander	1852 (34)	manufacturer	'night school'	HO clerk; factory sub-inspector	CB
KINCAID, John, Sir	1850 (63)		Polmont School	army officer (captain); prisons inspector	
BAKER, Robert	1858 (54)			doctor; factory sub-inspector	CB

Name	Date and age on appointment	Father's occupation	Education	Previous and relevant professional experience, and qualifications	Rank or honour gained apropos of work as inspector
MINES					
TREMENHEERE, Hugh S.	1842 (38)	naval officer	Winchester Oxford Inner Temple	commissioner inspecting education	CB
DICKINSON, Joseph	1850			mining engineer and viewer; FGS	
FOSTER, Clement Le Neve	1873 (32)			member geological survey, mining consultant; ARSM, FGS	KCB

Also: M. Dunn, C. Morton, H. Mackworth, T. Wynne, W. Alexander, R. Willis, W. Lancaster, J. J. Atkinson, J. Hedley, L. Brough, T. Evans, P. Higson, H. Longridge, R. Williams, J. P. Baker, R. Moore, T. E. Wales, A. Verner, G. W. Southern, F. N. Wardell, H. Hall, T. F. Evans (asst inspectors *not* included).

Name	Date and age on appointment	Father's occupation	Education	Previous and relevant professional experience, and qualifications	Rank or honour gained apropos of work as inspector
EXPLOSIVES					
MAJENDIE, Vivian D.	1875 (39)	army officer	Leamington College RMA	army officer (RA major); assistant superintendent, royal laboratory, Woolwich; (temporary) inspector of gunpowder works	KCB Col.
FORD, Arthur (assistant)	1875 (41)		Grosvenor College, Bath; Cambridge RMA	army officer (RA captain); assistant director artillery studies, RMA	CB Col.

Name	Date and age on appointment	Father's occupation	Education	Previous and relevant professional experience, and qualifications	Rank or honour gained apropos of work as inspector
PRISON					
WILLIAMS, William J.			grammar school	army officer (captain)	
HILL, Frederic	1835 (32)	headmaster	Hazelwood School, Birmingham	schoolmaster; political private secretary	
PERRY, John G.	1843 (41)		St Bartholomew's Hospital	surgeon, governor various London hospitals; FRCS, FRAS	
O'BRIEN, Donatus	1847			army officer (captain); political private secretary; secretary railway department, B of T	
KINCAID, John, Sir	1847 (60)	see under 'FACTORY'			
VOULES, Herbert, P.	1851 (47)		Eton	army officer (Bengal army); director of convict prisons	
BRISCOE, Henry	1869		Glasgow university	army doctor (RA)	
POWELL, T. F.	1869			army officer (captain); prison governor	

REFORMATORY AND INDUSTRIAL SCHOOLS

Name	Date and age on appointment	Father's occupation	Education	Previous and relevant professional experience, and qualifications	Rank or honour gained apropos of work as inspector
TURNER, Sydney	1857 (43)	solicitor and historian	Cambridge	clergymen (C of E); chaplain and master, Redhill Philanthropic Farm School (reformatory)	
ROGERS, Henry (assistant)	1868 (38)	clergyman	Tonbridge. Cambridge	secretary Redhill School (above); clerk to inspector of reformatory and industrial schools	
INGLIS, William	1875			army officer (major)	Col.
CONSTABULARY					
CARTWRIGHT, William	1856			army officer (lieutenant-general)	
WOODFORD, John	1856			army officer (lieutenant-colonel); chief constable, Lancs.	
WILLIS, Edward	1857 (52)	country gentleman	Charterhouse	army officer (captain); chief superintendent, Manchester police	
KINLOCH, John	1858			army officer (colonel)	

Name	Date and age on appointment	Father's occupation	Education	Previous and relevant professional experience, and qualifications	Rank or honour gained apropos of work as inspector
ELGEE, William P.	1867 or 8			army officer (captain)	
COBBE, C. A.	1869			army officer (colonel); chief constable West Riding, Yorkshire	
CARNEGIE, Charles	1872 (39)			army officer (lieutenant); MP (Liberal)	
ANATOMY					
SOMERVILLE, James C.	1832			LRCS	
CRAIGIE, David	1832 (39)		Ed. University	lecturer in clinical medicine, Ed. university; physician to Ed. Royal Infirmary; FRCP (Ed.), FRS (Ed.)	
BACOT, John	1842 (61)	'medic'		army doctor retired to private practice; member GBH; MRCS, FRCS, member Apothecaries Co.	
ALCOCK, Rutherford, Sir	1842 (33)		King's College, London	army doctor and medical adviser to army; FRCS	
WOOD, Andrew	1842 (32)		Ed. university	surgeon Heriot Trades and Merchant Maiden Hospitals, Ed.; FRCS (Ed.)	

Name	Date and age on appointment	Father's occupation	Education	Previous and relevant professional experience, and qualifications	Rank or honour gained apropos of work as inspector
CURSHAM, George	1844 (49)	clergyman	Repton Paris	physician Brompton Hospital, London; FRCP	
HAWKINS, Charles	1858 (46)	doctor	Charterhouse	surgeon St George's Hospital, London; FRCS	
OGLE, John W.	1872 (48)		Oxford	lecturer in anatomy and physician St George's Hospital, London; FRCP	

BURIAL GROUNDS

Name	Date and age on appointment	Father's occupation	Education	Previous and relevant professional experience, and qualifications	Rank or honour gained apropos of work as inspector
SUTHERLAND, John	1852 (44)		Ed. university	doctor in private practice; medical inspector GBH; LRCS (Ed.)	
GRAINGER, Richard D.	1853 (52)	surgeon	grammar school	professor of anatomy and physiology St Thomas's Hospital, London; medical inspector GBH; FRS, FRCS	
HOLLAND, Philip H.	1853			medical inspector GBH; FRCS	

CRUELTY TO ANIMALS

Name	Date and age on appointment	Father's occupation	Education	Previous and relevant professional experience, and qualifications	Rank or honour gained apropos of work as inspector
BUSK, George	1876 (69)	merchant		surgeon and professor of medicine; FRS, FRCS, FZS	

Name	Date and age on appointment	Father's occupation	Education	Previous and relevant professional experience, and qualifications	Rank or honour gained apropos of work as inspector
SALMON FISHERIES					
fFENNELL, William	1861 (62)			chairman River Suir Preservation Society; Irish fisheries inspector	
EDEN, Frederick	1861			Irish fisheries commissioner	
BUCKLAND, Francis T.	1867 (41)	Dean of Westminster	Winchester Oxford	assistant surgeon, army; editor (with fFennell) *Land and Water* (naturalists' journal)	
WALPOLE, Spencer	1867 (28)	politician	Eton	political private secretary; clerk WO	

Appendix E

Numbers and salaries of Home Office inspectors in 1856, 1876, and 1914

Inspectorate	1856 Total nos	1856 Maximum salary (of chief)	1876 Total nos	1876 Maximum salary (of chief)	1914 Total nos	1914 Maximum salary (of chief)
Factory	19	£1,000	55	£1,000	223	£1,200
Mines	('Commr' +) 12	(£1,000) £700	26	£1,000	92	£1,500
Explosives	–	–	2	£1,000	4	£1,000
Prison	4	£800	2	£750	7	£750
Constabulary	2	£700	4	£850	3	£850
Reformatory and industrial schools	–	–	2	£750	9	£1,000
Aliens	–	–	–	–	1	£700
Anatomy	3	£100*†	3	£100*	2	unknown
Burial grounds	2	3 gns per day*	1	3 gns per day*	–	–
Inebriates	–	–	–	–	1	£700
Cruelty to animals	–	–	1	£105*	4	£800
Fisheries	–	–	2	£700	–	–

† the metropolitan inspector received £200 in addition for the distribution of dead bodies

* part-time

Sources: *British Imperial Calendar*; annual civil service estimates; inspectors' annual reports

Bibliography

Sources are arranged under the following heads: A. Manuscript sources (i) records of government departments; (ii) private papers; B. Official papers (i) parliamentary papers; (ii) parliamentary proceedings; C. Newspapers and periodicals; D. Works of reference; E. Memoir and biographical material; F. Essays, articles and theses; G. Other works.

A. *Manuscript Sources*
(i) Records of government departments
The collection of official departmental records at the Public Record Office has been one of the prime sources. The following classes of papers were used and all appear in the Notes without the initial 'PRO' reference:

Home Office (HO):

HO OS	=	old series of registered papers (up to 1871)
HO 34	=	out-letters to government departments 1836–98
HO 45	=	registered papers 1839–1949
HO 82	=	accounts and estimates entry books 1752–1903
HO 85	=	burials entry books 1854–1921
HO 87	=	factories entry books 1836–1921
HO 95	=	mines entry books 1855–71
HO 137	=	reformatories entry books 1873–1909
HO 144	=	supplementary registered papers 1868–1947
HO 173	=	HO entry books 1899–1921

Files, ESG/60 8/11/1 and HO 253239, and HO Printed Memoranda, Vol. XVI, were seen at the Home Office.

Civil Service Commission (CSC):

CSC 2/7	=	correspondence with the HO about recruitment
CSC 4	=	reports, orders in council, minutes and circulars
CSC 10	=	examinations, tables of marks and results

Labour and employment departments (LAB):

LAB 14	=	safety, health and welfare, general, 1878–1969
LAB 15	=	H.M. factory inspectorate 1836–1959

Treasury (T):

T1	=	Treasury Board papers 1557–1920
T2	=	registers of papers 1777–1920
T3	=	skeleton registers 1783–1920
T13	=	out-letters to HO 1835–1920

In addition, one or two cabinet papers (CAB) were consulted.

Apart from the above abbreviations, the following will be found in the Notes:

S of S   = secretary of state
FO   = Foreign Office
CO   = Colonial Office
LGB   = Local Government Board

(ii) Private papers
Asquith Papers Papers of H.H. Asquith, Earl of Oxford and Asquith,
  Bodleian Library, Oxford
Chilston Papers Papers of Aretas Akers-Douglas, first Viscount Chilston,
  Kent Archives Office, County Hall, Maidstone, Kent
Cross Papers Papers of R. A. Cross, first Viscount Cross, British Library
Du Cane Papers Papers of Sir Edmund Du Cane, Bodleian Library,
  Oxford
Visc. Gladstone Papers Papers of H. J. Gladstone, first Viscount
  Gladstone, British Library
W. E. Gladstone Papers Papers of W. E. Gladstone, British Library
Harcourt Papers Papers of W. V. Harcourt, Bodleian Library, Oxford
Maconochie Diary Unpublished diary of Alexander Maconochie, 1864–5,
  in the private possession of Mr Kenneth Maconochie
Ruggles-Brise Papers Papers of Sir Evelyn Ruggles-Brise, in the private
  possession of Sir John Ruggles-Brise
Salisbury Papers Papers of the third Marquess of Salisbury, Hatfield
  House, in the private possession of the present Marquess of Salisbury

B. Official papers
(i) Parliamentary papers
The following are arranged in date order with the title of the paper
succeeded by the date, sessional number (in brackets) or command number
(in square brackets), volume number and, in the Notes, relevant page
number (printed pagination) or – if minutes of evidence – question number.
All are House of Commons papers unless House of Lords (HL) is indicated.
In the Notes those papers referred to more than once or twice are
abbreviated. These are indicated below with an asterisk.

A Supplementary Report on the Results of a Special Inquiry into the
  Practice of Interment in Towns by Edwin Chadwick, PP 1843 [509] XII.
**Report of the Select Committee on Miscellaneous Expenditure*, PP 1847–8
  (543) XVIII(1).
Report on a General Scheme for Extramural Sepultre, PP 1850 [1158] XXI.
**Report of the Select Committee on Official Salaries*, PP 1850 (611) XV.
**Report on the Organization of the Permanent Civil Service*, PP 1854 [1713]
  XXVII.
Papers Relating to the Reorganization of the Permanent Civil Service, PP
  1854–5 [1870] XX.
Judicial Statistics 1857, PP 1857–8 [2407] LVII.
**Report of the Select Committee on Civil Service Appointments*, PP 1860
  (440) IX.
Report of the Royal Commission appointed to Inquire into Salmon Fisheries
  (England and Wales), PP 1861 [2678] XXIII.
Parliamentary Return of all the Notices for the Discontinuance of Burials

within the Metropolis issued by the Secretary of State, etc., PP 1861 (143) LXI.

*Report of the Select Committee on Prison Discipline, PP (HL) 1863 (499) IX.

Correspondence with the Inspectors of Prisons on the Subject of Carrying into Effect the Provisions of the Prisons Act, 1865, PP 1866 (72) LVIII.

Report of the Select Committee on Mines, PP 1867 (496) XIII.

Report of the Select Committee on Salmon Fisheries, PP 1870 (368) VI.

*Report of the Select Committee on Civil Service Expenditure, PP 1873 (352) VII.

Reports on the Necessity for the Amendment of the Law relating to Gunpowder and other Explosives, etc., PP 1874 [C. 977] LII.

*First Report of the Civil Service Inquiry Commission, PP 1875 [C. 1113] XXIII.

*Report of the Royal Commission appointed to Inquire into the Working of the Factory and Workshop Acts, etc., PP 1876 [C. 1443] XXIX.

Report of the Royal Commission on the Practice of Subjecting Live Animals to Experiments for Scientific Purposes, PP 1876 [C. 1397] LXI.

Instructions of the Secretary of State for H.M. Inspectors under the Coal Mines Regulation Act, 1872, PP 1878 [C. 1987] LXI.

Return of the Names, Ages and previous Occupations or Professions of the Inspectors of Factories appointed since 1 January 1867, etc., PP 1880 (371) XL(2).

Third Report of the Official Statistics Committee, PP 1881 (39) XXX.

Lower Division Clerks (Copy of Correspondence between the Treasury and Colonial Office with regard to the Petition of certain Lower Division Clerks as to their position and prospects under the Order of Her Majesty in Council of 12 February 1876), PP 1884 (227) XLVII.

Report of the Royal Commission on Reformatory and Industrial Schools, PP 1884 [C. 3876] XLV.

Report of the Committee to Inquire and Report as to the Origin and Character of the Disturbances which took place in the Metropolis on Monday 8 February, etc., PP 1886 [C. 4665] XXXIV.

*Second Report of the Royal Commission on Civil Establishments, PP 1888 [C. 5545] XXVII.

Second Report of the House of Lords Select Committee on the Sweating System, PP 1888 (HL448) XXI.

Fifth Report of the Royal Commission on Labour (Part II), PP 1894 [C. 7421-1] XXXV (Summaries of Evidence).

First Annual General Report upon the Mineral Industry of the United Kingdom, etc., PP 1894 [C. 7953] XXII.

Report of the Departmental Committee on Factory Statistics, PP 1895 [C. 7608] XIX.

*Report of the Departmental Committee on Prisons, PP 1895 [C. 7702] LVI.

Judicial Statistics, England and Wales, 1893 with *Report of the Departmental Committee Appointed to Revise the Criminal Portion of the Judicial Statistics*, PP 1895 [C. 7725] CVIII.

Report of the Departmental Committee on Mining and Mineral Statistics, PP 1895 [C. 7953] XLII.

Report of the Departmental Committee on the Civil Judicial Statistics, PP 1896 [C. 8263] XCIV

*Report of the Departmental Committee on Reformatory and Industrial Schools, PP 1896 [C. 8204] XLV.

*Report of the Committee of Inquiry into the Case of Mr Adolph Beck, PP 1905 [Cd. 2315] LXII.

Report of the Departmental Committee on the Provision of Funds for Reformatory and Industrial Schools, PP 1906 [Cd. 3143] LIV.

(Factory Inspectors) *Return of the Names, Previous Occupations or Professions of (a) the Inspectors, (b) the Inspectors' Assistants and the Lady Inspectors who are now serving*, etc., PP 1907 (172) LXXVI.

Report of the Royal Commission on Vivisection, PP 1907 [Cd. 3326] XLI.

Papers Relating to the Case of George Edalji, PP 1907 [Cd. 3503] LXVII.

First Report of the Royal Commission on Mines, PP 1907 [Cd. 3548] XIV.

Minutes of Evidence before the Royal Commission on Mines (Vol. III), PP 1908 [Cd. 4349] XX.

Report of the Departmental Committee on Factory Accidents in Places under the Factory and Workshop Acts, PP 1911 [Cd. 5535] XXIII.

First Report of the Royal Commission on the Civil Service, PP 1912-13 [Cd. 6209] XV; *Minutes of Evidence* [Cd. 6210].

Second Report of the Royal Commission on the Civil Service, PP 1912-13 [Cd. 6534] XV; *Minutes of Evidence* [Cd. 6535].

Report of the Departmental Committee on Reformatory and Industrial Schools, PP 1913 [Cd. 6838] XXXIX.

Fourth Report of the Royal Commission on the Civil Service, PP 1914 [Cd. 7338] XVI; *Minutes of Evidence* [Cd. 7339] and [Cd. 7340].

Report of the Royal Commission on the Civil Service, PP 1930-1 [Cmd. 3909].X; *Minutes of Evidence* published separately by HMSO.

Report of the Committee on the Civil Service, 1966-68, Vol. I, PP 1967-8 Cmnd. 3638 XVIII.

General:
Annual Reports of the Civil Service Commission
Annual Estimates for the Civil Service
Annual Reports of the Inspectors (later Chief Inspector) of Factories (and Workshops)
Annual Reports of the Inspectors of Mines
Annual Reports of the Inspector(s) of Explosives
Annual Reports of the Inspectors of Prisons (after 1877 the Commissioners of Prisons)
Annual Reports of the Inspectors of Constabulary
Annual Reports of the Inspector of Reformatory and Industrial Schools

(ii) Parliamentary proceedings
Hansard, *Parliamentary Debates*, Third, Fourth and Fifth Series, 1848-1914. The series number is given first, then follows the volume number, column numbers and date of speech.

Acts of Parliament, 1848-1914.

C. Newspapers and periodicals
Civilian
Civil Service Gazette
Civil Service Times
Evening News
Illustrated London News
Journal of the Statistical Society of London
Lancet
London Gazette
Nineteenth Century
The Times

D. Works of reference
Annual Register
Army Lists
Boase, F., *Modern English Biography*
British Imperial Calendar and Civil Service List
Burke's Family Records (1897)
Burke's Landed Gentry
Burke's Peerage, Baronetage and Knightage
Catalogue of Fellows, Candidates etc. of the Royal College of Physicians
Crockford's Clerical Dictionary
Dictionary of National Biography
Dod, C. R., *The Parliamentary Pocket Companion*
Foster, Joseph, *Men at the Bar* (1885)
Haydn, Joseph, *Book of Dignities* (1894)
Kelly's Handbook to the Titled, Landed and Official Classes
Kelly's Handbook to the Upper Ten Thousand
List of Members of the Royal College of Surgeons
London Post Office Directory
Phillimore, W. P. W., and Fry, E. A., *Index to Changes of Name 1760–1901* (1905)
Registers of all well-known public schools of the period
Registers of all British universities (and Oxford and Cambridge colleges) of the period
Vincent, J., and Stenton, M., *McCalmont's Parliamentary Poll Book of all Elections 1832–1918* (1971)
Who's Who
Who Was Who

E. Memoir and biographical material
Abbott, A., and Campbell, C., *Life and Letters of Benjamin Jowett*, 2 vols (1897).
Aberdare, first Lord, *Letters of the Rt Hon. Henry Austin Bruce, GCB, Lord Aberdare of Duffryn*, 2 vols (privately printed, 1902).
Anderson, Sir Robert, *The Lighter Side of My Official Life* (1910).
Armytage, W. H. G., *A. J. Mundella 1825–97: The Liberal Background to the Labour Movement* (1951).
Asquith, H. H., Earl of Oxford and Asquith, *Fifty Years of Parliament*, 2 vols (1926).
Asquith, H. H., Earl of Oxford and Asquith, *Memories and Reflexions, 1852–1927*, 2 vols (1928).
Broadhurst, Henry, *Henry Broadhurst M.P.: The Story of his Life from a Stonemason's Bench to the Treasury Bench told by Himself* (1901).
Butler, Sir Harold B., *Confident Morning* (1950).
Childers, E. S. E., *The Life and Correspondence of the Rt Hon. Hugh C. H. Childers 1827–1896* (1901).
Cross, R. A., Viscount Cross, *A Political Memoir* (privately printed, 1903).
Faber, Geoffrey, *Jowett: A Portrait with a Background* (1957).
Finer, S. E., *The Life and Times of Sir Edwin Chadwick* (1952).
Gardiner, A. G., *The Life of Sir William Harcourt*, 2 vols (1923).
Graves, A. P., *To Return to all That* (1930).
Guillemard, Sir Laurence N., *Trivial Fond Records* (1937).
Hill, Constance (ed.), *Frederic Hill: an Autobiography of Fifty Years in Times of Reform* (1894).
Jenkins, Roy, *Asquith* (1964).

Kempe, Sir John Arrow, *Reminiscences of an old Civil Servant 1846–1927* (1928).
Lambert, Royston, *Sir John Simon 1816–1904 and English Social Administration* (1963).
Leslie, Shane, 'Henry Matthews, Lord Llandaff', *Dublin Review*, 168 (January-June 1921), pp. 1–22.
Leslie, Shane, *Sir Evelyn Ruggles-Brise: A Memoir of the Founder of Borstal* (1938).
Liddell. Adolphus G. C., *Notes from the Life of an Ordinary Mortal* (1911).
Lyell, Katherine (ed.), *Memoir of Leonard Horner, F.R.S., F.G.S.* (1908).
Mallet, C. E., *Herbert Gladstone* (1932).
Martin, A. P., *Life and Letters of the Right Honourable Robert Lowe, Viscount Sherbrooke*, 2 vols (1893).
Martin, Bernice, 'Leonard Horner: A Portrait of an Inspector of Factories', *International Review of Social History*, 14 (1969), pp. 412–43.
Morley, John, *The Life of William Ewart Gladstone*, 3 vols (1905).
Redmayne, Sir R. S., *Men, Mines and Memories* (1942).
Samuel, Sir Herbert Louis, *Memoirs* (1945).
Scott, Sir Harold R., *Your Obedient Servant* (1959).
Trollope, Anthony, *An Autobiography, 1800–1875* (1883).
Ward, C. H. Dudley, and Spencer, C. B., *The Unconventional Civil Servant: Sir Henry H. Cunynghame* (1938).
Webb, R. K., 'A Whig Inspector', *Journal of Modern History*, 27 (December 1955), pp. 352–64.
West, Sir Algernon, *Contemporary Portraits* (1920).

F. Essays, articles and theses
Bailey, Victor, 'The Metropolitan Police, the Home Office and the threat of Outcast London', in Victor Bailey (ed.), *Policing and Punishment in Nineteenth-Century Britain* (1981).
Bartrip, P. W. J., 'Safety at Work: the Factory Inspectorate in the Fencing Controversy', Centre for Socio-Legal Studies, Wolfson College, Oxford, Working Paper No. 4, March 1979.
Bartrip, P. W. J., and Fenn, P. T., 'The Administration of Safety: the Enforcement Policy of the Early Factory Inspectorate, 1844–1865', *Public Administration*, 58 (1980), pp. 87–102.
Brebner, J. B., 'Laissez-faire and State Intervention in Nineteenth-Century Britain', *Journal of Economic History*, Supplement VIII (1949), pp. 59–73.
Brown, K. D., 'John Burns at the Local Government Board 1886–1909: a Reassessment', *Journal of Social Policy*, 6 (1977), pp. 157–70.
Clark, G. Kitson, 'Statesmen in Disguise: Reflexions on the History of the Neutrality of the Civil Service', *Historical Journal*, II (1959), pp. 19–39.
Compton, J. M., 'Open Competition and the Indian Civil Service 1854–1876', *English Historical Review*, 83 (1968), pp. 265–84.
Craig, M. E., 'Bureaucracy and Negativism: the Local Government Board 1886–1909', unpublished MA thesis, University of Edinburgh (1975).
Cromwell, Valerie, 'Interpretations of Nineteenth-Century Administration: an Analysis', *Victorian Studies*, IX (1966), pp. 245–55.
Crossick, Geoffrey, 'The Emergence of the Lower Middle Class in Britain', in G. Crossick (ed.), *The Lower Middle Class in Britain* (1977).
Davidson, R., and Lowe, R., 'Bureaucracy and Innovation in British Welfare Policy 1870–1945', in W. J. Mommsen (ed.), *The Emergence of the Welfare State in Great Britain and Germany 1850–1950* (1981).

Dwyer, F. J., 'The Rise of Richard Assheton Cross and his work at the Home Office', unpublished B Litt thesis, University of Oxford (1954).

Eade, Susan Margaret, 'The Reclaimers: A Study of the Reformatory Movement in England and Wales 1846-1893', unpublished PhD thesis, Australian National University (1975).

Hanham, H. J., 'The Sale of Honours in Late Victorian England', *Victorian Studies*, III (1960), pp. 277-89.

Harrison, Brian, 'State Intervention and Moral Reform in Nineteenth-Century England', in Patricia Harris (ed.), *Pressure from Without in Early Victorian England* (1974)

Hart, Jenifer, 'The County and Borough Police Act, 1856', *Public Administration*, 34 (1956), pp. 405-17.

Hart, Jenifer, 'Nineteenth-Century Social Reform: A Tory Interpretation of History', *Past and Present*. XXXI (1965), pp. 39-61.

Hughes, Edward, 'Sir Charles Trevelyan and Civil Service Reform', *English Historical Review*, 64 (1949), pp. 53-88 and 206-34.

Lewis, Brian, 'The Home Office, the Metropolitan Police and Civil Disorder 1886-1893', unpublished M Phil thesis, University of Leeds (1975).

MacDonagh, Oliver, 'The Nineteenth-Century Revolution in Government: a Reappraisal', *Historical Journal*, I (1958), pp. 51-67.

MacLeod, Roy, 'The Alkali Acts Administration, 1863-84: The Emergence of the Civil Scientist', *Victorian Studies*, IX (1965), pp. 85-112.

MacLeod, Roy, 'Government and Resource Conservation: the Salmon Acts Administration, 1860-1886', *Journal of British Studies*, 7 (1967-8), pp. 114-50.

MacLeod, Roy, 'The Edge of Hope: Social Policy and Chronic Alcoholism 1870-1900', *Journal of the History of Medicine and Allied Sciences*, XXII (1967), pp. 215-45.

Mayer, Arno J., 'The Lower Middle Class as a Historical Problem', *Journal of Modern History*, 47 (September 1975), pp. 409-36.

Morris, R. M., 'The Metropolitan Police Receiver in the XIXth Century', *The Police Journal*, XLVII (1974).

Parris, Henry, 'The Nineteenth-Century Revolution in Government: a Reappraisal Reappraised', *Historical Journal*, III (1960), pp. 17-37.

Parris, Henry, 'The Home Office and the Provincial Police in England and Wales: 1856-1870', *Public Law* (1961), pp. 230-55.

Parris, Henry, *Constitutional Bureaucracy: The Development of British Central Administration since the Eighteenth Century* (1969).

Pellew, J. H., 'The Home Office and the Explosives Act of 1875', *Victorian Studies*, XVIII (1974), pp. 175-94.

Pellew, J. H., 'Administrative Change in the Home Office: 1870-96', unpublished PhD thesis, University of London (1976).

Perkin, Harold, 'Individualism versus Collectivism in Nineteenth-Century Britain: a False Antithesis', *Journal of British Studies*, XVII (1977), pp. 105-18.

Roach, J. P. C., 'Victorian Universities and the National Intelligentsia', *Victorian Studies*, III (1959), pp. 131-50.

Sutherland, Gillian, 'Recent Trends in Administrative History', *Victorian Studies*, XIII (1970), pp. 408-11.

Tomlinson, M. Heather, ' "Not an Instrument of Punishment": Prison Diet in the mid-Nineteenth Century', *Journal of Consumer Studies and Home Economics*, 2 (1978), pp. 15-26.

Williamson, A., 'Some retarding factors on penal reform 1895-1914', unpublished MA thesis, University of Edinburgh (1976).

G. Other works

Anderson, Gregory, *Victorian Clerks* (1976).

Ashworth, W., *An Economic History of England, 1870-1939* (1960).

Barker, Sir Ernest, *The Development of the Public Services in Western Europe 1660-1930* (1944).

Blakeley, Brian L., *The Colonial Office 1868-1892* (1972).

Bowring, J. (ed.), *Constitutional Code* in *The Works of Jeremy Bentham* (1843).

Brown, R. G. S., *The Administrative Process in Britain* (1970).

Burn, W. L., *The Age of Equipoise: A Study of the Mid-Victorian Generation* (1964 pb. edn 1968).

Burnett, John (ed.), *Useful Toil* (1974).

Carr, Sir Cecil T., *Delegated Legislation* (1921).

Clark, G. Kitson, *The Making of Victorian England* (1962).

Clarke, P. F., *Lancashire and the New Liberalism* (1971).

Cohen, E. W., *The Growth of the British Civil Service 1780-1939* (1965).

Crook, J. M., and Port, M. H., *The History of the King's Works, vol. 6, 1782-1851* (1973).

Crossman, R. H. S., *The Diaries of a Cabinet Minister*, 3 vols (1964-70).

Dale, H. E., *The Higher Civil Service of Great Britain* (1941).

Dicey, A. V., *Lectures on the Relations Between Law and Public Opinion in England during the Nineteenth Century* (first pub. 1905; pb. E. C. S. Wade (ed.), 1962).

Dickens, Charles, *Little Dorrit* (1867-8).

Ensor, R. C. K., *England 1870-1914* (1936).

Finer, Herman, *The Theory and Practice of Modern Government* (1951).

French, Richard D., *Antivivisection and Medical Science in Victorian Society* (1975).

Halévy, Elie, *The Growth of Philosophic Radicalism* (first pub. 1928; pb. trans. Mary Morris, 1972).

Hanes, David G., *The First British Workman's Compensation Act 1897* (1968).

Harris, José, *Unemployment and Politics: A Study in English Social Policy 1886-1914* (1972).

Harris, José, *William Beveridge: a Biography* (1977).

Hobhouse, L. T., *Liberalism* (first pub. 1911, pb. 1964).

Humphries, B. V., *Clerical Unions in the Civil Service* (1958).

Jones, Ray, *The Nineteenth-Century Foreign Office: an Administrative History* (1971).

Kellner, P., and Crowther-Hunt, Lord, *The Civil Servants: An Inquiry into Britain's Ruling Class* (1980).

Kelsall, R. K., *Higher Civil Servants in Britain* (1955).

Lewis, Roy, and Maude, Angus, *Professional People* (1952).

Lewis, Roy, and Maude, Angus, *The English Middle Classes* (1953).

MacDonagh, Oliver, *A Pattern of Government Growth 1800-60: The Passenger Acts and their Enforcement* (1961).

MacDonagh, Oliver, *Early Victorian Government 1830-1870* (1977).

McDowell, R. B., *The Irish Administration 1801-1914* (1964).

Mack, E. C., *Public Schools and British Opinion, 1780-1860: an Examination of the Relationship between Contemporary Ideas and the Evolution of a British Institution* (1938).

MacLeod, Roy, *Treasury Control and Social Administration: A Study of Establishment Growth at the Local Government Board 1871-1905* (1968).

Mill, J. S., *Principles of Political Economy* (first pub. 1848; pb. Donald Winch (ed.), 1970).

Mitchell, Brian R., and Deane, Phyllis, *Abstract of British Historical Statistics* (1962).

Moses, Robert, *The Civil Service of Great Britain* (1914).

Nelson, R. A., *The Home Office 1782–1801* (1969).

Newsam, Sir Frank, *The Home Office* (New Whitehall Series, 1954).

Parris, Henry, *Constitutional Bureaucracy: The Development of British Central Administration since the Eighteenth Century* (1969).

Perkin, Harold, *The Origins of Modern English Society* 1780–1880 (1969).

Reader, W. J., *Professional Men: the Rise of the Professional Classes in Nineteenth-Century England* (1966).

Rhodes, Gerald, *Inspectorates in British Government: Law Enforcement and Standards of Efficiency* (1981).

Roach, John, *Public Examinations in England 1850–1900* (1971).

Roberts, David, *The Victorian Origins of the British Welfare State* (1960).

Roseveare, Henry, *The Treasury: the Evolution of a British Institution* (1969).

Routh, Guy, *Occupation and Pay in England 1906–60* (1965).

Sabine, G. H., *A History of Political Theory* (1937).

Sainty, J. C., *Home Office Officials 1782–1870* (Office-Holders in Modern Britain, V. 1975).

Salter, James Arthur, Lord, *Memoirs of a Public Servant* (1961).

Simon, Brian, *Studies in the History of Education 1780–1870* (1960).

Smith, Paul, *Disraelian Conservatism and Social Reform* (1967).

Strutt, Sir Austin, *The Home Office 1870–1896: the Modernization of an Office* (privately printed, 1961).

Sutherland, Gillian (ed.), *Studies in the Growth of Nineteenth-Century Government* (1972), in particular:
    Davidson, Roger, 'Llewellyn Smith, the Labour Department and government growth 1886–1909', pp. 227–62;
    Donajgrodzki, A. P., 'New Roles for Old: the Northcote-Trevelyan Report and the Clerks of the Home Office 1822–48', pp. 82–109.

Sutherland, Gillian, *Policy-making in Elementary Education 1870–1895* (1973).

Troup, Sir Edward, *The Home Office* (Whitehall Series, 1925).

Webb, S. and B., *English Prisons under Local Government* (1922).

Wright, Maurice, *Treasury Control of the Civil Service 1854–74* (1969).

Notes

For key abbreviations used in Notes, see Bibliography pp. 225-6.

Preface

1 R. A. Nelson, *The Home Office, 1782-1801* (1969).
2 A. P. Donajgrodzki, 'New roles for old: the Northcote-Trevelyan Report and the clerks of the Home Office 1822-48', in Gillian Sutherland (ed.), *Studies in the Growth of Nineteenth-Century Government* (1972), pp. 82-109.
3 J. C. Sainty, *Home Office Officials 1782-1870* (Office Holders in Modern Britain, V, 1975).
4 Austin Strutt, *The Home Office 1870-1896: the Modernization of an Office* (1961).
5 Edward Troup, *The Home Office* (Whitehall Series, 1925); Frank Newsam, *The Home Office* (New Whitehall Series, 1954).

Chapter 1

1 Troup, *The Home Office*, p. 19.
2 Much of this paragraph is derived from Sainty, *Home Office Officials 1782-1870*, pp. 3-5. The process of paying officials fixed salaries occurred in different government offices at different times; Emmeline W. Cohen, *The Growth of the British Civil Service 1780-1939* (1965), pp. 56 ff.
3 Herman Finer, *The Theory and Practice of Modern Government* (1951), p. 765.

Chapter 2

1 Sainty, *Home Office Officials 1782-1870* p. 12.
2 See list of home secretaries at Appendix A.
3 *Sel. Cttee on Misc. Expenditure*, 1847-8; *Mins of Ev.*, 2834.
4 *Sel. Cttee on Official Salaries*, 1850; *Mins of Ev.*, 2882.
5 Ibid., 2883.
6 Ibid., 2880.
7 *Sel. Cttee on Misc. Expenditure*, 1847-8; *Mins of Ev.*, 4136.
8 'Docketing' meant summarizing the contents of a letter on its jacket.
9 *Sel. Cttee on Misc. Expenditure*, 1847-8; *Mins of Ev.*, 2874.
10 Ibid., 3036.
11 A. J. Eagleston, 'The Secretary of State's Office under Elizabeth', HO45 18563/808993/1.
12 Donajgrodzki, 'New roles for old; the Northcote-Trevelyan Report and the clerks of the Home Office 1822-48', in Sutherland (ed.), *Studies in the Growth of Nineteenth-Century Government*, pp. 104-5.
13 *Sel. Cttee on Misc. Expenditure*, 1847-8; *Mins of Ev.*, 3033, 3035, 3041.
14 See above, p. 2.
15 *Sel. Cttee on Official Salaries*, 1850; *Mins of Ev.*, 2883.

16 *Sel. Cttee on Misc. Expenditure*, 1847–8; *Mins of Ev.*, 4158, 4172–9.
17 Ibid., 1136.
18 Maurice Wright, *Treasury Control of the Civil Service 1854–74* (1969), pp. 111, 194 ff.
19 Report of Committee of Inquiry into HO, 1848, HO45 9483/1782M/1. For a fuller account see Sainty, pp. 6–7.
20 Report of Committee of Inquiry into HO, 1848, and subsequent minutes and letters, HO45 9483/1782M/1, 2.
21 *Rep. on Organization of Perm. C. S.*, 1854.
22 W. J. Reader, *Professional Men: the Rise of the Professional Classes in Nineteenth-Century England* (1966), pp. 53–72.
23 E. C. Mack, *Public Schools and British Opinion, 1780–1860: an Examination of the Relationship between Contemporary Ideas and the Evolution of a British Institution* (1938), p. 323; John Roach, *Public Examinations in England 1850–1900* (1971), pp. 56–7.
24 J. M. Compton, 'Open Competition and the Indian Civil Service 1854–1876', *English Historical Review*, 83 (1968), p. 265.
25 *Rep. on Organization of Perm. C.S.*, 1854, p. 1.
26 Ibid., pp. 15–16.
27 Letter by Jowett accompanying *Rep. on Organization of Perm. C.S.*, 1854.
28 *Papers on the Reorganization of the C.S.*, PP 1854–5 [1870], XX, p. 76.
29 Ibid., p. 74.
30 Ibid., pp. 383–402.
31 For details see Edward Hughes, 'Sir Charles Trevelyan and Civil Service Reform', *English Historical Review*, 64 (1949), pp. 53–88, 206–34.
32 Order in council, 21 May 1855, see *1st Rep. of CSC*, PP 1856 [2083], XXII, pp. iii-iv.
33 Minute by CSC, 21 January 1865, CSC2/7.
34 HO to CSC, 28 April 1856, CSC2/7. Not all departments were as co-operative: the CSC found the FO and the Post Office difficult: Ray Jones, *The Nineteenth-Century Foreign Office: an Administrative History* (1971), p. 48; *5th Rep. of CSC*, PP 1860 [2631], XXIV, p. 132.
35 See tables maintained from 1863 by CSC (in reports) showing the numbers of competent and incompetent candidates for each vacancy.
36 Roach, *Public Examinations in England 1850–1900*, pp. 202–3.
37 *Sel. Cttee on C.S. Appointments*, PP 1860 (440), IX, *Mins of Ev.*, 3015.
38 Appendix B contains a list of HO established officials of the rank of third class or junior clerk and above, showing their backgrounds and careers.
39 A. P. Graves, *To Return to All That* (1930), p. 150.
40 Henry Roseveare, *The Treasury: the Evolution of a British Institution* (1969), pp. 172–3; Brian L. Blakeley, *The Colonial Office 1868–1892* (1972), p. 13.
41 Brian Simon, *Studies in the History of Education 1780–1870* (1960), pp. 294–7.
42 HO-T Report on the HO, 22 July 1856, T1 6258A/13006.
43 Grey's 'Instructions', 1856, T1 6258A/13006.
44 T to HO, 25 February 1860, T13/5.
45 For a fuller account see Wright, pp. 215–20.
46 HO-T correspondence, January–May 1860, T13/5 and T1 6258A/13006.

47 T to HO, 25 January 1866, T13/7.
48 HO to T, 26 January 1866, T1 6661B/19489.
49 HO to T, 10 March 1868, T1 6821A/17942; T to HO, 14 March 1868, T13/8.
50 There is a distinction between a Treasury Minute, which was a formal statement of Treasury policy, often circulated to other departments, and a Treasury minute which was merely a departmental comment on, say, an incoming letter.
51 Bruce to Gladstone, 19 October 1869, W. E. Gladstone Papers, Add. MSS, 44086, f. 44.
52 Geoffrey Faber, *Jowett: a Portrait with a Background* (1957), p. 404.
53 A. Abbott and L. Campbell, *Life and Letters of Benjamin Jowett* (1897), vol. 1, pp. 271-2.
54 L. N. Guillemard, *Trivial Fond Records* (1937), pp. 12-13.
55 Algernon West, *Contemporary Portraits* (1920), p. 150.
56 Charles Dickens, *Little Dorrit* (1867-8 edn), chapter X.
57 Robert Anderson, *The Lighter Side of My Official Life* (1910), p. 42.
58 West, *Contemporary Portraits*, p. 151.
59 T to HO, 23 December 1869, T13/8.
60 HO to T, 19 February 1870, T1 6971A/7615.
61 Lingen to Lowe, 20 November 1870, T1 7025A/22423, quoted Wright, p. 91.
62 *Sel. Cttee on C.S. Expenditure*, 1873, *Mins of Ev.*, 4306.
63 Memo by Maconochie, March 1875, HO45 9283/1782MB/4.
64 *Sel. Cttee on C.S. Expenditure*, 1873, *Mins of Ev.*, 4306; minute by Lingen, 10 March 1871, T1 7121B/18378.
65 HO to T, 5 September 1873, T1 7317/17728A.
66 T minute, 6 September 1873, T1 7317/17728A.
67 Report, 'HO Organization', 9 December 1870, HO45 9283/1783MA/4.
68 Ibid.
69 Wright, p. 140.
70 T Minute, 8 December 1869, T1 6971A/7615.
71 Report, 'HO Organization', 9 December 1870, HO45 9283/1782MA/4.
72 Ibid.
73 S of S's directive, December 1870, HO45 9483/1782M/15.
74 Ibid.
75 See below, p. 96 ff.
76 T to HO, 21 March 1871, T13/9.
77 Memo by Rutson, undated (1871), HO 45 9283/1782MA/7.
78 Anderson, *The Lighter Side of My Official Life*, p. 43.
79 Graves, *To Return to All That*, p. 150.
80 J. A. Kempe, *Reminiscences of an Old Civil Servant 1846-1927* (1928), p. 35.
81 Blakeley, *The Colonial Office 1868-1892*, p. 54.
82 See below, p. 73.
83 HO to T, January 1876, T1 7121B/18378.
84 T to HO, 21 March 1871, T13/9; HO to T, 25 August 1871, T1 7121B/18378.
85 Lushington to Cross, 13 October 1875, HO45 9892/B17626; T to HO, 24 March 1876, T13/12.
86 *1st Rep. of C.S. Inquiry Commission*, 1875.
87 Another part of the commissioners' scheme, the establishment of a clearly defined higher division, common to the whole civil service, was only put into effect in a few public offices.
88 See below, chapter 5.

89 HO to T, 15 March 1876, T1 75531B/19254.
90 From 1847 the HO had been situated with the Privy Council Office and Board of Trade about half way along Whitehall on the Horse Guards side. In 1875 it was moved to the other side of Downing Street, towards Parliament Square, where it shared offices with the FO and CO, J. M. Crook and M. H. Port, *The History of the King's Works, Vol. 6, 1782–1851* (1973), pp. 550–1.
91 HO to T, 14 June 1876, T1 7553B/19254.
92 T to HO, 24 June 1876, T13/12.
93 T to HO, 9 August 1876, T1 7553B/19254.
94 T to HO, 2 June 1876, T1 7553B/19254.
95 HO to T, 10 August 1876, and T minutes, T1 7553B/19254.
96 See tables pp. 6 and 23.
97 Treasury officials privately acknowledged different categories of department. The HO, with the Treasury itself, FO and CO, came within the prime category and this was reflected in its upper division salary scales; Wright, *Treasury Control of the Civil Service*, p. 234.
98 *Sel. Cttee on Official Salaries*, 1850, *Mins of Ev.*, 2873.

Chapter 3

1 Guillemard, *Trivial Fond Records*, p. 13.
2 This change of name was authorized by order in council, 15 August 1890.
3 See Appendix B.
4 *4th Rep. of R.C. on C.S.*, 1914, pp. 41–2.
5 Simon, *Studies in the History of Education* 1780–1870, pp. 298–9; in addition the wealth of rich colleges, which had a tradition of providing scholarships, was severely reduced by the effects of the agricultural depression, see J.P.C. Roach, 'Victorian Universities and the National Intelligentsia', *Victorian Studies*, 3 (1959), pp. 131–50.
6 G. Kitson Clark, *The Making of Victorian England* (1962), pp. 273–4; W. L. Burn, *The Age of Equipoise: a Study of the Mid-Victorian Generation* (pb. edn. 1968) p. 266.
7 *2nd Rep. of R.C. on C.S.*, 1912–13, *Mins of Ev.*, 5050.
8 In 1880 the salary scales of junior clerks or their equivalents were as follows: Treasury £250 × £20 – £600; HO £200 × £20 – £600; Post Office £150 × £10 – £250.
9 Reports of CSC, in particular CSC4/21–33 and 10/428; See Appendix B.
10 For the resentment by some departments of these departmental differences see *2nd Rep. of R.C. on Civil Establishments*, 1888, *Mins of Ev.* (Secretary of the Post Office), 17,942a; Roy MacLeod, *Treasury Control and Social Administration: A Study of Establishment Growth at the Local Government Board 1871–1905* (1968), pp. 14–16.
11 Samuel Ruggles-Brise to W. V. Harcourt, 26 May 1881; John Lubbock to Harcourt, 3 June 1881, Evelyn Ruggles-Brise papers.
12 Shane Leslie, *Sir Evelyn Ruggles-Brise: A Memoir of the Founder of Borstal* (1938), pp. 76–7.
13 3 Hansard 313, 1241–4 (19 April 1887).
14 *Evening News*, 13 March 1922.
15 Guillemard, pp. 13–14.
16 Leslie, *Sir Evelyn Ruggles-Brise: A Memoir of the Founder of Borstal*, p. 32.
17 A. W. L. Hemming, quoted Blakeley, *The Colonial Office 1868–1892*, p. 171.

18 Minute by Knyvett, 24 January 1885, HO45 9611/A7070B/1b.
19 *Rep. of Sel. Cttee on C.S. Expenditure*, 1873, *Mins of Ev.*, 4304.
20 Minute by Maconochie, 29 October 1878, HO45 9483/1782M/38.
21 Campbell to Lushington, 14 April 1881, HO45 9611/A7070/1A.
22 Erskine to Liddell, 25 June 1881, HO45 9611/A7070/1B.
23 Paul Smith, *Disraelian Conservatism and Social Reform* (1967), p. 202.
24 Erskine to Liddell, 25 June 1881, HO45 9611/A7070/1B.
25 Draft, Harcourt to T, 30 December 1881, HO45 9614/A10549/2.
26 *Rep. of Sel. Cttee on C.S. Expenditure*, 1873, *Mins of Ev.* (Liddell), 4304.
27 Memo by Troup, 19 January 1885, HO45 9611/A7070B/1.
28 Harcourt to Gladstone, 14 May 1882, W. E. Gladstone papers, Add. MSS 44197, f. 36.
29 Minutes by Deffell and Harcourt, 6 and 7 April 1885, HO45 9653/A39184/1a, 1.
30 In 1889 this work was transferred to the new Board of Agriculture.
31 The registry recorded 44,541 incoming papers for 1880, 43,236 for 1889 and 43,621 for 1891.
32 Memo by Troup and minute by Campbell, 19 and 20 January 1885, HO45 9611/A7070B/1, 1C.
33 Memo by Lushington, 9 February 1885, HO45 9648/A37252B/5C.
34 A. G. Gardiner, *The Life of Sir William Harcourt* (1923), Vol. 1, p. 392.
35 HO to T, 3 May 1890, T1 8522A/16825; the HO, however, did agree to the concession of lowering the ceiling of the junior clerks' salary scale from £600 to £500.
36 Minute by Knyvett, 24 January 1885, HO45 9611/A7070B/1b.
37 Minute by Troup, 14 August 1885, HO45 9611/A7070B/2a.
38 Minute by Lushington, 8 March 1886, HO45 9611/A7070B/2e.
39 *Second Rep. of R.C. on Civil Establishments*, 1888, *Mins of Ev.*, 12,078.
40 Guillemard, p. 19.
41 See below, chapters 6 and 7, for a detailed account of the development of the inspectorates.
42 Du Cane to Cross, 17 August 1877, HO45 9554/65747.
43 Minute by Maconochie, 15 November 1877, HO45 9554/65747/13.
44 Minute by Lushington, undated (1877), HO45 65747/13; the inspector of explosives – also unsuccessfully – tried to do the same thing.
45 *Dept. Cttee on Prisons*, 1895 pp. 41-2.
46 Leslie, pp. 86-7; Anderson, *The Lighter Side of My Official Life*, pp. 80-1.
47 Correspondence and papers by Du Cane, Liddell and Hornby, November 1878 to June 1881, Du Cane papers, C. 648, ff. 148-76, C. 649, ff. 7-15; *Dept. Cttee on Prisons*, 1895, p. 7.
48 Correspondence between Du Cane and HO, July 1880 to September 1888, Du Cane papers, C. 649, ff. 7-8, 86-91, 179-89.
49 Letters, Lushington to Du Cane and Du Cane (draft) to Lushington, Du Cane papers, October 1888, C. 649, ff. 80-91.
50 Draft, Du Cane to Matthews, February 1891, Du Cane papers, C. 650, ff. 6-9.
51 Draft, Du Cane to Harcourt, undated (1893), Du Cane papers, C. 650 ff. 44-7.
52 See, for example, the *Daily Chronicle*, 23, 25 and 29 January 1894, where Du Cane was held personally responsible for many flaws in the system.

53   *Dept. Cttee on Prisons*, 1895 *Mins of Ev.*, 11,397–8.
54   *Report of the Committee to Inquire and Report as to the Origin and Character of the Disturbances which took place in the Metropolis on Monday 8 February etc.*, PP 1886 [C. 4665] XXXIV.
55   *Report of the Committee etc. to Inquire into the Administration and Organization of the Metropolitan Police Force*, PP 1886 [C. 4894] XXIV; Brian Lewis, 'The Home Office, the Metropolitan Police and Civil Disorder 1886–1893', unpublished MPhil thesis, University of Leeds (1975), pp. 66–72.
56   R. M. Morris, 'The Metropolitan Police Receiver in the XIXth Century', *The Police Journal*, XLVII (1974), p. 65.
57   Minute by Lushington, 10 July 1887, HO144/208 A48043/1; papers on HO144/198 A46998.
58   Papers on HO144/203 A47600; HO144/190 A46472B; HO144/200 A47288; HO144/190 A46472C.
59   Minute by Lushington, 10 July 1887, HO144/208 A48043/1.
60   Memo by Lushington, 9 November 1888, HO144/198 46998/34; few commissioners of the metropolitan police would have considered their department a mere sub-department of the HO and even Lushington thought it prudent not to refer to it as such in official documents.
61   Matthews to Warren (clearly drafted by Lushington), 30 October 1887, HO144/208 A48043/1.
62   Victor Bailey, 'The Metropolitan Police, the Home Office and the Threat of Outcast London', in Victor Bailey (ed.), *Policing and Punishment in Nineteenth-Century Britain* (1981), pp. 108–11.
63   3 Hansard 322, 1879–1954 (1 March 1888); 3 Hansard 323, 35–134 (2 March 1888).
64   Police Order, 19 July 1887, HO45 9964/X15633/1.
65   3 Hansard 318, 364 (28 July 1887).
66   Minute by Lushington, 1 August 1887, HO45 9964/X15633/1.
67   Papers on HO45 9678/A47459; HO-metropolitan police relations continued to cause the department embarrassment until Sir E. Bradford became commissioner in 1890.
68   Anderson, p. 126.
69   Matthews to Salisbury, 4 June 1887, Salisbury papers, correspondence with Henry Matthews.
70   Memo by Lushington, 10 November 1887, HO45 9780/B2369/1.
71   This committee had been set up in 1884 following a report of the Select Committee on Police and Sanitary Regulations. In January 1885, accepting a HO plea of overwork, the Treasury allowed the LGB representative to take over HO duties towards the committee; T to HO, 8 January 1885, HO45 9648/A37252/2.
72   Memo by Troup (undated), HO45 9785/B2956C/1; the bill was later dropped.
73   Minutes by Troup and Matthews, 8 and 14 March 1892, HO45 9846/B12087/1.
74   Although Redgrave had attended the fourth session of the International Statistical Congress in London in 1860, no further direct connection between the HO and this society can be ascertained until 1890 when Grosvenor delivered to it a somewhat misleading paper on crime.
75   *Third Report of the Official Statistics Committee*, PP 1881 (39) XXX, Appendix A.
76   Secretary, Statistics Inquiry Committee, to HO, 18 August 1882, HO45 R620/1.

77 Harcourt to Gladstone, 14 January 1885, W. E. Gladstone papers, Add. MSS 44199, ff. 146–8.
78 Memo by Grosvenor, minutes by Knyvett and Lushington, 10 and 13 April 1888, HO45 17780/R12102/3.
79 Minutes and memo by Simpson, Troup and Lushington, 31 October, 19 and 21 November 1890, HO45 17780/R12102/9.
80 *Fifteenth Report of the Commissioners of Prisons*, PP 1892 [C. 6738] XLII, pp. 1–6.
81 Memo by Troup, 23 November 1892, HO45 10424/R19175/4.
82 *Judicial Statistics, England and Wales, 1893*, with *Report of the Departmental Committee Appointed to Revise the Criminal Portion of the Judicial Statistics*, PP 1895 [C. 7725] CVIII.
83 *Introduction to the Judicial Statistics for 1893*, PP 1895 (300) CVIII, p. 3.
84 *Report of the Departmental Committee on the Civil Judicial Statistics*, PP 1896 [C. 8263] XCIV.
85 Memo by Simpson, November 1893, HO45 9877/B15358/1.
86 See below, p. 155.
87 *Report of the Departmental Committee on Mining and Mineral Statistics*, PP 1895 [C. 7609] XLII.
88 Minute by Troup, 26 October 1894, HO45 9877/B15358/12.
89 Minute by Stapleton, 9 February, 1887, HO45 9768/B904.
90 Minute by Lushington, 19 July 1881, HO45 9611/A7070/1a.
91 Minute by Troup, 3 May 1892, HO45 10122/B12457/1.
92 Quoted in T minute by Mowatt, 8 March 1893, T1 8763A/15502.
93 Gladstone to Asquith, 18 July 1893, Visc. Gladstone papers, Add. MSS 45989, ff. 9–15.
94 Asquith to Gladstone, 19 January 1894, Visc. Gladstone papers, Add. MSS 46090, f. 17.
95 Memo by Troup, Simpson, Byrne, Legge and Dryhurst to Lushington, 30 November 1894, HO ESG/60 8/11/1 (paper 1); much of the information in the subsequent three paragraphs comes from this HO file.
96 Minute by Lushington, 4 December 1894, HO ESG/60 8/11/1 (paper 2).
97 HO to T and T (draft) to HO, 13 and 16 January 1896, T1 9004B/908; in a veiled riposte from Digby to Mowatt, the formal HO letter to the Treasury was worded as though the HO agreed to go ahead with internal reorganization now that the Treasury had consented to requested staff changes.
98 Figures are taken from the annual estimates, 1877–8 and 1896–7, and include private secretary allowances.

Chapter 4

1 The actual drafting of government bills was done by the parliamentary counsel to the Treasury.
2 Notes on HO business, March 1907, Visc. Gladstone papers, Add. MSS 46096, f. 81.
3 HO to Office of Works, 15 July 1903, 28 October 1903 and 18 February 1904, HO173/1.
4 For a while, however, there were four principal clerks. Deffell, although never head of a department, was promoted to a principal clerkship when he became registrar of the imperial service order in 1902.
5 HO to T, 2 August 1904, T1 10137/B13664.
6 In the event the new division did not take over work from the

employment of children act.
7 T to HO, 28 December 1906, T13/26.
8 Draft HO to T, December 1906, HO45 10351/148128.
9 Ibid.
10 Ibid.
11 *Cttee of Inquiry into Beck Case*, 1905; appendix to cabinet paper by Akers Douglas, 7 December 1904, CAB 37/73 (1904).
12 *The Times*, 19 August 1904, p. 7 and 9 September 1904, pp. 4–5; *Cttee of Inquiry into Beck Case*, 1905, *Mins of Ev.*, 343; see *Daily Mail*, 16 July 1904, p. 3.
13 Chalmers to Akers Douglas, 14 October 1904, Chilston papers, U564/C119/2.
14 Cabinet paper by Akers Douglas, 7 December 1904, CAB 37/73 (1904).
15 *Cttee of Inquiry into Beck Case*, 1905, Appendix.
16 *Cttee of Inquiry into Beck Case*, 1905, p. vii.
17 Ibid., p. xv.
18 Harold Scott, *Your Obedient Servant* (1959), p. 61.
19 See above, p. 60.
20 Cabinet paper by Akers Douglas, 7 December 1904, CAB 37/73 (1904).
21 4 Hansard 143, 688–701 (21 March 1905).
22 Scott, *Your Obedient Servant*, pp. 61–2.
23 Draft HO to T, 10 March 1906, HO45 10343/140508/1.
24 The finger-print system was introduced for the identification of criminals in 1902 at Scotland Yard by (Sir) Edward Henry, assistant commissioner of CID.
25 4 Hansard 154, 1003 (27 March 1906).
26 *Papers relating to the case of George Edalji*, PP 1907 [Cd. 3503] LXVII.
27 Draft memo by Simpson, 19 December 1904, HO45 10918/B20218/8.
28 Indeed, a contemporary official alleged that by 1910 fewer officials were being called to the bar after entry into the HO than previously, Scott, pp. 30–31.
29 Chalmers to Gladstone, 30 March 1907, Visc. Gladstone papers, Add. MSS 45993, f. 53.
30 Waller to Gladstone, 8 September 1907, Visc. Gladstone papers, Add. MSS 45994, ff. 34–5.
31 Troup to Gladstone, 18 December 1907, Visc. Gladstone papers, Add. MSS 45993, f. 113.
32 Cunynghame to Asquith, December 1907, enclosed in Asquith to Gladstone, 23 December 1907, Visc. Gladstone papers, Add. MSS 45989, ff. 171–2.
33 *The Times* 6 May 1935, p. 14.
34 Ibid.
35 C. H. Dudley Ward and C. B. Spencer, *The Unconventional Civil Servant: Sir Henry H. Cunynghame* (1938), pp. 241–6.
36 Arthur Ponsonby to Blackwell, 11 November 1907, and Asquith to Gladstone, 6 December 1907, Visc. Gladstone papers, Add. MSS 45993, ff. 315–16, and 45989, f. 163.
37 There is a disappointing lack of non-official sources on Troup's ideas, character and life.
38 Scott, p. 28.
39 Harold Butler, *Confident Morning* (1950), p. 69.
40 Strutt, *The Home Office 1870–1896: the Modernization of an Office*, p. 146.
41 HO to T, 29 November 1870, T1 7028A/22564; T to HO, 7 December

1870, T13/9; at first this clerk was to be available for the general business of the office when not needed by the home secretary but by 1876 his post had become a full-time appointment.

42 The precise date of this appointment is not clear; but provision for it was first made in the annual estimates for 1865–6. Although this too was formally a full-time appointment the parliamentary under-secretary's private secretary seems to have had time to spare out of the parliamentary session for departmental work.

43 Paper on the HO establishment (circa 1893), Visc. Gladstone papers, Add. MSS 46090, f. 22 ff.

44 These were R. S. Mitford, Ruggles-Brise, F. J. Dryhurst and Waller.

45 Leslie, *Sir Evelyn Ruggles-Brise: A Memoir of the Founder of Borstal*, p. 37.

46 Harcourt to Sir Samuel Ruggles-Brise, 19 May 1884, Ruggles-Brise papers.

47 Guillemard, *Trivial Fond Records*, p. 171.

48 Correspondence Waller to Gladstone, Visc. Gladstone papers, Add. MSS 45994.

49 Legge to Gladstone, 29 January 1894, Visc. Gladstone papers, Add. MSS 45990, ff. 198–9.

50 *2nd Rep. of R.C. on C.S.*, 1912–13, *Mins of Ev.*, 4952, 4957.

51 Waller to Gladstone, 17 July 1907, Visc. Gladstone papers, Add. MSS 45994, f. 125.

52 Waller to Gladstone, 23 December 1909, Visc. Gladstone papers, Add. MSS 45994, ff. 242–3.

53 HO to T, 14 November 1911, T1 11441/13483; T to HO, 21 November 1911, T13/28.

54 Registered incoming papers were, of course, not the only papers dealt with in the office but they were usually taken as the best indication of the increasing burden on it.

55 Figures taken from a breakdown of registered incoming papers in HO B.27590, submitted to the Treasury and now in T1 11272/4765.

56 Minutes by Troup and Pedder, 9 February 1910 and 15 January 1909, T1 11272/4765 (HO B.27590).

57 Minute by Chalmers, 22 January 1908, T1 11272/4765 (HO B.27590).

58 Minutes by Byrne and Troup, January 1909, T1 11272/4765 (HO B.27590); at this period heads of department seem to have been putting in work reports regularly every January.

59 House of Commons committee office (circular letter), 7 February 1913, HO45 19202/204404/2.

60 Minutes by Pedder and Delevigne, 18 January and 5 February 1910, T1 11272/4765 (HO B.27590).

61 Minute by Gladstone, 9 February 1910, T1 11272/4765 (HO B.27590).

62 Notes on HO legislation and other work, 1906–9, Visc. Gladstone papers, Add. MSS 46096, f. 269.

63 Scott, pp. 24–5.

64 Butler, *Confident Morning*, pp. 48–9.

65 Memo by Aitken, 23 March 1910, T1 11272/4765 (HO B.27590).

66 Memos by Aitken and Pedder, 23 March and 13 April 1910, T1 11272/4765 (HO B.27590).

67 Memo by Byrne, 7 October 1910, T1 11272/4765 (HO B. 27590).

68 See below, p. 174.

69 Memo by Byrne, 7 October 1910, and HO to T, 1 November 1910, T1 11272/4765 (HO B.27590).

70 T to HO, 5 December 1910, T13/27; the Treasury also agreed to the

addition of a second division clerk, two assistant clerks and one boy clerk.

71 See above, p. 70.
72 Minute by Troup, 1 July 1913, HO45 11095/B27590/30.
73 Minute by Troup, 1 July 1913, HO45 11095/B27590/1; for more details on this departmental committee see below, Chapter 7, p. 175.
74 See Appendix C for full details of the work and staffing of the six divisions after 7 November 1913.
75 HO to T, 12 and 27 June 1913, T1 11588/24025.
76 T to HO, 13 and 30 June 1913, T13/28; Troup's reason for this change in title was that Delevigne's 'relations to employers of labour and to officers having similar functions in other Departments make it desirable that he should have a distinctive title'.
77 The cost of the June 1913 changes, for example was around £750 in mean terms. This is not to say, however, that the HO got its way on other financial matters, see below, p. 163-4.
78 Cawston to Byrne, 22 September 1910, T1 11272/4765.
79 J. S. Bradbury to Troup, 17 October 1913, T1 11588/24025.
80 HO to T, 3 December 1913, T1 11588/24025; T to HO, 5 December 1913, T13/28.
81 Memo by McKenna, 10 December 1913, HO45 11095/B27590/9.
82 Figures are taken from the annual estimates 1896-7 and 1914-15.
83 C. E. Mallet, *Herbert Gladstone* (1932), p. 208.
84 Ibid., p. 203.
85 Butler, p. 77.
86 Troup, *The Home Office*, p. 54.
87 Memos by Troup, 21 and 24 October 1911, in HO 'Confidential Memoranda and Reports', HO45 10658/212470.
88 See papers on HO45 11138/186474.
89 See the account by Roy Jenkins, *Asquith* (1964), pp. 189-93, which the author derives from the Asquith papers. Documents in the Visc. Gladstone papers give an illuminating account of Troup's role. See also Mallet, *Herbert Gladstone*, pp. 217-19.
90 One example was an annual procession at Arundel.
91 Troup to Gladstone, 8 September 1908, Visc. Gladstone papers, Add. MSS 45993, ff. 137-8.
92 Ibid.
93 Troup to Gladstone, 9 September 1908, Visc. Gladstone papers, Add. MSS 45993, ff. 139-45.
94 Ibid.
95 Jenkins, *Asquith*, pp. 190-91.
96 Archbishop of Westminster to Asquith and Gladstone to Archbishop of Westminster, 10 September 1908, HO45 11138/186474/1.
97 Troup to Gladstone, 12 September 1908, Visc. Gladstone papers, Add. MSS 45993, ff. 153-4.
98 Troup to Gladstone, 13 September 1908, Visc. Gladstone papers, Add. MSS 45993, ff. 157-60.
99 Jenkins, p. 192.
100 Memo by Troup, 23 September 1908, Visc. Gladstone papers, Add. MSS 45993, f. 184 ff.
101 Troup to Gladstone, 25 September 1908, Visc. Gladstone papers, Add. MSS 45993, f. 203 ff.
102 José Harris in *Unemployment and Politics: A study in English Social Policy 1886-1914* (1972), p. 11, for example, mentions H. Llewellyn Smith (first Commissioner for Labour, Board of Trade, 1893-1903)

and W. Beveridge (Board of Trade, Ministry of Munitions, and Ministry of Food, 1908–19).

103 For example, R. H. S. Crossman, *The Diaries of a Cabinet Minister*, Vols. 1–3 (1975–7); P. Kellner and Lord Crowther-Hunt, *The Civil Servants: An Inquiry into Britain's Ruling Class* (1980).
104 Three random examples are reports of committees on file cutting regulations (1903 [Cd. 1658]), brass-casting factories (1908 [Cd. 4154]) and florists' workshops (1909 [Cd. 4932]).
105 Cecil T. Carr, *Delegated Legislation* (1921), p. 1.
106 Papers on HO45 10644/208925; Bryce later objected to the HO blocking of another similar bill whereupon the department withdrew its objections, but the bill received insufficient Commons support to succeed; Bryce to McKenna, 27 October 1911, HO45 10644/208882/2.
107 J. H. Pellew, 'Administrative Change in the Home Office: 1870–96', unpublished PhD thesis, University of London (1976), p. 275 ff.; David G. Hanes *The First British Workmen's Compensation Act, 1897* (1968).
108 A. Williamson, 'Some retarding factors on penal reform 1895–1914', unpublished MA thesis, University of Edinburgh (1976), p. 23.
109 Butler, p. 78.
110 Herbert Louis Samuel, *Memoirs* (1945), p. 55.
111 K. D. Brown, 'John Burns at the Local Government Board 1886–1909: a Reassessment', *Journal of Social Policy*, 6 (1977), pp. 157–70; M. E. Craig, 'Bureaucracy and Negativism: The Local Government Board 1886–1909', unpublished MA thesis, University of Edinburgh (1975).
112 Gillian Sutherland, *Policy-making in Elementary Education 1870–1895* (1973), p. 191.
113 R. Davidson and R. Lowe, 'Bureaucracy and Innovation in British Welfare Policy 1870–1945'; in W. J. Mommsen (ed.), *The Emergence of the Welfare State in Great Britain and Germany 1850–1950* (1981).
114 Samuel, *Memoirs*, p. 52.
115 R. S. Redmayne, *Men, Mines and Memories* (1942), p. 141.
116 Ibid., p. 140.
117 Harris, *Unemployment and Politics: A Study in English Social Policy 1886–1914* p. 81.
118 Butler, p. 50.
119 Waller to Gladstone, 11 August 1910, Visc. Gladstone papers, Add. MSS 45994, ff. 260–1.
120 Minute by Troup, 17 August 1911, HO45 10654/212470/68.
121 E.g. minute by Troup, 21 August 1911, HO45 10654/212470/112.
122 Memo by Troup, (May or June) 1912, HO144/121/223877.

Chapter 5

1 Memo by Maconochie, 30 August 1873, HO45 9283/1782MA/9.
2 *30th Rep. of CSC*, PP 1886 [C. 4753], XX, Appendix, p. 36.
3 Ibid. (Report), p. v.
4 *2nd Rep. of R.C. on Civil Establishments*, 1888, *Mins of Ev.*, 12,160.
5 *1st Rep. of R.C. on C.S.*, 1912–13, Appendix III, p. 134.
6 *1st Rep. of R.C. on C.S.*, 1912–13, Appendix, pp. 130–1.
7 See above, pp. 28 ff.
8 *2nd Rep. of R.C. on Civil Establishments*, 1888, *Mins of Ev.*, 12,195.
9 Memos by Maconochie, January–March 1871 and 15 November 1875, HO45 9483/1782M/16b, 18, 18a, and HO45 9283/1782MA/14.
10 Butler, *Confident Morning*, p. 71.

11 T Minute, 7 April 1880, HO45 9591/92728/1a.
12 Memo by Boehmer, 28 May 1902, HO45 10245/B38128/1.
13 A. J. Eagleston, 'The Secretary of State's Office under Elizabeth' (1938), HO45 18563/808993/1.
14 Minutes by Wheeler, 28 December 1889, 23 September and 13 October 1890, HO45 9832/B9548/1; minutes by Moran, 27 October 1890 and 21 October 1892, HO45 9832/B9548/1, 5.
15 Eagleston, 'The Secretary of State's Office under Elizabeth', p. 11.
16 *2nd Rep. of R.C. on C.S.*, 1912–13, *Mins of Ev.*, 4914, 5058.
17 Papers on HO45 10510/B20762.
18 Memo by Moran, 13 October 1894, HO45 9832/B9548D/1.
19 Draft HO to T and T to HO, 13 and 19 November 1894, HO45 9832/E9548D/1, 2.
20 Strutt, *The Home Office 1876–1896: the Modernization of an Office*, p. 127.
21 Minute by Murdoch, 24 February 1896, HO45 10175/B28787/15.
22 'Report of the Committee on the Home Office Registry', 3 November 1898, HO45 13624/B27360/2.
23 Minutes and memos, 1898–9, HO45 13624/B27360/7 ff.
24 Butler, p. 72. See also Scott, *Your Obedient Servant*, p. 29.
25 Memo by Locke, 18 March 1901, HO45 13624/B27360/24.
26 Minute by Boehmer, 19 March 1901, HO45 13624/B27360/24.
27 One example of a useful index, probably compiled by the registry noter at a slightly later date, is entitled 'Suffragettes: Index of Names and Persons Arrested 1900–1914'. Derived from information originally written on index cards, it was first started 'with a view to facilitate the tracing of cases – both male and female – which had come before the HO, and proved of considerable value in linking up earlier and later convictions of the same person'; minute, 6 May 1922, on HO 253239/27.
28 Memo, HO to Royal Commission on Public Records (1913), HO45 17784/B31038/17.
29 Memo by Boehmer, 28 May 1902, HO45 10245/B38128/1.
30 Memo by Boehmer, 31 March 1908, HO45 10175/B28787/28. By this time it was virtually only the staff clerks who made personal applications for salary rises since all the others (except for a few specialist titled clerks in the inspectors' offices) were in some grade whose salary was fixed generally.
31 Minute by Troup, 10 September 1908, HO45 10175/B28787/28.
32 Papers on HO45 10152/B21297/60.
33 Papers on HO45 13624/B27360/41.
34 Papers on HO45 13624/B27360/46.
35 Scott, p. 29; see also Butler, p. 71.
36 T to HO, 14 March 1868, HO45 10510/B20762/24; see above, p. 19.
37 The Treasury drew a distinction between the two different kinds of accounting responsibilities in its Minute of 14 August 1872, HO45 9305/11855/1a.
38 HO to T, 8 February 1870, T1 7028A/22564.
39 The Patriotic Fund, started in 1854 to aid dependents of those killed in the Crimean War, was extended in 1866–8 to include dependents of anyone killed on active service.
40 Memo by Liddell, 10 January 1884, HO45 9640/A34334/1.
41 CSC to T, 28 January 1884, and draft T to CSC, 1 February 1884, T1 8128C/17798.
42 *2nd Rep. of R.C. on Civil Establishments*, 1888, *Mins of Ev.*, 11,151.

43 This vote probably related to metropolitan police superannuation and certain contributions towards provincial police funds.

44 Draft HO to T, 22 December 1888, HO45 9801/B5456/1.

45 Minute by Tripp, 29 October 1890, HO45 9770/B1137/15.

46 Minute by Tripp, 20 October 1904, HO45 10222/B36029/3; minute by Tripp, 1 March 1907, HO45 10510/129054/26.

47 Minute by Digby, 3 February 1896, HO45 10918/B20218/5.

48 Minute by Troup, 25 January 1908, HO45 10918/B20218/11.

49 Minute by Troup, 8 December 1909, HO45 10918/B20218/12.

50 Ibid.

51 Draft HO to T, 8 December 1909, and T to HO, 14 January 1910, HO45 10918/B20218/12, 13.

52 Draft T to HO, 28 August 1912, HO45 10918/B20218/20.

53 Memo by Grunwald, 2 August 1912, HO45 10918/B20218/20; for 'certifying surgeons' see below, Chapter 6, p. 125.

54 T to HO, 12 September 1912, HO45 10918/B20218/22.

55 See above, pp. 53–7.

56 See above, p. 56–7 and below, p. 155–7.

57 T to HO, 8 December 1896, T13/14; four assistant clerks were also added to the branch at that time.

58 *Report of the Departmental Committee on Mining and Mineral Statistics*, PP 1895 [C. 7953], XLII, p. 13.

59 *First Annual General Report upon the Mineral Industry of the United Kingdom etc.*, PP 1894 [C. 7953], XXII.

60 *2nd Rep. of R.C. on C.S.*, 1912–13, *Mins of Ev.*, 5023.

61 Memo by Farrant, 17 April 1917, HO 45 17788/B32589/73.

62 Ibid.

63 Ibid.; also *2nd Rep. of R.C. on C.S.*, 1912–13, *Mins of Ev.*, 5023.

64 Memo by Farrant, 5 October 1916, and following minutes, HO45 10908//R410.

65 Minute by Byrne, 20 January 1908, HO45 17787/B32589/26a; in fact, employers did not always submit individual returns because they were allowed to submit information through insurance companies which sent in collective returns.

66 Memo by Farrant, 17 April 1917, HO45 17788/B32589/73.

67 Memo by Pedder and Aitken, 21 July 1911, HO45 17788/B32589/64.

68 Draft HO to T and report by Byrne and Tripp, December 1909, HO45 17787/B32589/46.

69 Report on the HO statistics branch, by Byrne and Tripp, 16 December 1909, HO45 17787/B32589/46.

70 T to HO, 25 January 1910, HO45 17787/B32589/51; Farrant was not happy about this, having requested a maximum of £700. He was obliged to accept £550 but continued to press his case.

71 *2nd Rep. of R.C. on C.S.*, 1912–13, *Mins of Ev.*, 4904.

72 Minute by Delevigne, 19 December 1905, HO 45 10918/B20218/9.

73 *2nd Rep. of R.C. on C.S.*, 1912–13, *Mins of Ev.*, 4904.

74 Memo by Farrant, 17 April 1917, HO45 17788/B32589/73.

75 Draft HO to T, 20 October 1910, HO45 11095/B27590/25.

76 Minute by Delevigne, 5 February 1910, HO45 11095/B27590/25.

77 Draft HO to T, 20 October 1910, HO45 11095/B27590/25.

78 Scott, p. 83.

79 T to HO, 5 December and 21 December 1910, T13/27.

80 *Civil Service Gazette*, 14 October 1876, p. 666.

81 The HO had become a '7-hour' (as opposed to a '6-hour') office and its lower division clerks therefore started at £90.

82 T to HO, 17 November 1886, T13/19.
83 HO to T, 1 August 1881, 31 July 1882 and 21 May 1886, HO45 9483/1782M/43, 45, 50.
84 *Civil Service Gazette*, 19 November 1870, p. 742.
85 See B. V. Humphries, *Clerical Unions in the Civil Service* (1958), Chapters III, IV, V; Cohen, *The Growth of the British Civil Service 1780–1939* (1965), pp. 141–2; on individual departments see Blakeley, *The Colonial Office 1868–1892*, Chapter VII; MacLeod, *Treasury Control and Social Administration: A Study of Establishment Growth at the Local Government Board 1871–1905*, pp. 27–8.
86 Lower division clerks to T, June 1880, and T to CO, 8 July 1881, *Correspondence between the Treasury and Colonial Office with regard to the petition of certain lower division clerks etc.*, PP 1884 (227), XLVII, pp. 13–16.
87 Petition, HO lower division clerks to S of S, 18 August 1883, T1 8102A/10706.
88 T to CO, 19 June 1884, *Correspondence between the Treasury and Colonial Office with regard to the petition of certain lower division clerks etc.*, PP 1884 (227), XLVII, p. 2.
89 *2nd Rep. of R.C. on Civil Estalishments*, 1888, Appendices, p. 525.
90 Ibid., p. 527.
91 Minute, lower division clerks to Knyvett, 17 January 1887, HO45 9760/B661/11.
92 *2nd Rep. of R.C. on Civil Establishments*, 1888, *Mins of Ev.*, 12,205 ff.
93 Ibid., 11,243, 11,866, 10,980, 11,765 and 11,872.
94 Ibid., 10,889, 11,265, 11,307, 11,896 and 12,005.
95 Welby to Lushington, 6 November 1890, HO45 9801/B661F/1.
96 HO to T, 3 May 1890, HO45 10410/B661A/7.
97 T to HO, 12 September 1891, T13/22.
98 Geoffrey Crossick, 'The Emergence of the Lower Middle Class in Britain', in Crossick (ed.), *The Lower Middle Class in Britain* (1977), p. 34.
99 Gregory Anderson, *Victorian Clerks* (1976), p. 68.
100 Ibid., p. 25.
101 *2nd Rep. of R.C. on Civil Establishments*, 1888, Appendix, p. 434.
102 Also their chances of promotion outside the HO were lessened by the ending of the restriction of metropolitan police court clerkships to HO clerks; *2nd Rep. of R.C. on C.S.*, 1912–13, *Mins of Ev.*, 5101.
103 A group of assistant clerks in 1912 claimed that 28/- a week was the bare minumum cost of lodgings in the 'well known lodging centres for clerks' plus 'other purely subsistence expenses'; *2nd Rep. of R.C. on C.S.*, 1912–13, Appendix VII, p. 498.
104 Crossick, 'The Emergence of the Lower Middle Class in Britain', p. 33.
105 John Burnett (ed.), *Useful Toil* (1974), p. 161.
106 Mrs Simpson to Lushington, 8 November 1887, HO45 9640/A34334/7.
107 The *Civilian*, 28 September 1901, p. 370.
108 See above, p. 103.
109 This act necessitated the employment of large staffs very quickly; Humphries, *Clerical Unions in the Civil Service*, p. 61.
110 Ibid.
111 The Second Division Clerks' Association – forerunner of the modern Society of Civil and Public Servants – eventually declined affiliation to the Civil Service Federation which failed in its original aim of promoting the common rights of the various clerical classes.

248 *The Home Office 1848–1914*

2112 Humphries, p. 71.
113 HO second division clerks to S of S, 2 October 1893, HO45 10410/B661A/20.
114 *2nd Rep. of R.C. on C.S.*, 1912–13, *Mins of Ev.*, 5511–12.
115 Ibid., 5088.
116 Ibid., 5101–3.
117 Scott, p. 69.
118 *2nd Rep. of R.C. on C.S.*, 1912–13, *Mins of Ev.*, 5027–31.
119 Ibid., 5145.
120 These figures were quoted in parliament from evidence to the Macdonnell Commission; 5 Hansard 35, 2206–7 (21 March 1912).
121 *1st Rep. of R.C. on C.S.*, 1912–13, Appendix, pp. 119–20.
122 *2nd Rep. of R.C. on C.S.*, 1912–13, *Mins of Ev.*, 5208.
123 Scott, p. 62.

Chapter 6

1 David Roberts, *The Victorian Origins of the British Welfare State* (1960), p. 132.
2 Ibid., p. 110.
3 For biographical details of HO inspectors, 1848–76, see Appendix D; for details of their numbers and salaries, see Appendix E.
4 Oliver MacDonagh, *Early Victorian Government 1830–1870* (1977), p. 66.
5 P. W. J. Bartrip, 'Safety at Work: the Factory Inspectorate in the Fencing Controversy', Centre for Socio-Legal Studies, Wolfson College, Oxford, Working Paper No. 4, March 1979, p. 13.
6 Bernice Martin, 'Leonard Horner: A Portrait of an Inspector of Factories', *International Review of Social History* (1969), p. 431.
7 *Report of the Inspector of Factories to the Secretary of State, December 1849*, PP 1850 [1141] XXIII, pp. 4–5.
8 MacDonagh, *Early Victorian Government 1830–1870*, p. 72.
9 The factory acts extension act of 1867, for example, added blast furnaces, copper mills, forges, paper mills, glass factories, letterpress printers and book-binders to the works already covered.
10 Martin, 'Leonard Horner: A Portrait of an Inspector of Factories', p. 430.
11 Bartrip, 'Safety at Work: the Factory Inspectorate in the Fencing Controversy'; P. W. J. Bartrip and P. T. Fenn, 'The Administration of Safety: the Enforcement Policy of the Early Factory Inspectorate, 1844–1865', *Public Administration*, 58 (1980), pp. 87–102.
12 *Rep. of R.C. on Factory and Workshop Acts*, 1876, p. lxxxix.
13 Ibid., p. lxxxviii.
14 Ibid., p. lxxxix.
15 Ibid., p. xc.
16 Papers on HO45 OS 8000 and HO45 OS 8002.
17 Edward Baines MP to Bruce, 7 January 1869, HO45 OS 8002.
18 Bartrip and Fenn, 'The Administration of Safety: the Enforcement Policy of the Early Factory Inspectorate, 1844–1865', p. 44.
19 Report, Horner to S of S, November 1859, HO45 OS 6757, p. 2.
20 *Rep. of R.C. on Factory and Workshop Acts*, 1876, p. xciii.
21 Martin, p. 413; Katherine Lyell (ed.), *Memoir of Leonard Horner, FRS, FGS* (1890).
22 Martin, p. 428.
23 *Rep. of R.C. on Factory and Workshop Acts*, 1876, *Mins of Ev.*, 566.
24 Although Baker had become a sub-inspector long before Redgrave, he

succeeded to an inspectorship later.

25 T-HO report, 9 December 1867, T1 6833A/19090, p. 2.

26 Memo by Maconochie, 7 July 1874, and draft, S of S to T, 11 July 1874, HO45 9360/32214/15.

27 *Return of the names, ages and previous occupations or professions of the inspectors and sub-inspectors of factories appointed since 1 January 1867*, etc., PP 1880 (371) XL(2).

28 MacDonagh, *Early Victorian Government 1830-1870*, p. 82.

29 Unsigned memo, November 1892, HO45 9771/B1137J/1a.

30 *Report of the Select Committee on Mines*, PP 1867 (496) XIII, *Mins of Ev.*, 563.

31 Papers concerning HO estimates for 1893-4, Visc. Gladstone Papers Add. MSS 46090, f. 28.

32 MacDonagh, *Early Victorian Government 1830-1870*, p. 66.

33 Ibid., p. 92.

34 Ibid., p. 78.

35 HO to Carrington, 27 May 1864, HO95/3.

36 *Reports of the Inspectors of Mines to Her Majesty's Secretary of State for the Year 1867*, PP 1867-8 [4063] XXI, p. 3.

37 J. H. Pellew, 'The Home Office and the Explosives Act of 1875', *Victorian Studies*, XVIII (1974), pp. 175-94.

38 Roy MacLeod, 'The Alkali Acts Administration, 1863-84: The Emergence of the Civil Scientist', *Victorian Studies*, IX (1965), pp. 85-112.

39 L. Horner, *On the Employment of Children in Factories*, etc. (1840), see Martin, p. 433.

40 R. K. Webb, 'A Whig Inspector', *Journal of Modern History*, XXVII (1955), p. 356.

41 Papers on HO45 OS 7259.

42 These do not include convict prisons which were centrally administered.

43 Roberts, *The Victorian Origins of the British Welfare State*, p. 47.

44 Throughout the period one inspector reported to the home secretary on Scottish prisons but the control of these prisons was vested in the General Board of Prisons for Scotland from 1839 to 1860 after which they were administered by the managers of Scottish prisons. In Ireland central inspection of local prisons was in operation before the end of the eighteenth century, and in 1822 the lord lieutenant was empowered to appoint two inspectors-general regularly to report on gaols and bridewells. R. B. McDowell, *The Irish Administration 1801-1914* (1964), pp. 145-50.

45 *Rep. of Sel. Cttee on Prison Discipline*, PP(HL) 1863 (499) IX, *Mins of Ev.*, 27.

46 Ibid., 18.

47 3 Hansard 113, 274 (25 July 1850).

48 M. Heather Tomlinson, ' "Not an Instrument of Punishment": Prison Diet in the Mid-Nineteenth Century', *Journal of Consumer Studies and Home Economics*, 2 (1978), pp. 17-18.

49 Roberts, p. 246; S. and B. Webb, *English Prisons under Local Government* (reprint, 1963), pp. 117-33.

50 *Fourteenth Report of the Inspectors of Prisons to the Secretary of State* (District II), PP 1849 [1033] XXVI; Constance Hill (ed.), *Frederic Hill: an Autobiography of Fifty Years in Times of Reform* (1894), pp. 256-7.

51 S. and B. Webb, *English Prisons under Local Government*, pp. 155-6.

52 Prisons inspectors to S of S, 19 January 1846, HO45 OS 541; *Rep. of*

Sel. Cttee on Prison Discipline, 1863, p. xii.
53 Ibid., p. xiv.
54 Ibid., Mins of Ev., 36.
55 Ibid., Mins of Ev., 1907.
56 3 Hansard 113, 275 (25 July 1850).
57 Rep. of Sel. Cttee on Prison Discipline, 1863, Mins of Ev., 2271.
58 Ibid., p.. xiv.
59 3 Hansard 177, 217 (13 February 1865).
60 Correspondence with the Inspectors of Prisons on the subject of carrying into effect the Provisions of the Prisons Act, 1865, PP 1866 (72) LVIII, p. 1.
61 Separate prison acts were passed for Scotland and Ireland whose prisons were to be administered by boards equivalent to the English Prison Commission.
62 This is not including the inspector of reformatory and industrial schools, see below p. 137.
63 Hill, Frederic Hill: an Autobiography of Fifty Years in Times of Reform.
64 Following the 1857 Scottish counties and burghs police act, an inspector for Scotland reported to the home secretary.
65 Reports of the Inspectors of Constabulary for the Year Ending 29 September 1857, etc. (District I), PP 1857–8 (20) XLVII, p. 6.
   Here too centralization had come first in Ireland where, from 1863, there was a single police force (which later became the Royal Irish Constabulary), inspected and controlled by the government. McDowell, The Irish Administration 1801–1914, p. 138.
66 Reports of the Inspectors of Constabulary for the Year Ending 29 September 1857, etc. (District I), PP 1857–8 (20) LVIII, p. 6; see also Jenifer Hart, 'The County and Borough Police Act, 1856', Public Administration, 34 (1956), pp. 405–17.
67 Henry Parris, 'The Home Office and the Provincial Police in England and Wales: 1856–1870', Public Law (1961), p. 243.
68 Ibid., p. 231.
69 Memo by Murdoch, 5 December 1888, HO45 10016/A52889/1.
70 Parris, 'The Home Office and the Provincial Police in England and Wales: 1856–1870', p. 233.
71 See e.g. First Report of the Inspector of Reformatory Schools to the Secretary of State, PP 1857–8 [2426] XXIX, p. 6.
72 Susan Margaret Eade, 'The Reclaimers: A Study of the Reformatory Movement in England and Wales 1846–1893', unpublished PhD thesis, Australian National University (1975), p. 204.
73 A Supplementary Report on the Results of a Special Inquiry into the Practice of Interment in Towns by Edwin Chadwick, PP 1843 [509] XII, p. 84.
74 Report on a General Scheme for Extramural Sepultre, PP 1850 [1158] XXI.
75 Royston Lambert, Sir John Simon 1816–1904 and English Social Administration (1963), p. 221.
76 3 Hansard 122, 874 (17 June 1852).
77 HO outgoing letters on burial matters from April 1854, HO85/1–8.
78 Parliamentary Return of all the notices for the discontinuance of burials within the Metropolis issued by the Secretary of State, etc., PP 1861 (143) LXI.
79 Report of the Royal Sanitary Commission, PP 1868–9 [4218] XXXII, Mins of Ev., 8144.

80 2 & 3 Will. IV Cap. 75, sect. 1.
81 Minute by Winterbotham, undated, HO45 9341/22233/1.
82 *Report of the Royal Commission on the Practice of Subjecting Live Animals to Experiments for Scientific Purposes*, PP 1876 [C. 1397] LXI, p. xvi.
83 For a comprehensive account see Richard D. French, *Antivivisection and Medical Science in Victorian Society* (1975).
84 The *Lancet*, 31 December 1831, p. 481; by 1858 the metropolitan inspector was receiving an additional £200 a year above his salary for distributing unclaimed bodies for dissection.
85 *The Times*, 12 July 1876, p. 9; 3 Hansard 231, 892–3 (9 August 1876).
86 Brodie to Graham, 27 September 1842, HO45 OS 189.
87 *Report of the Royal Commission appointed to Inquire into Salmon Fisheries* (England and Wales), PP 1861 [2678] XXIII.
88 For a full account of the development of this inspectorate see Roy MacLeod, 'Government and Resource Conservation: the Salmon Acts Administration, 1860–1886', *Journal of British Studies*, 7 (1967–8), pp. 114–50. The freshwater fisheries act of 1878 extended the scope of the inspectorate beyond salmon to freshwater fish.
89 *Report of the Select Committee on Salmon Fisheries*, PP 1870 (368) VI.
90 J. Bowring (ed.) *Constitutional Code* in *The Works of Jeremy Bentham* (1843), p. 24.
91 Elie Halévy, *The Growth of Philosophic Radicalism* (first published 1928; pb. trans. Mary Morris, 1972), p. 431.
92 A. V. Dicey, *Lectures on the Relations Between Law and Public Opinion in England during the Nineteenth Century* (first published 1905; pb. E. C. S. Wade (ed.), 1962), Lecture VI.
93 An early powerful challenge came from J. B. Brebner in 'Laissez-faire and State Intervention in Nineteenth-Century Britain', *Journal of Economic History*, Supplement VIII (1948), pp. 59–73; for a bibliography of literature on the subject see V. Cromwell, 'Interpretations of Nineteenth-Century Administration: an analysis', *Victorian Studies*, IX (1966), pp. 245–55, and Gillian Sutherland, 'Recent Trends in Administrative History', *Victorian Studies*, XIII (1970), pp. 408–11.
94 Oliver MacDonagh, 'The Nineteenth-Century Revolution in Government: a Reappraisal', *Historical Journal*, I (1958), pp. 52–67; see also Oliver MacDonagh, *A Pattern of Government Growth 1800–60: The Passenger Acts and their Enforcement* (1961).
95 J. Hart, 'Nineteenth-Century Social Reform: a Tory Interpretation of History', *Past and Present*, XXXI (1965), pp. 39–61; Henry Parris, 'The Nineteenth-Century Revolution in Government: a Reappraisal Reappraised', *Historical Journal*, III (1960), pp. 17–37; see also Henry Parris, *Constitutional Bureaucracy: The Development of British Central Administration since the Eighteenth Century (1969)*.
96 Harold Perkin, 'Individualism Versus Collectivism in Nineteenth-Century Britain: a False Antithesis', *Journal of British Studies*, XVII (1977), pp. 105–18.
97 MacDonagh, 'The Nineteenth-Century Revolution in Government: a Reappraisal', pp. 58–61.
98 Brian Harrison, 'State Intervention and Moral Reform in Nineteenth Century England', in Patricia Harris (ed.), *Pressure from Without in Early Victorian England* (1974), p. 316.
99 Martin, p. 415.
100 Hill, p. 48.

101 J. S. Mill, *Principles of Political Economy* (Donald Winch (ed.) 1970), p. 314.
102 *Reports on the Necessity for the Amendment of the Law relating to Gunpowder and other Explosives*, etc., PP 1874 [C. 977] LII, p. 7.
103 *Fifth Report of the Inspector of Reformatory and Industrial Schools*, PP 1862 [5069] XXVI, pp. 20–1.
104 Redgrave to S of S, 16 March 1867, HO45 OS 7886/29.
105 *Reports on the Necessity for the Amendment of the Law relating to Gunpowder and other Explosives*, etc., PP 1874 [C. 977] LII, p. 7.
106 Minutes by Erskine, Majendie, Campbell and Selwin Ibbetson, 29 October to 16 November 1875, HO45 9505/15848/122.
107 Roberts, p. 126.
108 *Rep. of Sel. Cttee on Prison Discipline*, 1863, *Mins of Ev.*, 2271.
109 *Report of the Select Committee on Mines*, PP 1867 (496) XIII, *Mins of Ev.*, 1274.
110 G. Kitson Clark, 'Statesmen in Disguise: Reflexions on the History of the Neutrality of the Civil Service', *Historical Journal*, II (1959), pp. 19–39.

Chapter 7

1 For an account of central government's half-hearted attempts to legislate and administer the law on this unpopular subject see Roy MacLeod, 'The Edge of Hope: Social Policy and Chronic Alcoholism 1870–1900', *Journal of the History of Medicine and Allied Sciences*, XXII (1967), pp. 215–45.
2 41 Vict. cap. 16.
3 This, and later figures, includes salaries, travelling allowances, fees to surgeons, cost of prosecutions and incidental expenses.
4 MacDonagh, *Early Victorian Government: 1830–1870*, p. 48.
5 Memorial, Parliamentary Committee of the TUC to HO, November 1878, HO45 9550/61697A/4.
6 Memo by Harcourt, 24 August 1884, HO45 9550/61697A/44.
7 This was J. D. Prior, aged forty, who had been secretary of the Amalgamated Society of Carpenters and Joiners.
8 Memo by Redgrave, 19 July 1884, HO45 9550/61697A/43.
9 *2nd Rep. of R.C. on C.S.*, 1912–13, *Mins of Ev.*, 5222.
10 Memo by Redgrave, 25 March 1887, HO45 9770/B1137/6.
11 *2nd Report of the House of Lords Select Committee on the Sweating System*, PP 1888 (HL448) XXI, *Mins of Ev.*, 16582–5.
12 Minute by Lushington, 26 May 1892, HO45 9770/B1137/42.
13 Minute by Matthews, 28 December 1890, HO45 9774/B1508A/1.
14 Minute by Matthews, 25 May 1891, HO45 9774/B1508A/4.
15 *Report of the Chief Inspector of Factories and Workshops etc. for the Year ending 31 October 1890*, PP 1890–1 [C. 6330] XIX, pp. 8ff.
16 (Draft) HO to T, 8 August 1892, HO45 9770/B1137/49.
17 Memo by Lushington, 9 November 1892, HO45 9771/B1137J/1a.
18 *The Times*, 25 January 1893, at HO45 9770/B1137/70.
19 *Report of the Chief Inspector of Factories and Workshops etc. for the Year ending 31 March 1879*, PP 1880 [C. 2489] XIV, pp. 98–100.
20 Minute by Lushington, 17 June 1890, HO45 9818/B8031/3.
21 Notices of parliamentary questions for 26 February, 23 June and 20 July 1891, HO45 9818/B8031/5, 6, 7.
22 Memo by Oram, 22 November 1893, HO45 9877/B15358/1.
23 Mundella to W. E. Gladstone, 9 June 1892, W. E. Gladstone papers, Add. MSS 44258, ff. 274–7. See Roger Davidson, 'Llewellyn Smith,

the Labour Department and government growth 1886–1909', in G.
Sutherland (ed.), *Studies in the Growth of Nineteenth-Century
Government*, pp. 227–62.

24 Notice of House of Commons resolution and motion, proposed for 3
   May 1892, HO45 10122/B12457/1.
25 *Fifth Report of the Royal Commission on Labour* (Pt. II), PP 1894
   [C. 7421–1] XXXV, *Summaries of Evidence*, 575.
26 Memo by Asquith, 12 December 1892, HO45 9771/B1137J/1a.
27 Asquith to H. Gladstone, 14 October 1892, Visc. Gladstone papers,
   Add. MSS 45989, f. 4.
28 J. H. Pellew, 'Administrative Change in the Home Office: 1870–1896',
   pp. 281ff.
29 Memos by Gladstone, Asquith and Lushington, November and
   December 1892, HO45 9771/B1137J/1a.
30 Memo by Asquith, 12 December 1892, HO45 9771/B1437J/1a.
31 Ibid.
32 (Draft) HO to T, 6 December 1893, HO45 9771/B1137J/46.
33 H. H. Asquith, *Fifty Years of Parliament*, Vol. 1 (1926), pp. 213–14.
34 See above, p. 56.
35 See above, p. 61.
36 Factory inspectorate circular, 9 November 1899, HO45 10042/
   A61612/1.
37 Papers (1902–7) on HO45 10043/A61612.
38 Memo by Whitelegge, 20 July 1904, HO45 10496/115515/4.
39 Memorial, factory inspectors to S of S, 13 February 1904, LAB 14/173,
   p. 2.
40 See above, p. 74.
41 Copy of examination of inspectors of factories, 1900, CSC3/321.
42 *Dept. Cttee on Factory Accidents*, 1911, *Mins of Ev.*, 993; *2nd Rep. of
   R.C. on C.S.*, 1912–13, *Mins of Ev.*, 5251.
43 Ibid., 5224.
44 *Return of the Names, Previous Occupations or Professions of (a) the
   Inspectors, (b) the Inspectors' Assistants*, etc., PP 1907 (172) LXXVI;
   Dept. Cttee on Factory Accidents, 1911, p. 49.
45 Minute by Delevigne, 16 November 1906, LAB 14/171.
46 *Dept. Cttee on Factory Accidents,* 1911, *Mins of Ev.*, 950; the *Imperial
   Calendar* shows that in fact nine inspectors' assistants were promoted in
   1906 or 1907, and another four before 1914.
47 See papers on LAB 14/171.
48 *Dept. Cttee on Factory Accidents*, 1911, p. 50.
49 Ibid., p. 60.
50 1 Edw. VII cap. 22.
51 Memo, Fabian Society to HO, March 1900, and *Report by Industrial
   Law Committee* (1900), HO45 9949/B31418/15, 16.
52 Digby to *The Times*, 11 June 1900, p. 3.
53 Cabinet paper by Ritchie, 28 January 1901, CAB 37/56 (No. 11), p. 2.
54 See e.g. Minute by Troup, 14 February 1900, HO45 9949/B31418/4.
55 Report of departmental committee on the factory inspectorate, 16
   January 1913, LAB 14/182, pp. 6–7.
56 Report of departmental committee on the factory inspectorate, 23
   December 1907, HO45 10553/164207.
57 *Dept. Cttee on Factory Accidents*, 1911, p. 1.
58 Ibid., pp. 21, 51.
59 Report of departmental committee on the factory inspectorate, 16
   January 1913, LAB 14/182.

60 HO to T, 18 January 1913, LAB 14/182.
61 T to HO, 28 January 1913, LAB 14/182.
62 Minute by Delevigne, 29 January 1913, LAB 14/182.
63 In the event ten new districts were formed, two abolished and seventeen altered in 1913.
64 For reasons of space this section concentrates on the financial problems of these schools. For discussion of other administrative issues and the ideals underlying their foundation up to 1893, see Eade, 'The Reclaimers: A Study of the Reformatory Movement in England and Wales 1846–1893'.
65 See above, p. 138.
66 Figures taken from memo by Lushington, 5 October 1880, CAB 37/4 (No. 70).
67 29 & 30 Vict. cap. 117 and 29 & 30 cap. 118.
68 Figures taken from memo by Lushington, 5 October 1880, CAB 37/4 (No. 70). (The residue of the expense fell on the school managers.)
69 *Report of the Royal Commission on Reformatory and Industrial Schools*, PP 1884 [C. 3876] XLV, *Mins of Ev.*, 1534.
70 By 1880 six school boards had established day industrial schools to which the Treasury also contributed.
71 Memo by Lushington, 5 October 1880, CAB 37/4 (No. 70).
72 There was no clear age distinction between inmates of the two types of school. At reformatory schools they had to be over ten unless previously convicted by a court of quarter sessions or assizes, or previously charged with an offence punishable with imprisonment. They could not be over sixteen when admitted, nor could they be detained more than five years. The age range, therefore, tended to be from eight or nine to twenty-one. At industrial schools inmates had to be over five and under fourteen when admitted and none could be detained involuntarily after the age of sixteen.
73 *Dept. Cttee on R. and I. Schools*, 1896, Appendix XXXII.
74 Ibid., Appendix XXXIII.
75 3 Hansard 256, 1279 (4 September 1880).
76 Memo by Lushington, 21 February 1882, HO45 9617/A13312/15a.
77 Harcourt to *The Times*, 18 September 1880, p. 12.
78 HO views on the latter point had been made clear in an earlier brief inter-departmental report (February 1881), signed by government representatives from Local Government Board, Treasury, Education Department and Home Office; see HO45 9607/A2720/1. No action on this had been taken in view of the appointment of the royal commission.
79 *Report of the Royal Commission on Reformatory and Industrial Schools*, PP 1884 [C. 3876] XLV.
80 3 Hansard 437, 194 (11 April 1889).
81 Memo by Lushington, 1890, HO45 9801/B5314C/1.
82 Minutes by Lushington, 6 and 25 August 1890, in papers and correspondence concerning the departmental committee on the reformatory and industrial schools inspectorate, HO45 9830/B9213/8.
83 Eade, pp. 327 ff.
84 Report on the reformatory and industrial schools inspectorate, 25 June 1891, Appendix II, HO45 9830/B9213/8. ('Industrial schools' includes the separately listed 'day industrial schools'.)
85 Ibid.
86 Draft HO to Office of Works, April 1895, HO45 9831/B9213A/14.
87 *40th Report of the Inspector of Reformatory and Industrial Schools of*

Great Britain, PP 1897 [C. 8566] XLI, p. 5.

88 These included J. E. Dorington MP, Rev. Brooke Lambert, Charles Bill MP and Rev. J. B. Richards.

89 *Report of the Departmental Committee on Reformatory and Industrial Schools*, PP 1896 [C. 8204] XLV, Memorandum A; this was signed by Lushington, Hugh Hoare, Emma Cons and Margaret Eve.

90 A further memorandum (C) was signed by Lushington, Cons and Eve.

91 *Dept. Cttee on R. and I. Schools*, 1913, p. 69.

92 Minute by Legge, 3 April 1903, HO45 10222/B36029/4. The Board of Education replaced the Education Department in 1899.

93 The relative contributions towards reformatory and industrial schools' incomes from the Treasury and from local authorities in 1890 and 1906 were as follows:

	reformatory schools		industrial schools	
	1890	1906	1890	1906
Treasury	66%	60%	53%	36%
Local authorities	20%	26%	31%	42%

These and subsequent figures taken from the *Rep. of the Dept. Cttee on R. and I. Schools*, 1913, p. 70.

94 Minute by Legge, 16 April 1901, HO45 10222/B36029/1.

95 Memo by Legge, August 1904, HO45 10222/B36029/4.

96 Notes on a meeting between S of S and a deputation from the National Association of Certified Reformatory and Industrial Schools, 30 April 1901, HO45 10222/B36029/2.

97 Minutes by Chalmers and Akers-Douglas, 21 November and 23 December 1904, HO45 10222/B36029/4.

98 *Report of the Departmental Committee on the Provision of Funds for Reformatory and Industrial Schools*, PP 1906 [Cd. 3143] LIV.

99 Papers, September–December 1906, on HO45 10510/129054/6.

100 T to HO, 23 January 1907, HO45 10510/129054/6.

101 Notes on meeting between S of S and deputation from National Association of Certified Reformatory and Industrial Schools, November 1907, HO45 10510/129054/48.

102 Minute by Byrne, 18 November 1907, HO45 10361/154821/7.

103 8 Edw. 7 cap. 67.

104 *Dept. Cttee on R. and I. Schools*, 1913, *Mins of Ev.*, 7.

105 This figure includes salaries, travelling expenses, cost of legal proceedings and incidental expenses.

106 *Dept. Cttee on R. and I. Schools, 1913, Mins of Ev.*, 485–7.

107 *Dept. Cttee on R. and I. Schools*, 1913, p. 15.

108 Minute by Legge, 5 December 1898, HO45 10464/B25779A/3.

109 Robertson to S of S, 24 December 1898, HO45 10934/173838/1.

110 *Dept. Cttee on R. and I. Schools*, 1913, *Mins of Ev.*, 42.

111 *Dept. Cttee on R. and I. Schools*, 1913, p. 7.

112 *Dept. Cttee on R. and I. Schools*, 1913, *Mins of Ev.*, 50–7. There was no chief inspector of prisons because the work was geographically divided but (leaving aside the women inspectors) each prison inspector earned more than each inspector and assistant inspector serving under the chief inspector of reformatory and industrial schools.

113 *Dept. Cttee on R. and I. Schools*, 1913, p. 13.

114 See above, p. 80.

115 HO to T, 6 December 1913, HO45 10705/239280/4.

116 *58th Report of the Chief Inspector of Reformatory and Industurial Schools of Great Britain*, PP 1914–16 [Cd. 8091] XXXIV, p. 13.
117 Troup, *The Home Office*, p. 131.
118 G. H. Sabine, *A History of Political Theory* (1951 edn), p. 615.
119 Ibid., p. 619.
120 Sir Robert Anderson and Sir Charles Warren are two examples.
121 A. V. Dicey, *Lectures on the Relations between law and Public Opinion in England during the Nineteenth-Century* (1963 pb. edn), p. 290.
122 See above, p. 154.
123 *Report of the Royal Commission on Mines*, PP 1907 [Cd. 3548] XIV, *Mins of Ev.*, 9095.
124 See above, p. 145.
125 Waller to Gladstone, 15 October 1907, Visc. Gladstone papers, Add. MSS 45994, ff. 41–4; for the growth of the inspectorates, see Appendix E.
126 Roseveare, *The Treasury: the Evolution of a British Institution*, p. 186.
127 Standing order by Cross, 16 December 1878, HO45 9567/74589/29.
128 See above, p. 42–3.
129 Minute by Lushington, 31 July 1881, HO45 9611/A7070/3.
130 *Dept. Cttee on R. and I. Schools*, 1913, *Mins of Ev.*, 7.
131 See R. C. K. Ensor, *England 1870–1914* (1936), p. 207.
132 Gerald Rhodes, *Inspectorates in British Government: Law Enforcement and Standards of Efficiency* (1981).

Chapter 8

1 G. Kitson Clark, *The Making of Victorian England*, pp. 260–62.
2 Harold Perkin, *The Origins of Modern English Society 1780–1880* (1969), p. 254.
3 A. V. Dicey (*Fortnightly Review*, 1867), quoted by Reader, *Professional Men: the Rise of the Professional Classes in Nineteenth-Century England*, p. 159.
4 See above, p. 11–12.
5 Although many 'specialist' clerks were brought into line with the more regularly classified clerks, there always remained some posts on the HO establishment which had specific salaries attached to them, particularly in the lower class of clerks.
6 T to HO, 2 June 1868, T13/8.
7 T to HO, 8 November 1872 and 3 June 1875, T13/9 and T13/11.
8 *Sel. Cttee on Misc. Expend.*, 1847–8, *Mins of Ev.*, 2969.
9 See unpublished diary of Alexander Maconochie, 1864–5.
10 *2nd Rep. of R.C. on Civil Establishments*, 1888, *Mins of Ev.*, 11,166.
11 Grey had tried in vain to impose attendance books on the office in the 1850s.
12 Memo by Troup, 19 January 1885, HO45 9611/A7070B/1.
13 *2nd Rep. of R.C. on Civil Establishments*, 1888, *Mins of Ev.*, 10,902.
14 T Minute, 'Premature Publication of Official Publications', 13 March 1884, HO45 9831/B7315A/1.
15 Salisbury to Cross, 30 June 1885, Cross papers, Add. MSS 51263, ff. 91–2. Salisbury's choice was Sir Henry Maine who was actually appointed but could not take up the post because of ill-health.
16 T Minute, 'Civil Servants under the Control of the Treasury who are Candidates for Seats in the House of Commons', 12 November 1884, PP 1884–5 [C. 4229] XLV.
17 Law Officers' Opinion, 1 August 1885, HO45 9655/A40433/2.
18 3 Hansard 324, 51 (22 March 1888).

19 T Minute, 30 November 1868, HO45 9473/B2745/1.
20 HO to T, 30 April 1868, T1 6943A/21356.
21 Guillemard, *Trivial Fond Records*, p. 16.
22 Roy Lewis and Angus Maude, *Professional People* (1952), pp. 55–6.
23 W. Ashworth, *An Economic History of England, 1870–1930* (1960), p. 240.
24 L. T. Hobhouse, *Liberalism* (first pub. 1911, pb. 1964), p. 107; Ashworth, *An Economic History of England, 1870–1939*, p.248.
25 Reader, p. 202.
26 Exceptions to this rule were made as, for example, in the case of Pemberton who retired in 1894, aged seventy.
27 *2nd Rep. of R.C. on Civil Establishments*, 1888, *Mins of Ev.*, 10,952.
28 H. J. Hanham, 'The Sale of Honours in Late Victorian England', *Victorian Studies*, III (1960), p. 278.
29 See above, p. 187.
30 Matthews to Salisbury, 22 April 1887 and 3 May 1892; McDonnell to Salisbury, 29 April 1890 and 4 May 1892, Salisbury papers.
31 Arthur Ponsonby to Blackwell, 11 December 1907, Visc. Gladstone papers, Add. MSS 45993, ff. 315–16.
32 Searches in the *London Post Office Directory* and *Kelly's Handbook* of 1910 and 1914 show that at that time by far the majority of HO first division clerks of senior clerk level and above (i.e. old enough to have settled somewhere fairly permanent) lived in central London, mostly in Kensington.
33 Scott, *Your Obedient Servant*, p. 25.
34 *2nd Rep. of R.C. on Civil Establishments*, 1888, *Mins of Ev.*, 11,830.
35 Report on HO statistics branch, 16 December 1909, HO45 17787/B32589/46.
36 'Report of the Committee on the HO Registry', 3 November 1898, HO45 13624/B27360/2.
37 *2nd Rep. of R.C. on Civil Establishments*, 1888, *Mins of Ev.*, 12,289.
38 *Civil Service Gazette*, 6 October 1888, p. 9.
39 Arno J. Mayer, 'The Lower Middle Class as a Historical Problem', *Journal of Modern History*, (47) September 1975, pp. 418 ff.
40 Memorial by Wheeler, 24 December 1894, HO45 9832/139548D.
41 The *Civilian*, 6 April 1912, p. 377.
42 Crossick, 'The Emergence of the Lower Middle Class in Britain', in Crossick (ed.), *The Lower Middle Class in Britain 1870–1914*, pp. 21–2, 25, 32.
43 Clark, *The Making of Victorian England*, p. 260.
44 See above p. 34.
45 W. L. Burn, *The Age of Equipoise: A Study of the Mid-Victorian Generation* (pb. edn 1968), p. 267.
46 Crossick, 'The Emergence of the Lower Middle Class in Britain', pp. 39–40; see also P. F. Clarke, *Lancashire and the New Liberalism* (1971).
47 The constabulary and prisons inspectors were officially crown appointments made by royal warrant.
48 'Instructions by the Secretary of State for H.M. Inspectors of Factories and Workshops', 1894, HO45 9772/B1137AF/1.
49 (Draft) S of S to Redgrave, 1896, HO45 OS8002/22.
50 3 Hansard 330, 637–8 (8 November 1888), 1035–8 (13 November 1888), 1519–20 (19 November 1888).
51 HO minute, 27 May 1879, HO144 208/A48043/3.
52 Papers, November 1888, on HO144 208/A48043.

53 Whitelegge to S of S, 22 August 1900, HO45 9954/B32558.
54 Circular to factory inspectors, 1896, LAB 15/9.
55 *Instructions of the S of S for H.M. Inspectors under the Coal Mines Regulation Act, 1872*, etc., PP 1878(C. 1987] LXI.
56 *Report of the Royal Commission on Mines*, Vol. III, PP 1908 [Cd. 4349] XX, *Mins of Ev.*, 21,387.
57 *Report of the Royal Commission on Vivisection*, PP 1907 [Cd. 3326] XLI, *Mins of Ev.*, 1237–46.
58 Dr Mary Gordon to Mrs Pethwick-Lawrence, 26 October 1908, HO45 10552/163497/6.
59 HO minutes, 1914, HO45 10552/163497/6.
60 See Appendix E and Table 6, p. 81 above.
61 Papers, 1907–8, on HO45 10553/164207.
62 Papers, 1912–16, on HO 10552/163497.
63 The salary of the principal lady inspector, for example, £400 × £20 – £500, was less than any of the men specialist inspectors and had a ceiling no higher than ordinary men factory inspectors.
64 Herman Finer, *The Theory and Practice of Modern Government* (1951), p. 772.
65 See, for example, Robert Moses, *The Civil Service of Great Britain* (1914).
66 R. K. Kelsall, *Higher Civil Servants in Britain* (1955), p. 127, Table 17.
67 R. H. Crossman's criticism (1935) is quoted by Finer, *The Theory and Practice of Modern Government*, p. 772.
68 Finer, p. 774.
69 See e.g. J. A. (Lord) Salter, *Memoirs of a Public Servant* (1961), pp. 51ff; José Harris, *Unemployment and Politics: a Study in English Social Policy 1886–1914*, p. 11; José Harris, *William Beveridge: a Biography* (1977), pp. 144ff.
70 Moses, *The Civil Service of Great Britain*, pp. 216–17.
71 Quoted by Kelsall, *Higher Civil Servants in Britain*, p. 45.
72 *Report of the Royal Commission on the Civil Service*, 1930–1, *Mins of Ev.*, (HMSO), 2152.
73 R. G. S. Brown, *The Administrative Process in Britain* (pb. edn 1971), p. 51.
74 *Report of the Royal Commission on the Civil Service*, 1930–1, *Mins of Ev.* (HMSO), 2152–3.
75 Finer, p. 774; H. E. Dale, *The Higher Civil Service of Great Britain* (1941), p. 192; Roy Lewis and Angus Maude, *The English Middle Classes* (pb. edn 1953), pp. 78–9.
76 Redmayne, *Men, Mines and Memories*, pp. 141–2.
77 *Report of the Royal Commission on the Civil Service*, PP 1930–1, Cmd. 3909 X, p. 52.
78 *Report of the Committee on the Civil Service, 1966–8*, PP 1968, Cmnd. 3638 XVIII, Vol. I.
79 Professor A. F. Pollard, quoted by Ernest Barker, *The Development of the Public Services in Western Europe 1660–1930* (1944), p. 29.

Index

second division (contd)
  salaries of staff clerks in, 30, 94
Stephen, Sir James (permanent
  under-secretary of Colonial
  Office), 13
Streatfield, J. (HO clerk, see
  Appendix B, p. 209), 15
suffragette movement, 83, 198-9
superintendent of registry, *see*
  registry of HO
supplementary clerks of HO, 93,
  111, 115
  number and salaries of, 23, 30,
    94-5
  position regularized, 17-18
  work of, 23-4
Sutherland, John (burial grounds
  inspector, see Appendix D, p.
  222), 138-40, 145, 149

telephone, first use of in HO, 98
Thane, G. D. (cruelty to animals
  inspector from 1899), 198
Thring, Henry (HO counsel,
  1861-9), 19
Tomlin Commission (Royal
  Commission on the Civil
  Service, 1930-31), 202-3, 204
Treasury, 16, 35, 42, 60, 78, 102,
  103, 104, 181, 183, 205
  committees on HO
    establishment, (1848) 11-12,
    (1856) 16-18, (1876) 29,
    (1910) 79, (registry, 1911)
    101
  and control of government
    departments, 4, 11, 24, 40,
    through Minutes etc., 184,
    187, 192
  democratic process, impedes,
    177-8
  and HO factory inspectorate,
    151, 152, 154, 157, 161, 164,
    180
  grants-in-aid, 123, 134, 135-7
  gratuities, refuses to grant, 185
  and lower/second division
    discontent, 110-14, 116-19
  and open competition, 20-21, 25

overtime, dislikes, 191
and reformatory and industrial
  schools, 164-76
reforms itself, 12
and HO reorganization,
  (1870-76) 25-31, (1896) 61,
  (1904-6) 65-6, (1913-14)

Tremenheere, H. S. (mines
  inspector, see Appendix D, p.
  218), 128, 131, 149
Trevelyan, Sir Charles (assistant
  secretary of the Treasury), 4,
  10-14, 201
Tripp, G. H. (HO clerk in charge
  of accounts, 1887-1909),
  102-4, 107, 111, 116, 118, 172,
  192, 193
Troup, Sir Edward (HO permanent
  under-secretary, see Appendix
  B, p. 208), 45, 75, 76, 79, 80,
  87, 88, 91, 101, 152, 163, 188,
  189, 190, 198, 199, 201
  appointment to HO and
    background of, 33-4
  and Beck case, 68-9
  and corporate feeling within HO,
    118
  and departmental
    responsibilities, 52-3
  effective minutes of, 90
  and law and order problems,
    82-6, 91-2
  memoir sources, lack of, *x*
  (possible) narrowness of vision,
    203
  and parliamentary work, 52
  promoted to senior clerkship,
    36-7
  to headship of industrial and
    parliamentary department,
    61, 157, 161, 180
  to permanent under-
    secretaryship, 71-3
  and promotion of career
    officials, 59-61
  prototype of modern generalist
    official, 205
  and reform of HO statistics,